Women on the Verge

Asia-Pacific:

Culture, Politics, and Society

Editors: Rey Chow, H. D. Harootunian,

and Masao Miyoshi

Women on the Verge

Japanese Women, Western Dreams

KAREN KELSKY

Duke University Press ≈ *Durham and London 2001*

© 2001 Duke University Press   All rights reserved

Printed in the United States of America on acid-free paper ∞

Typeset in Scala by Keystone Typesetting, Inc.

Library of Congress Cataloging-in-Publication Data

appear on the last printed page of this book.

For Taro, Miyako, and Seiji

Contents

Illustrations

Acknowledgments

It is my pleasure to thank the many people who made this book possible. For their close and critical readings of early chapter drafts in a variety of forms, I wish to extend my gratitude to Kären Wigen, Jennifer Robertson, Marilyn Ivy, Niko Besnier, Ken George, Mark McLelland, Lisa Yoneyama, John Treat, John Russell, Masao Miyoshi, Peggy Pascoe, Eric Cazdyn, and Alan Cole. I owe a special debt of gratitude to Anne Allison, who gave generously of her time and support in countless ways, large and small, and who encouraged me with her enthusiasm, energy, and perspicuity. Others whose comments I took to heart, in perhaps unanticipated ways: Akhil Gupta, Purnima Mankekar, Louisa Schein, Ted Swedenberg, Faye Ginsberg, and Dan Segal.

At the University of Oregon I am indebted to Jeff Hanes for his generosity of spirit and ferocity of expectations. Colleagues at the Anthropology Department at Oregon pushed me to write with clarity. I thank Terry O'Nell, Lynn Stephen, Diane Baxter, and Aletta Biersack. From the University of Hawai'i, I wish to thank Kathy Ferguson, Jocelyn Linnekin, Alan Howard, Dru Gladney, and Takie Lebra. Rob Wilson has my enduring gratitude for sustaining me through a difficult time and showing me the provocations and possibilities of critical interdisciplinary work in borderland places. I also want to thank Geoff White, of the University of Hawai'i and the East-West Center, for being the kind of mentor and friend every scholar needs. At the University of the Sacred Heart in Tokyo, I am indebted to Takahashi Keiko-sensei, who lent her unfailing enthusiasm and energy to my fieldwork travails. At Duke University Press I am grateful to Reynolds Smith and Sharon Parks Torian. Finally, a fond thank you to Fosco Maraini for the wonderful photographs.

I am also grateful to friends who kept the spirit from wilting over the years: Tracy Palmgren, Susan Schultz, LeeRay Costa, Gretchen Riess, Louisa Cameron, Maram Epstein, and Betsy Wheeler. Anna Watson generously maintained my supply of grist for the mill. And the people of Oshika village, whom I thank not only for giving us a home, superlative food, and an idyllic place to write a dissertation, but for continuing to have us back: Miyazaki Fumihito and Yasuko, Iwamoto Jun'ichi and Masami, Yanagishita Shūhei and Toshiko, Matsuda Morio and Kikue, and Simon Piggott and Nakamura Masako.

And thanks most of all to the women in Japan, particularly Shōyama Noriko and Maeda Yukiko, who gave of their time and their ideas, and with their thoughtfulness on so many levels made this book possible.

I cannot finish without thanking my family. I am indebted to my parents, Albert and Kathleen Kelsky, for passing on to me a love of learning and encouraging me throughout. Finally, this book is dedicated to my husband, Iwata Tarō, daughter Miyako, and son Seiji. How could I have done it without you?

Fieldwork was funded by the National Science Foundation Graduate Fellowship, the East-West Center Graduate Fellowship, and the Japan Foundation Doctoral Dissertation Fellowship. Writing was supported by the National Endowment for the Humanities, the Social Science Research Council Sexuality Research Program, and the Oregon Humanities Center. The University of Oregon Center for Asian and Pacific Studies generously assisted with the indexing.

Parts of this book were previously published in *Cultural Anthropology* and the *International Journal of Politics, Culture and Society*.

Every effort has been made to trace the copyright of the illustrations reproduced in this book. Unfortunately, in some cases this has proved to be impossible. The author and the publisher would be pleased to hear from any copyright holders whom they have been unable to contact and to print due acknowledgments in the next edition.

Note on Japanese Names and Terms

Japanese names are written following the Japanese practice: surname first, given name second. The only exceptions to this rule are the names of Japanese authors who have published in English using Western name order or who, for any reason, have chosen to reverse their name order when publishing in Japanese.

Japanese terms are transcribed with diacritics, except in those cases where a place-name (for example, Tokyo or Kyoto) is well-known in English.

Introduction

When life in Japan becomes too constricting, I simply flee abroad, like a goldfish coming to the surface for air.—ARIYOSHI SAWAKO, "NOBODY ni tsuite" (About nobody)

How [do] we engage the complex politics of pleasure and of "resistance" when nothing is beyond commodification or beyond the dominant . . . ?—DORINNE KONDO, *About Face: Performing Race in Fashion and Theater*

Occidental Longings The 1980s and 1990s saw a series of profound and far-reaching transformations in Japanese gender relations, transformations that are still in process and that have yet to be fully grasped in their implications. It was during this time that the birthrate first began its precipitous slide downward, reaching 1.57 births per woman in 1989, well below the minimum 2.2 births required to sustain the present population. This development so stunned the public that it earned the name "the 1.57 shock" and inspired impassioned media debate as well as government directives to women to bear more children (these were ineffective, and by 1997 the rate had plummeted to 1.39; Kōseishō 2000a). Meanwhile, it was during this time that Japanese began marrying considerably later in life: By the late 1990s the average age of first marriage had risen to almost twenty-nine for men and almost twenty-seven for women, the highest in the industrialized world (Kōseishō 2000b). Single Japanese men now began to suffer seriously from the effects of *kekkon-nan* (marriage difficulty), as a large proportion of young single marriage-age women first deserted rural areas and farming life for the large cities and then, even within the large cities, spurned men employed in the blue-collar sector for the urban, middle-class ideal of the white-collar *sararīman* (salaryman). At the same time, backed by the high yen and the overvalued economy, young women began traveling abroad in ever-increasing numbers, eventually surpassing, by 1990, the number of young men engaging in foreign travel by a margin of 2 to 1. As one offshoot of this overseas craze, *ryūgaku* (study abroad) for periods ranging from one month to several years became an accepted and even common career move for middle-class single women in their twenties and thirties. By the early 1990s, almost 80 percent of Japanese study-abroad students were female. Finally, it was in 1986 that the much-anticipated Equal Employment Opportunity Law (EEOL) was implemented as Japan's belated effort to show progress on women's status before the end of the U.N. Decade for Women. The EEOL was updated in 1997.

At first glance, these various phenomena seem only distantly related: What has the 1.57 shock to do with women's ryūgaku boom? The "de-feminization" of the countryside with the EEOL? As I hope to show, very much indeed. I argue that by turning away from (what they label) "traditional" lifestyles, resisting the expectations of (what they label) "traditional" Japanese men, refraining from having children, and traveling, studying, and working abroad, more and more Japanese women are exploiting their position on the margins of corporate and family systems to engage in a form of "defection" from expected life courses.

This book focuses on one form of this defection: young women's personal and professional investment in what I call the realm of the foreign, through means such as foreign language study, study abroad, work abroad, employment in international organizations and foreign-affiliate firms (*gaishikei*), and romantic or sexual involvement with foreign men.[1] This book sets this investment against the backdrop of the social changes mentioned above to explore the meanings that the foreign option carries for some internationally active Japanese women. I argue that the turn to the foreign has become perhaps the most important means currently at women's disposal to resist gendered expectations of the female life course in Japan. Indeed, the space of the foreign as site of professional opportunity, personal liberation, and romantic or erotic self-expression offers those women inclined to use it, and whose personal circumstances of age, class, marital status, and place of residence enable them to do so, the means to radically challenge persistent gender ideologies that make authentic Japanese womanhood (and the stability of the Japanese nation) contingent on women's continued subordination to Japanese men and "traditional" gender roles. The subject of *Women on the Verge* is the narratives of internationalism which some Japanese women use to justify their shift of loyalty from what they call a backward and "oppressive" Japan to what they see as an exhilarating and "liberating" foreign realm.

Internationalist narratives tell a story of mobility and hinge on a gender reversal. They argue that if women are blocked from the safe and secure paths of male professional achievement within Japan, women also, as a result of these very exclusions, enjoy a special freedom to explore alternative life choices, such as devoting several years to studying a foreign language, experimenting with foreign firms, working or studying abroad, or engaging with foreigners in Japan and the world outside. What in the high-growth era of the national economy was simply discrimination becomes available for other interpretations in the age of transnational flux and instability. Indeed, women all but monopolize an international niche in the economy for interpreters, translators, bicultural and bilingual consultants, international public servants, and other facilitators of Japan's business, media, and cultural relations with the world. Ultimately, by staking their claim in the realm of the foreign, Japanese women claim to be moving beyond narrow and declining national interests into dynamic transnational worlds of finance, technology, international aid, and the arts, competing successfully, for the first time, against Japanese men. This international niche that women occupy, however, is itself marginal to the mainstream economy, and the results of women's claims on it are mixed.

Yet the foreign option encompasses far more than professional advancement: time spent overseas or in the (intimate) company of foreigners provides women with a foreign-inflected vocabulary for a sustained critique of Japan's gender relations, as well as the means to circumvent or reject them. By collapsing the foreign with the West (I return to this below), women's narratives of internationalism advocate the absorption of the West into the female self, yielding a "new self" (*atarashii jibun*) that represents a detachment of woman's subjectivity from the Japanese nation-state. Women's narratives of internationalism depend on two sets of rhetorical contrasts: between a progressive West and a backward Japan, and internationalized Japanese women and "feudalistic" Japanese men. The narratives argue a "natural" alliance between Japanese women and Western interests against the insular and wrongheaded Japanese male establishment. They construct the West as a site of rescue for Japanese women whose ambitions and abilities are thwarted in Japan. They take as their agenda the project to remake Japan in the West's image.

In this way women's "defection" is not precisely to the West, but to an idea of the West, which is synonymous with the international. In their most utopic forms, narratives of internationalism argue for an alliance with the "universal" ideals of Western modernity and require not so much women's physical displacement overseas as an absorption of that modernity into Japan. Thus, whereas the encroachment of Western modernity has often been viewed in Japan as a traumatic event of the first order—in philosopher Takeuchi Yoshimi's view, nothing but the "devastation" of being deprived of an independent subjectivity (in Sakai 1989, 117)—for some women, internationalist modernity is seen as offering them (and potentially Japanese men too) their very first chance at unfettered freedom.

In *Women on the Verge* I explore some of the ways the trope of Western modernity exerts a pull on the minds and bodies of those educated and ambitious Japanese women who are engaged in projects of resistance against Japan. I approach this Western power to attract as an eroticized and racialized power, in which the liberatory potential of the West is intertwined with desire for the white man as fetish object of modernity. I want to show how individual women as actors deploy these pervasive, subversive, and performative discourses of complaint and desire, sometimes championing them, at other times rejecting them. My goal in this book is to consider ways that desire for the West is a potentially transgressive and transformative force, and at the same time a deeply compromised one politically when it elides a recognition of the transnational, postcolonial racial, gender, class, and sexual politics that constitute it. Finally, I explore the implications of such transnationally mediated fetishizations of a global West as site of desire and imaginative icon for anthropological understandings of "the field."

Three points are critical to address at the outset. The first: How many Japanese women can really be called internationalist? The scale of women's international exodus is impossible to grasp in a strictly demographic sense. Certainly internationalism as an active practice is by and large limited to a relatively small number of women. Countless women—as well as men—adhere to longstanding Japanese racial ideologies that make both foreign countries and foreign bodies sites of contamination and danger (see Russell 1998, Buckley 1997a, and Wagatsuma 1967). The individuals treated in this book were predominantly highly educated, urban, mostly single career women between the ages of twenty and forty-five, with extensive study abroad or work abroad experience and English-language expertise. These women generally lived alone and worked at foreign-affiliate firms or international organizations. Women I interviewed for this research included bilingual secretaries and securities traders in British and American investment firms, grants officers at the United Nations University in Tokyo, international journalists, and professional interpreters—certainly constituting a minority in the Japanese female labor market. Yet nearly 140,000 women study abroad each year, and millions travel overseas for tourism purposes, at a rate that dwarfs such travel by Japanese men. Unlike in many other countries, this mobility is not an elite phenomenon but is grounded firmly in the middle classes. Overseas travel has become so common among middle-class young women that certain locations, such as Hawai'i are now dismissed as vulgar and passé.

Thus, the problem of naming arises. George Marcus has observed that one of the dilemmas for anthropology of global-local topics is that they "defy conventional practices of bounding and naming the cultural subject of study" (1995, 425). For the sake of brevity, I have chosen to call the women this book treats "internationalist Japanese women," although "internationalist" in Japanese translation (*kokusaiteki, kokusaijin*) is a term that the women I knew rarely employed to describe themselves, due to its association in Japanese with the state-sponsored project of "internationalization" (*kokusaika*), a nationalistic project that, as Marilyn Ivy has written, advocates "the thorough domestication of the foreign and the dissemination of Japanese culture throughout the world" (Ivy 1995, 3). Kokusaika represents a distinct project from these women's vision of a Japan transformed according to Western liberal values. Nevertheless, because their vision adheres so closely to the meaning of the *English* term "internationalism" (see Malkki 1994), I have chosen to employ it throughout. Elsewhere,

where I have simply used the term "Japanese women," I do not do so to imply that all Japanese women are internationally oriented. In some cases, I mean to refer in a demographic sense to the young, single, urban women with international opportunities and experience that I describe above. More often, however, I am referencing the discursive construct "Japanese women" that women themselves depend on within their internationalist narratives, which essentialistically posits all Japanese women as possessed, whether exercised or not, of a "natural" potentiality and aptitude for international pursuits (I return to this below).

Second, I wish to be clear that the geographic boundaries of the "realm of the foreign" are not coterminous with any borders that can be fixed on the map. As I have indicated, when women speak of "the foreign" as the object of their desires, it is almost invariably "the West" that they mean. Yet, this is not a West divided into specific countries, but rather a generic "West" that is made to contrast with what they consider a backward and benighted "Japan."

In practice, America is the country most powerfully associated with the West. To be sure, there are significant contingents of internationalized women who are devoted Anglophiles, Francophiles, or fans of Italy, Canada, or other Western countries, and they make their appearance in the pages that follow. England seems to hold a special place in women's internationalist narratives as the home of a truly sublime sophistication, an apotheosis of "class," that is contrasted favorably to the "coarseness" of the United States. There are also women who have turned their attention in recent years to the booming economies of Asia, especially Hong Kong, although here again, as I show, it is the "Westernized" aspects of these sites that attract. However, not only do the overwhelming majority of internationally inclined women ultimately make their way to America for study or work, but more important, even for women who remain in Japan, at the level of cultural imaginary the United States reigns supreme. Because of Commodore Perry and his Black Ships, because of Pearl Harbor, Hiroshima, and the Occupation, U.S.-Japan trade, the war brides, *Father Knows Best,* Hollywood movies, and the rest of the postwar inundation of American popular culture into Japan—in other words, because of a century and a half of intensive mutual enmeshment at military, political, economic, and cultural levels—America still dominates Japan's image of the West.

Even so, women's narratives of Occidental longing persistently refuse to clearly differentiate among America, the West, and a generic realm of the foreign.[2] An early internationalist writer remarked in 1941, "To me, as to most of the Japanese people of the time, the West was a luminous world where we could hardly distinguish Europe from America and the different nations in them" (Mishima S. 1941, 87). Despite the vastly increased quantity of information about foreign countries in Japan today, as well as the considerable cosmopolitanism of internationalist women themselves, it seems that something of this tendency remains. "The West" as trope, like the tropes of "Japan" and "Japanese tradition," becomes a constantly expanding and contracting discursive axis around which women speak, write, and act, and a fluid basis for a dynamic narrative of internationalist becoming. Thus, in this book, although I make efforts to distinguish the United States, England, and other countries where this is necessary and possible (especially in chapter 1, where I trace some particular histories of women's contact with the United States before and after World War II), throughout the book I preserve the slippage between and among these places on the map, for the slippage is the very point: this is the "mythological" West, the West as (somebody else's) fantasy.

Finally, the economy. As economic conditions in Japan have worsened in the post-1990 recession, and as the phallocentric nationalistic euphoria over the "victorious" mid-1980s "bubble economy" recedes into distant memory before the steady encroachment of a renewed American economic hegemony, some young Japanese men have begun following in women's internationalist footsteps, seeking a solution to reduced domestic prospects in careers that take them outside of Japan. What in the 1980s and early 1990s emerged as a subterranean women's oppositional praxis, now appears to be in the process of possible appropriation by men. Although women's investments in the international sphere show no signs of abating, and indeed are intensifying with the worsening female domestic job market, this space may become in the next decade subject to renewed masculine control.

I incorporate some material on this recent male trajectory throughout *Women on the Verge*. However, at the same time, I wish to emphasize that the gradual entry of young men into what women have been claiming for years as an exclusively female space has not significantly altered the gendered politics of that space, but rather has served to foreground the nature of women's continued investment in it. For what distinguishes women's turn to the foreign/Western realm is that it resonates profoundly into personal realms as well, reflecting a wider state of disjuncture between Japanese men and women that is at odds with long-standing notions of Japan's gender complementarity and mutually reinforcing labor (Edwards 1989). Although the new "internationalized male" is increasingly valorized in the media as a dynamic young freethinker who challenges the conventions of a hidebound "Japan Inc.," in almost no case is the idea of the global career linked, for men, to a questioning of Japanese gender, marital, or family conventions. It is safe to say that rarely is the idea of the global career associated, for men, with the pursuit of a Western wife.

By contrast, women's internationalist narratives rarely take the notion of career in isolation; following distinct conventions, they almost always begin in tones of desperation and rage, narrate a broad ideological allegiance to Western modernity, and sometimes Western men, and end in a profound critique of Japanese "feudalism," which they take as exemplified by the family structure, the corporation, and, above all, by Japanese men themselves. In some cases, such as among the "yellow cab" subculture I discuss in chapter 3, the West offers opportunities for sexual experimentation and flamboyant defiance of sexual norms. In most cases, defiance is more muted and less overtly sexual than pervasively eroticized. For, as I argue throughout the book, in women's narratives of the international, white Western men are idealized for their exemplification of the modern, romanticized for their alleged sensitivity (*yasashisa*), and fetishized as signifiers of success and gatekeepers of social upward mobility in the world. In this way, white Western men as potential lovers or husbands become one of the most alluring means, for heterosexual Japanese women so inclined, to effect a potential escape from Japanese social constraints into the embrace of the "outside" world.[3]

The other distinctive element of women's internationalism is that it is posited, essentialistically, as the result of an inherent or "inborn" female adaptability, derived from women's very exclusions from family and corporate structures. Whereas Japanese men are increasingly urged to acquire training to respond to the immediate economic imperative of a global economy, women, it is claimed, instinctively know how to do it, because they were never adequately socialized as Japanese in the first place. This is a striking claim in light of Japanese women's persistent deployment as the ultimate signifiers of Japanese tradition and the burden laid on them over the course of Japan's modernization to maintain, in the absence of overworked men, both the sanctity of the family and the incorporation of succeeding generations of children into the labor force (Allison 2000).[4] A number of scholars have argued that woman as mother is the centerpiece both of the contemporary economic system (Allison 2000) and of nostalgic patriarchal imaginings of the generative native place of tradition (Robertson 1998b, 124–25). Yet, as Jennifer Robertson has remarked, this very nostalgia for the "traditional woman" has served to deflect attention from the real instability of patriarchal categories.

For ironically, internationally active women explain their marginality by reference to patriarchal Japanese tradition itself. That is, they argue that precisely because women, under the terms of traditional patrilocal marriage, are forced to leave their natal homes and enter their husband's after marriage; because girls are not as indulged as boys but forced to develop their own "inner resources"; because girls are not required to devote themselves to academic success but are left free to explore their own interests; because they do not bear the burden of parents' expectations for present success and future care; because they are excluded from avenues of advancement in the Japanese corporation—for all these reasons, women insist, they are inherently marginal compared to men to the structures of the Japanese family and economy and possessed of an innate "adaptability" that allows them to quickly and painlessly mold themselves to the expectations of the Other.

Marilyn Ivy has observed that in the context of Japan National Railway advertising campaigns of the 1980s, women as travelers were persistently imagined by male ad designers as culturally marginal and inauthentic compared to the native, authentic male: According to the designers, whereas men use travel to find the true Japanese self, women use it to seek an "other" self (1995, 29–54): "A woman must leave home, realize home as essentially lacking, in order to display and thus discover herself in the eyes of the other" (39). Far from criticizing this exclusionary conception of women, internationalist women, as well as a number of Japanese feminist scholars, have appropriated it, taking it even further to argue that all women are imagined in Japan as already "partially foreign," and that where the foreign, particularly the Western, is posited by Japanese men, it is superimposed on the minds, voices, and bodies of Japanese women (Tajima 1993; Mizuta 1993). A host of media and advertising images bear out this claim, which I analyze in chapter 3. What is even more striking is the degree to which internationalist women themselves have embraced this exclusion, relying on terms such as "refugee" (*nanmin*), "defector" (*bōmeisha*), and "foreigner" (*gaijin*) to describe their "alien-ated" position in Japan.

However, if these narratives are essentializing, the goal of *Women on the Verge* is to show that the internationalist identity is not innate, but the product of specific historical, economic, and political motivations. There are forces that direct Japanese women and men into different routes and relationships to the nation and the world, trajectories of gender and privilege that make women's and men's relations with the foreign far from inherent proclivities, but rather considered responses to the distinct social and economic conditions they face. In short, there are reasons Japanese women choose the West and reasons they then explain and justify that choice by reference to a natural and inborn propensity.

At the same time, I argue that women's agency in "choosing" is always mediated by larger forces of attraction and repulsion that increasingly operate through the mechanisms of the global marketplace. "Normative discourses," as Elizabeth Povinelli and George Chauncey have observed, "interpellate individuals into hegemonic gendered social orders that produce . . . the trajectory of their desire" (1999, 444). Foucault reminds us that desire is always an expression of power: "Where there is desire, the power relation is already present" (1978, 81). Women's desires for the Occident are embedded in, indeed constituted by, power relations between Japan and the West (exemplified most often by the United States), in an ongoing dialectic of modernity that makes the West the inevitable destination in a unilineal tale of progress. Now, however, such desires are also anticipated and indeed to some extent produced by globally circulating images of the West that are currently "sold" to women through countless means both domestically and internationally. The lures of the glittering global career/lifestyle/romance are regularly featured in women's magazines, from *Cosmopolitan Japan* to the businesswoman's *Nikkei Woman*. To attract the mainstream female market, television and magazine advertising, the multimillion-dollar-a-year "ladies comic" industry, and other mass media persistently exploit the trope of the sophisticated globe-trotting woman, often as the lover/muse of the white man. Meanwhile, women's desires are incited by transnationally circulating Western media—most commonly, American movies—that make America and the West not simply glamorous locales but the very center of the universe (what Lavie and Swedenberg call "the Eurocenter," 1996, 1) and the inevitable destination for those fleeing the "backward" places of the world. Women are well attuned, too, to the persistent racialized imagery flowing out of the West of the Asian female–white male romance as both fantasy and fact.

In this way, women's fantasies of escape are inextricably bound up with prior fantasies of (in both senses) the Western Other, so that the *direction*, if not the degree, of women's outward trajectories are to a large extent determined before they ever leave home. At the same time, this interpellation is not simply a crude effect of a global culture industry. Rather, women's subject position as internationalized, cosmopolitan, or flexible is itself dependent on and derivative of a larger Eurocentric discourse of modernity and progress that, under the conditions of transnational capitalism, has become a mode for the absorption of mobile, elite, global subjects into a now shared, multicultural imaginary emanating from the West.

In this way, normative discourses of West-centrism circulate globally, drawing out the imaginative energies of dispersed subjects, detaching subjectivity from the state. Following Mayfair Yang, I am interested in "the increasing cosmopolitanism of the homeland" (1997, 289) whereby "those who have stayed in the country have started to undergo a change in subjectivity that is perhaps just as dramatic as that of those who have traveled abroad" (311). Arjun Appadurai has written that even where people exist within stable communities and so-called traditional networks of kinship, friendship, work, and leisure, "the warp of these stabilities is everywhere shot through with the woof of human motion" (1991, 192). If this is so, then even Japanese women who do not work at foreign companies, study English conversation, or pursue an MBA at Harvard increasingly reflect on their lives through "the prisms of the possible lives offered by mass media" (Appadurai 1996, 54). This returns us to the question of the scale of women's internationalism. Because of their embeddedness in media forms and fantasies, such globalized phenomena are not narrowly quantifiable. For this reason, although the subject of this book is the population of internationally active women I described earlier, I show that different forms of "Occidental longings" color the perspective of a variety of women across many different sectors of the population in the increasingly deterritorialized space of Japan.

Emergent Cosmopolitanisms Transnationalism, globalization, deterritorialization, diaspora: terms proliferate as cultural critics seek a vocabulary to describe the accelerating global flows of people, goods, capital, information, and images across national borders, the reconfiguration of the world according to a new logic of flexibility and mobility (even as the sanctity of ethnic identity is reasserted in opposition). David Harvey has located the core of these changes in economic practices of flexible accumulation, which have resulted in what he has called "time-space compression," marked by vastly accelerated turnover time in production, exchange, and consumption (1989, 284–85). Time-space compression has resulted in a now global mobility of people, as well as goods and capital, and in turn has fundamentally altered the subjectivities of the individuals caught up in these movements.

Drawing from Harvey's notion of flexible accumulation, Aihwa Ong has named this new form of identity and identification "flexible citizenship" (1999, 6). According to Ong, flexible citizenship refers to "the cultural logics of capitalist accumulation, travel, and displacement that induce subjects to respond fluidly and opportunistically to changing political-economic conditions" (6). It reflects the ways that transnationally mobile actors seek to "both circumvent *and* benefit from different nation-state regimes by selecting different sites for investments, work, and family relocation" (112). Thus, the new flexibility of capital has called forth, and indeed instituted, a new flexibility of identity, no longer unquestioningly embedded in the nation-state or ethnic group, but instrumentalizing and shifting according to the exigencies of the fluid global job market and the influences of an increasingly multifaceted (but centralized) global media and information network. Ong writes, "While mobility and flexibility have long been part of the repertoire of human behavior, under transnationality . . . flexibility, migration, and relocations, instead of being coerced or resisted, have become practices to strive for rather than stability" (19).

Obviously, the requirement of flexibility has not affected all people equally: as many have noted, the global economy has created its own class system. On the one hand, there are the temporary, contingent laborers who are drafted by multinational corporations locally or else compelled to migrate, as "transmigrants," from economic need (Glick-Schiller, Basch, and Szanton Blanc 1995). On the other hand, there are the new transnational professionals, or technocrats, who "administer" the new bureaucracy of flexibility. Ulf Hannerz, perhaps the dominant theorist (if not celebrant) of this latter class (which includes intellectuals), has called them "people with credentials [and] decontextualized cultural capital" (1996, 108). Some citizens are more flexible than others.

Yet identity is not merely a derivative of the job market. Appadurai and other anthropologists have been at pains to point out that global cultural flows move with a complexity that transcends a purely materialist analysis derived from Harvey's flexible accumulation model. As Povinelli and Chauncey observe, "A troubling aspect of the literature on globalization is its tendency to read social life off external social forms—flows, circuits, circulations of people, capital, and culture—without any model of subjective mediation" (1999, 445). Indeed, if there is a global economy, there is also an emergent global Imaginary, derived from the increasingly frenetic circulation of images through media ranging from American products like CNN, MTV, and the tireless output of Hollywood to the more dispersed media of Star TV (Australian media tycoon Rupert Murdoch's Asia-spanning satellite entertainment channel), endlessly recycled local and regional television programming, bootleg music and video recordings, the prolific output of movie industries in Bombay and elsewhere, and, of course, the Internet. This global Imaginary is productive of dispersed and disruptive desires that exceed the possibilities of the nation or, for that matter, the transnational media itself. As Appadurai has argued, "Fantasy is now a social practice: it enters, in a host of ways, into the fabrication of social lives for many people in many societies" (1996, 198). This is not simply depoliticized fantasy, a desire to briefly "forget" one's poverty, for example, by wallowing in a half-hour of the seductive fabulations of *Baywatch* reruns. Rather, imagination, inspired by but moving beyond received media images, potentially plays the critical role of providing the material of subversion. Nonini and Ong explain: "Imaginaries inspired by mass consumption, pastiche culture, fantasies of other places, and unruly desires can be disciplined either to support hegemonic views of regimes of truth . . . or to undermine them. . . . The concept of imaginaries therefore conveys the agency of diaspora subjects, who, while being made by state and capitalist regimes of truth, can play with different cultural fragments in a way that allows them to segue from one discourse to another, experiment with alternative forms of identification, shrug in and out of identities, or evade imposed forms of identification" (1997, 26). "The imagination," writes Appadurai, "is today a staging ground for action, and not only for escape" (1996, 7).

What both the material and the imaginative compulsions toward mobility and flexibility create are the conditions for cosmopolitanism, here defined not in the singular and abstract Kantian sense, but as multiplicitous and situated: an "actually existing cosmopolitanism" that is not "an ideal of detachment," but rather "a reality of (re)attachment, multiple attachment or attachment at a distance" (Robbins 1999, 3). This emergent form of cosmopolitanism has become the locus of intensive debate in recent years as perhaps the primary site of both new possibilities for self-making and resistance under conditions of globalization, as well as new impositions of dispersed modalities of governmentality (Ong 1999, 113). It has come to be cast as a potentially liberatory space, a locus of progressive politics and rejection of narrowly parochial nationalist/ethnicist positions. Paul Rabinow has famously written, "We are all cosmopolitans," and urges on intellectuals a critical cosmopolitanism as "an oppositional position . . . suspicious of sovereign powers, universal truths, overly relativized preciousness, local authenticity, moralisms high and low" (1986, 258). This progressive agenda is embedded in James Clifford's notion of "discrepant cosmopolitanisms" that has allowed cultural critics to finally abandon the "traveler/native" binary and attend to the "worldliness" of an increasing proportion of the world's population: those who move under compulsions as well as those elites, including scholars, who move by choice (1992, 108).

Despite Clifford's scrupulous efforts to enunciate a cosmopolitanism free from lingering auras of class, gender, and racial privilege, however, the term nevertheless applies awkwardly and incompletely to individuals who are not elite white men. If "we" are really all cosmopolitans, as Rabinow claims, when are we so, and in what ways? It is problematic to imagine the diasporic subject as homologous to the progressive cosmopolitan intellectual, and to assume he or she is radical (as the intellectual is radical) by virtue of sheer mobility. Put crudely, one can cross a border on a plane or in a car trunk.[5] Although growing numbers of people may have access to experiences classifiable as discrepant cosmopolitanisms, these experiences never operate independently of the histories of class, gender, and racial privilege that adhere to the original cosmopolitan category; they always fall short. It is this falling short, what Nonini and Ong have called the "impasses, contradictions, and pathos" of transnational subjects (1997, 13), that becomes the topic for sustained critical inquiry.

It is necessary to examine precisely how class, gender, racial, and sexual positionings (among others) both motivate and constrain an individual's transnational movements—not just vis-à-vis an oppressive nation-state, for example, but vis-à-vis deterritorialized fields of meanings and money, as well as prior and shifting social relationships locally and in the sites of travel and displacement. In this sense, the two-tiered transnational class system described above, of those who travel from need and those who travel by choice, is a false dichotomy; need and choice are hardly distinguishable in late capitalism when the seductions and compulsions of travel are so closely intertwined. For at least some transnational actors, pleasures may accompany exile.

At the same time, cosmopolitan experiences have the ability to reinforce precisely the relations of power that they appear to be undermining. This is the point of the widespread critique of cosmopolitan writers such as Salman Rushdie and Bharati Mukherjee. Timothy Brennan has argued that these writers function, precisely in describing the failures of the Third World nation, to reinforce the self-satisfied hegemony of the Western metropolitan reader's "dominant tastes" (1989, 39). Aijaz Ahmad has decried this kind of cosmopolitanism as "bourgeouisified," an "opportunistic Third-Worldism" (1992, 86), practiced by elite intellectuals who reap the rewards of the western high-end market for "difference." Cosmopolitanism, then, is not inherently subversive. Indeed, as Brennan has argued, the extraordinary recent scholarly consensus that cosmopolitanism *is* subversive should itself be grounds for suspicion: "Those who challenge the unalloyed goodness of the 'cosmopolitan' are working at a disadvantage" (1997, 19).

A brief discussion of the role of gender in globalization is illustrative here, especially the case of women who do seek inclusion in, or identify with, the cosmopolitan class. It has been almost axiomatic to assume women's victimization at the hands of globalization. Non-Western women in particular are frequently depicted as the ultimate local, the conscripted bearers of tradition against the onslaught of Western capital, or alternatively as laborer pawns in the hands of rapacious multinational corporations. Women are denied the appellation of cosmopolitan: they are rarely seen as cosmopolitan agents in their own right, but rather as the wives and daughters of cosmopolitan men (see Ong, 1999, 139–57); if they travel at all they are said to do so unwillingly, always anxious to maintain the traditions of home. Such representations are undoubtedly often warranted: many scholars have shown that women bear the brunt of symbolizing the sanctity of the nation, of both staying, and making, "home." Yet women, too, travel. They may travel alone or with families, with the goal of escaping or at least remaking tradition as much as preserving it. As Doreen Massey notes, "Many women have had to *leave* home precisely in order to forge their own version of their identities" (1994, 11).

Indeed, for relatively privileged strata of elite women (and perhaps for others as well), the cosmopolitan possibility is accompanied by, in Indian scholar Mary John's words, an almost inevitable "repudiation of the 'local'" in favor of "the geographical West . . . which represents the obvious goal in the pursuit of excellence" (1996, 10–11). She writes: "Some of the more ambitious among us have pushed for inclusion within the deceptively unmarked spaces of the new international class; given the often impossible complexities of our personal identities, we can experience the promise of modernity this class holds out, its 'independence' from gender and culture, as a special lure" (10). She concludes: "Everything can collude to bring us westward" (19).

The appeal of this westward journey is apparent in the proliferation of postcolonial women's writing, by authors such as Bharati Mukherjee, Jamaica Kincaid, and Jung Chang, that narrates a cosmopolitanism of apparently inevitable travel from a backward "premodern" cultural homeland to liberation in the West (often manifested in romantic or sexual relations with a white man).[6] Bruce Robbins, in a trenchant essay, has queried the meaning of this "upward mobility" of non-Western female agents toward an "advanced" or "developed" West (1994, 136). Deriving his central insight from Gayatri Chakravorty Spivak's analysis of *Jane Eyre* as double allegory of upward mobility for the British colonialist subject on the one hand and the bourgeois feminist critic on the other (Spivak 1985, 243–61), Robbins questions the popular success of stories by Kincaid and Mukherjee that "seem to flatter the metropolis as inevitable destination and saving source of freedom and happiness" (137): "In a sort of female Naipaulism, the personal trajectory from the Caribbean to the metropolis becomes paradigmatic of a Hegelian passage from primitive unselfconscious barbarism to universal civilization, thus relegating those who remain behind to a familiar sort of colonial statis and inferiority" (137).

Japan the International Robbins's (1994) argument raises important questions about the scope of Japanese women's agency, particularly sexual agency, within the postcolonial power relations that prevail between Japan and its various Western Others. Japan's prodigious economic resources have created a level of financial privilege obtained by Japanese women that enables them to command a wide range of cosmopolitan experiences, from traveling freely abroad as well-heeled tourists to conducting professional lives in New York, Paris, and Hong Kong. This emergent Japanese female cosmopolitanism is intimately linked to the flows of transnational capital, through global media, foreign tourism, and multinational job markets, in which highly educated middle-class Japanese women are not entirely marginalized but at times ambiguously empowered to imagine, and pursue, their own self-interest beyond Japan's borders. Scholarship that makes cosmopolitan Japanese women merely victims of serial patriarchies cannot account for the movements of this educated, elite or potentially elite, upwardly mobile group as they negotiate systems of education, employment, and social life in the West as well as Japan. Although they share with other globally mobile women experiences of discrimination and oppression in their homeland, it is not economic desperation that drives Japanese women overseas. Japanese women have the luxury of "choosing exile," if they so desire, for reasons that have less to do with immediate financial need than with lifestyle priorities. Yet economic privilege by no means translates simply into racial and gender privilege. As will be apparent in the pages that follow, Japanese women's efforts to include themselves in the class of transnational technocrats through a painstakingly acquired decontextualized cultural knowledge are not entirely successful; they are continually being put back in "their place" by continuing racial and gender hierarchies that serve to marginalize them even (or especially) in the internationalist venues they idealize. They must function in relation to a West that, as Naoki Sakai has written, is "an ambiguous and ubiquitous presence of a certain global domination" (1997, 61).

Yet this experience of marginalization too is not the final word. Japanese women rejecting Japan according to a logic of internationalist progress are often welcomed in the United States and other Western countries as ideal embodiments of an already feminized Japan (Simpson 1994), evidence of the universal desirability of the West over the Orient, legitimators of Western female feminism and Western male "sensitivity," and multicultural heroines in a Benetton era that sees white male–women of color romance and marriage as the increasingly valorized enactment of interracial harmony (*Pocahontas*), cultural diversity (cf. *The Joy Luck Club*), and economic alliance (see Figure 1). Japanese women in the West enjoy a precarious and ambivalent access to job opportunities and social networks through a newly reworked subject position as "Oriental woman," global signifier of exoticism and allure that has more recently evolved to include a new class-status prestige. Alan Rifkin's notorious piece in *Buzz* from 1993, "Asian Women, L.A. Men," is a paean to the Asian woman in Los Angeles as not just Hollywood trophy date but potential player sought out by the major studios. At a time when no newscast is complete without an Asian female coanchor, the Asian American women's magazine *Face* found it necessary to explain to its readers "Why White Men Love Us."

That the effects of this desirability are not entirely salutary should be obvious: as many Asian American feminist writers (Asian Women United of California 1989; Shah 1997; Esperitu 1997; C. Chow, 1998) have shown, objectification as the latest "hot commodity" is its own form of racism, against which Asian women struggle. However, at the same time, the state of being desirable (I return to this later) does produce its own opportunities, especially in a "multicultural" environment in the United States

He spoke *English.*
She spoke Japanese.
But the connection
was perfectly *clear.*

That's the power of technology behind 48% of all international calls.

Ericsson technology brings the world a little bit closer every day. Our digital switching system is the world's most successful with 128 million lines installed in 122 countries. Nearly 50% of all international calls are handled through it, as are 20% of all local calls. The same switching technology forms the platform for our mobile telephone systems, which carry 40% of all wireless calls around the world.

With 100,000 Ericsson employees developing solutions in 130 countries, we are truly a world leader in telecommunications. For further proof, just notice how clear your next overseas connection is – in any language.

That's the power of Ericsson.

ERICSSON

1. "He spoke English. She spoke Japanese. But the connection was perfectly clear."
Ericsson telecommunications advertisement. Source: *Business Week,* April 6, 1998.

2. "Relationships that endure." Citibank advertisement. Source: *Wall Street Journal*, 11 February 1997:A6.

3. Asia as the nubile young trading partner of elderly Uncle Sam, who turns his back on frumpy Europe. Editorial cartoon. Source: *Far Eastern Economic Review,* 6 June 1991:49.

in which racial acceptability and economic attainment have become intertwined. Recent advertising campaigns in the world of high finance suggest that Asian women increasingly are pictured, at least, as the anointed companions of white men's upward mobility, both the benefactees and the muses of their status cravings, the young new business partner for a multicultural world (see Figures 2 and 3). Certainly hegemonic images that collapse economic and erotic proximity to the white man do not reflect many Asian women's real economic status in the United States, but they do open up imaginative possibilities.

This becomes particularly apparent when the experiences of transmigrant Japanese women are juxtaposed with those of Japanese men. For if Japanese men still dominate the highest echelons of Japanese business investment in the United States, in the American *erotic* economy they are effortlessly vanquished by Japanese women. Once feared as too-successful corporate warriors, now dismissed as the ridiculous agents of a failed economic revolution, subsumed under long-standing racial stereotypes of Asian male emasculation, and anomalous figures within the current multicultural paradigm that seems determined to include every racial/gender group *except* Asian men (see Figure 4), Japanese men are effectively humbled through women's comparative ease of assimilation. The emasculated position of Japanese men in the United States is embedded in a Japanese aphorism about the U.S. Green Card: "To get the Green Card, women marry, men cook [gurīn kādo wo toru ni wa, onna wa kekkon, otoko wa kokku]." If both "options" here embed Japanese in a service economy to the white patriarchal state, again women at least achieve the fraught privilege of proximity.

This hierarchy is reaffirmed when women come to Western countries bearing a message of rejection of Japanese men. The internationalist narrative is characterized by a hyperbolic ridicule of Japanese men's "faults" in comparison with Western men. This repudiation of Japanese patriarchy and the (straw) figure of the Japanese man in turn produces its own politics of pleasure for a Western audience, always receptive to substantiation of the myth of the Oriental man as failure. *Women on the Verge* quotes extensively from such female discourses of repudiation of the Japanese man, as they are foundational to women's internationalist impulses. However, I ask the reader to remember that when I quote such narratives of ridicule, I am doing so not to record some transcendent "truth" about Japanese men, but to frame the narratives as one manifestation of the larger, globally circulating Orientalist discourse of masculinity that places the Japanese/Oriental man as the impotent opposite to the white man as racial icon. This discourse has been in place for two centuries and has dominated postwar U.S.–Japan relations in particular.

Meanwhile, this female ease of assimilation still is not the final word because women's investments in the West are not static but constantly shifting; many women returning home, by choice or not, come to reject blanket affiliations with the West, enunciating in some cases a renewed nationalistic identification with the Japanese state, and in other cases a vision of hybrid identity. Stuart Hall has written that the diasporic are always "producing themselves anew and differently . . . the products of several interlocking histories and cultures, belonging at the same time to several 'homes'—and thus to no one particular home" (1993, 362). Women are not inert subjects simply interpellated by the forces of global capital: they have agency, and they make choices over time. In practice, this means moving from various degrees of allegiance to the West to more skeptical

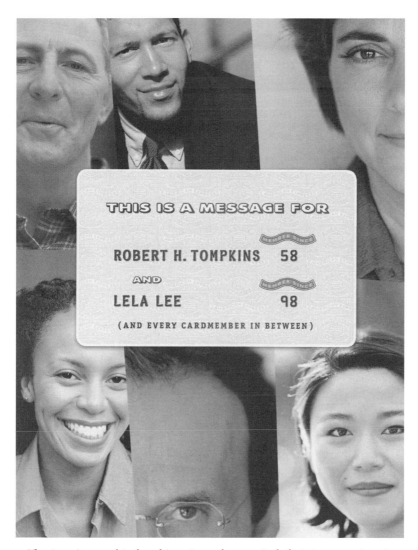

THIS IS A MESSAGE FOR

ROBERT H. TOMPKINS   58

AND

LELA LEE   98

(AND EVERY CARDMEMBER IN BETWEEN)

4. The American multicultural imaginary does not include Asian men. American Express advertisement. Source: *Harper's*, December 1998.

and ambiguous forms of resistance and accommodation to the claims of both the West and Japan on their bodies and minds. Theirs is a struggle toward finding a home, even if an untenable one.

There is a feminist imperative to honor the agency of internationalist Japanese women without losing sight of the overdetermined global conditions in which they act. In Hall's words, identity is "a 'production' which is never complete, always in process, and always constituted within, not outside, representation" (1994, 392). That is, agency is never pure or unmediated by power. This is particularly so under conditions of globalization. Marcus has observed that ethnographic studies of complex global-local processes "may require accounts of agency that are alien, and even repugnant, to anthropology's attachment to conditions of everyday life and the predicaments of particular human subjects so located" (1995, 424). I read Marcus as referring here in part to the tension between the humanist concerns of traditional anthropology (and feminism) and the antihumanist, deconstructive foundations of much contemporary cultural studies work, which replace assumptions of individual will with an insistence of subjectivities of persons as "the loci in which discourses intersect" (Godzich 1993, xiv). Yet I believe that these two positions do not necessarily have to be seen as entirely opposed. Particularly when feminist concerns come into play, critics often find themselves "in the paradoxical position of deploying . . . antihumanist discourse for humanist ends" (Kondo 1990, 301). Spivak famously summarized the deconstructive position as "saying an impossible no to a structure that one critiques, yet inhabits intimately" (1990b, 28). There is space for oppositionality here, if only of the impossible kind. If individual narratives "can be seen as both expressive and ideological in nature" (Visweswaran 1994, 40), then, as Kondo writes eloquently, "words like 'resistance' and 'accommodation' truly seem inadequate . . . [and] apparent resistance is constantly mitigated by collusion and compromise at different levels of consciousness, just as accommodation may have unexpectedly subversive effects" (1990, 299).

Thus, in *Women on the Verge* I sketch the trajectories of internationalist Japanese women within the multiple and scattered hegemonies of modern and postmodern economic, political, and ideological forces. Put another way, I wish to place their achievements and their dilemmas in a postcolonial perspective: privileged and yet subaltern, dependent on discourses of modernity that posit universal and transcendent truths, yet marginalized in their efforts to participate in these truths. The postcolonial optic, as Mary Louise Pratt (2000) has phrased it, is one that permits us to attend to the continuing adjustments and permutations of colonial power relations in the contemporary era; it requires us to analyze the ways that the power differentials embedded in older colonial projects still exert their effects even when the formal colonial relationship is gone. That Japan was never formally colonized by the West does not mean that it was free from the pull of Western imperialism as "ideological domination" (R. Chow 1993, 8). That Japan was also a colonial power in its own right, and is today an embattled economic power, makes it doubly imperative to see it as an idiosyncratic exemplar of the postcolonial dilemma, the "almost white but not quite" moment described by Homi Bhabha (1994) as the privilege and pathos of the elite postcolonial subject.

Thus, I contextualize women's discourses of Japan-West, tradition-modernity, oppression-emancipation within globally enacted hierarchies that permit some transnational subjects to gain privilege through certain strategic allegiances, while excluding others who resist (or are resisted by) them. I suggest that a careful attention to the discursive strategies that surround women's allegiance to an internationalist modernity reveals the increasingly complicated terrain of identity formation in transnationalized capitalist regimes among cosmopolitan, or would-be cosmopolitan, subjects. Women's claims to internationalist identity not only challenge patriarchal nationalism in Japan (and they do challenge it by giving women an unprecedented alternative to established female life courses), they implicate internationalized Japanese women in eroticized Western agendas of modernity and universalism and the emergence of a global cosmopolitan class that contains its own hierarchies of race, gender, and capital. Any Japanese female adoption of the universalizing claims of Western modernity both subverts and reinforces that universalism and the continuing Western hegemony that it serves. Internationalist Japanese women, perhaps more than any other transnationally mobile group, demonstrate the ambiguous and contradictory ways in which intersecting vectors of (domestic) economic disenfranchisement and (global) economic privilege, gendered discrimination and gendered opportunity, racial belonging and racial exclusions, sexual objectification and erotic desire operate simultaneously in systems of scattered hegemonies.

Questions of Methods and the Field In Japanese, the topic of this work can be encapsulated in a single term, *akogare,* which, translated variously as longing, desire, or idealization, is the word most often used both among and about women in Japan to describe women's feelings about the West. To have akogare (to *akogareru*) is to long for something that is unattainable. "Seiyō/Amerika ni akogare ga atta" (I had a longing for the West/America) was the phrase with which most women's narratives began. Akogare exemplifies the relations of teacher-student, dominant-subordinate that have characterized Western-Japanese interactions in the modern era: the West is the desired, always unattainable, Other. Of course, Akogare for the West, and the attitude of Japanese inferiority it perpetuates come in for a great deal of criticism in Japan, not just from right-wing nationalists but from many thoughtful people and, as I show, from internationalist women themselves. Indeed, akogare is always projected outward, away from the present self, from men onto women, from older women onto younger, and from younger women onto their even younger former selves. However, despite its disavowal—or because of it—akogare is the foundational premise of the internationalist narrative. If denial of akogare is where most internationalist narratives end, it follows that akogare, acknowledged or not, is where they begin.

What is suggestive about akogare is that it is a rather precise gloss, in an idiomatic register, of the term "desire" in Lacanian usage. Desire here, as Anne Allison explains, "is conditioned and structured by the very impossibility of attaining what one wishes for" (2000, 124). In Lacanian thought, desire arises from lack and finds expression in the fetish. The fetish substitutes for the thing that is desired but is impossible to obtain. Slavoj Žižek (1989) has shown the ways that the capitalist imaginary creates the hatching ground of commodity desire in late capitalist nations: docile postideological capitalist subjects fill their chronic sense of lack with consumption, and the economy functions to sell goods to these subjects through the phantasmatic promise of (phallic) fulfillment.

These kinds of desire and imagination, mediated by an impersonal market, are not quantifiable or reducible to the standard ethnographic legitimizing techniques. They float in space, alight unexpectedly, and resist institutionalization; above all, they function as much in their disavowal and denial as in their expression. "The terms of the negotiation between imagined lives and deterritorialized worlds are complex," Appadurai writes, "and they surely cannot be captured by the localizing strategies of traditional ethnography alone" (1996, 52). The "local," that is, no longer encompasses the anthropological "real."

How, then, do we write an ethnography of desire as a "social practice," of the lived enactments of imagination? Appadurai proposes a "cosmopolitan" ethnography that draws from cultural studies work on transnational media and literature as sites of self-making and resistance (51). Whereas anthropologists such as Nonini and Ong have rejected cultural studies approaches, which they claim have "diluted" ethnography by treating transnationalism as "a set of abstracted, dematerialized cultural flows" (1997, 13), I suggest that the textual attentiveness of cultural studies is indispensable for anthropology precisely because it expands anthropology's scope to include a greater attention to locally and/or globally circulating media imagery as inscription of deterritorialized regimes of fantasy and desire. These approaches enable us to see what Nonini, citing Deleuze and Guattari (1983), has called "the existence of collective imaginaries, or utopian fantasy-scripts for repertoires of practices: products of the imagination that transcend delimited spaces and the localizations of bodies by regimes of truth and power associated with these spaces" (Nonini 1997, 205–6).

To effect an ethnography of desire and imagination, an ethnography of akogare, I have based my analysis not in a spatially defined community— the mainstay of older anthropological inquiry—but rather in a set of discourses as they are enunciated across individual women and the people and media who observe, critique, represent, and market (to) them. *Women on the Verge* attends to women's own words, but depends equally on other dispersed sources, especially a genre of Japanese autobiographical writing and video, produced by so-called ordinary women for a female audience, about the promises and provocations of the West. It attends also to local and global images of Westernness and whiteness that work through larger media as a "pull" on women's imaginations. I show the ways that both women's autobiographical texts and local and global media forms all become the means through which knowledge about the West as site of women's deliverance is created, circulated, and eventually reproduced. As such, they cannot be distinguished from informants' words as sites of authoritative meaning; meaning here is dispersed, contingent. As I hope is apparent by now, there is no privileged "local" where "the truth about the West" resides.

This question of method raises the issue of normativity. I have been told that the actions of a small group of internationalized career women cannot be considered representative of "Japanese women" in general, or of Japan as a "culture." If the internationalist career women this book treats do, as I have written, constitute a minority of Japanese women, I believe that efforts to minimize their significance are problematic on several counts.

In the first place, as I wrote earlier, global conditions of deterritorialization have altered the subjectivity of even those people who remain "in familiar and ancestral places" (Gupta and Ferguson 1997b, 38). I argue that the belief that "there is no sexism in America" fundamentally shifts, even for women who do not leave Japan, their understandings of and responses to gender hierarchies at home. The West becomes not so much a source of critical comparative perspective (which can then be evaluated for its "accuracy," for example) as an imaginative simulacrum infinitely available for the production of discourses that motivate and explain resistance or accommodation.

More important, however, in *Women on the Verge* I wish to challenge the very notion of "representativeness" and the taken-for-granted virtues of normativity as a research goal in anthropology. Liisa Malkki has remarked that the persistent anthropological bias toward the stable and the ordinary makes uniqueness in subject matter "impl[y] a diminished scholarly weight for the evidence" (1997, 89): "In the face of long traditions of studying cultures as more or less stable, durable processes of order-making that retain and reproduce their constitutive elements over time, what do we do with fleeting, transitory phenomenon that are not produced by any particular cultural grammar? What should be the status of the material that has conventionally been cleaned off a finished ethnography—the freak occurrence, the anomaly, the unrepresentative figure, the nonrepeating pattern, the impermanent and unremarked cultural form?" (87). The status of the nonnormative is particularly vexed in the context of Japan anthropology, which to a large extent has depended on, and indeed tirelessly reproduced, normative constructs of "Japanese culture." Dorinne Kondo has called this "a tired ostinato of harmony, homogeneity, lifetime employment, and flattened, unidimensional portrayals of automaton-like workers happily singing the company song" (1990, 301). It is perhaps not surprising that to anthropology has fallen the task of stubbornly indigenizing a country that, in its peculiar juxtapositioning of an insistence on cultural premodernity with a global reach of economic postmodernity, provokes, as Ivy notes, "a profound categorical uneasiness" (1995, 1). Japan is a country that can elicit considerable anxiety in the West as the only non-Western First World power and an economic leader whose populace and practices yet seem shrouded in veils of "Oriental" inscrutability. As Allison has observed, this peculiarity extends to Japan's position in the academy; she remarks that Japan "lacks the scholarly prestige of cultures such as India and China for reasons not altogether clear . . . and sits uneasily in the academic imagination" (2000, 8). It seems that many anthropologists of Japan, anxious to assert the legitimacy of their fieldwork site according to older primitivist standards of the discipline, persist in taking the exotic angle, even finding premodern holdovers of village communitas, for example, in the practices of the multinational corporation. Analysis too often falls back on the tired *uchi-soto* (inside-outside) binary as all-purpose explanatory trope.

It seems that one ideological agenda behind such constructions of a bounded, spatially and temporally separate Japanese "culture" is undoubtedly to control the anxiety that Japan provokes as the Other that is not Other enough. A critical anthropology, by contrast, will, as Ivy suggests, reject the "fetishized simplicities of sheer cultural relativism" (1995, 8) and begin from the "dialectically entwined status of the United States (as the paradigm of the West) and Japan as national-cultural imaginaries" (3).

It is for this reason that my analysis resists the "domestication" argument that has prevailed in Japan studies, which posits that Japanese are never subject to cultural imperialism because they transform foreign objects and concepts (such as Disneyland, for example) into entirely Japanese, and hence benign, cultural forms. Such a perspective not only incarcerates Japanese in the safely exotic cultural space of Japan, eliding possibilities of mobility, but it also leaves intact the sanctity of the national/cultural border and presupposes a simple equivalence between nations and cultures that requires only an easy translation to render mutually intelligible. It posits a simplistic local or domestic agency that is entirely independent of histories of mutual enmeshment at ideological, as well as political and economic, levels.

Instead, I begin from the idea that the status of Japan as sovereign space is a construct dependent on intertwined histories of modernity. As Sakai argues, the very distinction between Japan and the foreign is one "whose relevance should be nil outside the contexts of the modern and present time" (1997, 46). That is to say, "Japan" itself is accorded ontological facticity, by both Japanese and Westerners, through its modern juxtaposition with the "outside." As Ivy writes, "Japan is literally unimaginable outside its positioning vis-à-vis the West" (1995, 4). This is what Sakai calls the schema of cofiguration:

> By the schema of cofiguration, I want to point out the essentially "imaginary" nature of the comparative framework of Japan and the West, since the figure in cofiguration is imaginary in the sense that it is a sensible image on the one hand, and practical in its ability to evoke one to act toward the future on the other. The figure invokes imagination by which desire for identity is produced, and is the central issue for the logic of imagination. . . . In the desire to want to know "Japanese thought," not only Japan but also the West has to be figured out: Japan and the West have to be cofigured. The desire to identify either with Japan or the West is, therefore, invariably a mimetic one, so that the insistence on Japan's originality, for instance, would have to be mediated by the mimetic desire for the West. (52)

We are returned again to the constitutive power of the imagination, as well as to its imbrication in global relations of power through mimetic desire. Cultural normativity, under these conditions, is a false positivism. What is needed is a cosmopolitan ethnography that accounts for spaces of agency and identity within *cofigured* regimes of truth.

Within the space of this particular ethnography it bears noting that internationalist Japanese women's knowledge about the West came not only from transnational media and women's own various forms of cosmopolitan experience, but also from the (American) anthropologist herself. That is to say, I became a medium of informants' knowledge about the West and the United States. The ethnographer's praxis, and presence, is another element of deterritorialization. If knowledge is no longer divided between here and there, between the modern West and the native Other, but rather consists of mutually owned and contested understandings, in this case about the place whence the ethnographer comes, then distinctions between the foreign and the native fall away: the ethnographer becomes a "native," and the informant her interlocutor. I do not of course mean to situate myself as a "native anthropologist" in the sense, so eloquently described by others (Abu-Lughod 1991; Daniel 1984; Kondo 1990; Narayan 1993; Visweswaran 1994), of an ethnographer who shares a national or ethnic identity with his or her informants. Rather, I mean to query the role of the Western ethnographer as native of a globally circulating West, a West that, in Ashis Nandy's evocative phrase, "is now everywhere" (1983, xi).

Yet the two positions are not entirely unrelated. As Gupta and Ferguson write of the "minorities, postcolonials, and 'halfies' for whom the anthropological project is not an exploration of Otherness," there is thrust on them "the responsibility of speaking their identity, thus inadvertently forcing them into the prison-house of essentialism" (1997b, 17). Throughout this particular fieldwork project, I was called on as a native to field questions and assertions about my native land; indeed, I was valued as a native informant who could confirm or refute women's understandings of the West/United States and its promised opportunities. As I discuss in the conclusion, my departures from, and failures in, this role of spokesperson for America were not entirely welcomed. At the same time, when I returned home and presented my research findings to American audiences, I again fielded assertions about Japan's egregious "sexism" that "forces talented women abroad." Because my research topic itself—Japanese women who reject Japan—seems to confirm some of the United States' most intractable stereotypes about Japan's "backwardness" in its treatment of women, I found myself in a painful spot, inadvertently bolstering (at least for inattentive audiences) precisely the West-centric discourses I was concerned to critique.

This was not all. My early work on the "yellow cabs" (a population of young women, discussed in chapter 3, who pursued short-term affairs with foreign men in places like Hawai'i and New York City during the late 1980s and early 1990s) continues to haunt me, carrying on an independent life of its own in the form of my published articles and conference abstracts that seem to float in perpetuity on the Internet. A result has been that since my earliest days working on the topic I have been approached, often over e-mail, by a series of white men apparently seeking to confess the sordid details of their intimacies with various Japanese women, perhaps in the hope that I can offer them some kind of expiation for the sin of cheap sex, or at least a therapeutic ear. Here too my American identity seems to have accorded me the role of mother confessor to these tortured souls: "Being that you are American I will be very direct," begins one e-mail. To say that I dislike this role would be an understatement. This is a field from which I cannot seem to escape.

And so both in Japan and at home I find I am continually fielding different agendas that are motivated by my research and my identity, as these intersect. I would like to propose, invoking a neologism, that more and more ethnographers are required to "field" multiple agendas in this way. Gupta and Ferguson (1997b) and many others have interrogated the new meanings of "the field" in anthropology under conditions of deterritorialization. They propose "to redefine the fieldwork 'trademark' not with a time-honored commitment to the *local* but with an attentiveness to social, cultural, and political *location* and a willingness to work self-consciously at shifting, or realigning, our own location while building epistemological and political links with other locations" (5). They call this practice "location-work." I propose that what location-work is to anthropology, fielding, the verb, is to ethnography, especially ethnographies of desire, imagination, and mutual imbrication, when the field travels with the ethnographer and is mediated by his or her work, speech, presence, and praxis. Gupta and Ferguson imagine the location-work of anthropological knowledge as a "form of situated intervention" (38). I can think of no better vision for anthropology. My hope for *Women on the Verge* is that it may serve as its own form of situated intervention in a variety of fields, querying American pieties of multiculturalism and diversity and deflecting self-serving Western perceptions of contemporary Japan and Japanese women from their well-worn tracks and teleologies into a more self-questioning, critically alert understanding.

Organization of the Book In chapter 1 I sketch the genealogy of women's akogare by inquiring into the antecedents of internationalism from the mid–nineteenth century through the postwar U.S. Occupation of Japan. Beginning with Tsuda Umeko, the first government-sponsored female study-abroad student, continuing through wartime female internationalist activists and writers, and ending with Occupation and immediate postwar women leaders and intellectuals, I trace the emergence of a discourse of women's "deliverance," at the hands of the United States, from what women insisted were the odious and intolerable oppressions of the patriarchal Japanese family system. I explore the ways women's narratives of Western rescue reflect back simultaneous American understandings of the Japanese woman as "she-who-must-be-saved" (T. Yamamoto 1999, 24), and constitute this rescue as an eroticized project authorized by white American men as lovers/husbands.

In chapter 2 I turn to the contemporary versions of women's gendered critique and their intensifying public search for alternative lifestyles (*ikikata*) that reference a Western-derived "individualism" (*ko toshite no ikikata*) as emancipatory project. Sketching the mechanisms by which women pursue access to the West, I trace the narratives of internationalism that internationally active Japanese women use to justify their turn abroad, and the meaning of the trope of the "new self" (*atarashii jibun*) as eroticized signifier of transformation and redemption.

Chapter 3 specifically takes up the erotic subtext of internationalist discourse in the present day, inquiring into the fetishization of the white man as signifier of social upward mobility in three women's texts spanning a twenty-year period, and also the deployment of the white man as signifier of racialized status anxiety in contemporary Japanese media culture. Throughout this discussion, my concern is with the transnational mutuality of attraction and desire, as women's narratives of the Occidental erotic meet and mediate long-standing Western male narratives of the "exotic" Oriental woman.

In chapter 4 I turn back to the difficulties women face in their efforts to carve out a life course on the borders between countries, constrained by the tangible requirements of jobs, visas, and personal commitments. I sketch women's disappointments with their position in the Japanese job market and their relations with Japanese and foreign men, and describe their efforts to negotiate continued social pressures regarding age, marital status, and proper behavior. Although many internationalist Japanese women who permanently settle in Japan claim to make, over time, a kind of delicate peace with that country, enunciating a hybrid identity that challenges both Japanese nativist identity claims and Western assimilationist impulses, I argue that this "peaceful resolution" forecloses possibilities for widespread social change, especially in its rejection of internationalist alliances with feminist activist movements in Japan or abroad.

The conclusion interrogates internationalism's dependency on Western masculinist authorizing mechanisms and enmeshment in Western rhetorical trajectories about multiculturalism, diversity, and inclusiveness. I explore the profoundly compromised nature of any cosmopolitan efforts toward liberation that operate through a (re)inscription of a unilinear time line of modernity that originates and ends in the West. Querying my own role in mediating Japanese and American understandings of Japanese women's place in an American assimilationist telos, I consider the work of ethnographers in fielding multiple and contradictory agendas in the pursuit of a deterritorialized anthropology.

1 ≋ The Promised Land:

A Genealogy of Female Internationalism

In the history of Japan's official contact with the West, Japanese women have played a minor role. A surprising number, however, emerge on the margins of the official encounters, serving over the past 150 years as informal, sometimes unwilling, mediators between a globally emergent Japan and the West. One of the first such women was Okichi, the "native wife" given over by the Japanese government to the first American consul to Japan, Townsend Harris, after his arrival in 1856. Over the years Okichi has been sanctified as the martyred symbol of Tokugawa-era Japan's subjection to American imperialist penetration into the Japanese national body (Leupp 1993, 10). Indeed, Okichi was not the first woman so offered; she followed in the wake of the Deshima prostitutes provided by the Tokugawa government on behalf of the Dutch traders who were confined to the island of Deshima during Japan's nearly three hundred years of Tokugawa-era isolation.[1] Okichi was in turn followed by the *rashamen,* the mistresses of foreigners in the late Tokugawa treaty ports. As John Dower writes, "Enlisting a small number of women to serve as a buffer protecting the chastity of the 'good' women of Japan was well-established policy in dealing with Western barbarians" (1999, 126).[2]

However, Japan's encounter with the West after the Meiji Restoration of 1868 yielded many more opportunities for an increasing number of merchant- and upper-class women to encounter firsthand the West and Westerners, particularly Americans, in elite educational or professional settings. These encounters profoundly altered women's own interpretations of their position in the family and nation and provided for the first time a *comparative* foundation for a gendered perspective on Japan. Such women include Tsuda Umeko (and other early female government-sponsored students to the United States), who used her American education, English fluency, and foreign contacts to found one of the first Japanese women's colleges; Sugimoto Etsu, whose lengthy residence in the United States during the last years of the Meiji era inspired an oeuvre of writing in English on the status of Japanese women; Katō (Ishimoto) Shizue, who championed Margaret Sanger and Western birth control practices in the Taishō and early Shōwa periods, and later became one of Japan's first female elected officials to the House of Representatives; hundreds of women students benefiting from a variety of public and private scholarship sources to study in the United States in the prewar and postwar periods; and finally, the thousands of women who, as employees, associates, friends, lovers, or future wives of U.S. Occupation soldiers, encountered the United States firsthand in ways that profoundly altered their own lives and helped shape the postwar relations between the two countries.

To be sure, each of these encounters occurred in its own specific historical, social, economic, political, and cultural context. Tsuda Umeko and the other early female study-abroad students were samurai daughters, educated at Japanese government expense in an effort to bring Japanese women in line with current Western standards of women's education. Katō Shizue and Sugimoto Etsu were aristocratic women who took upon themselves the role of intercultural interpreters to foster "international understanding" and Japan's democratization. The Deshima prostitutes, Okichi, and the official Occupation comfort women, by contrast, were generally lower-class women conscripted by the Japanese government as a "female floodwall" between "good" Japanese women and the invading foreign hordes (Molasky 1999, 105). Many of the other women involved, professionally or personally, with the Occupation were relatively well-educated middle-class women chosen by Westerners as the individuals most appropriate to represent their nation for rehabilitation, willing and eager democratic subjects who were singled out as the "best hope" of Japan after the treachery of Japanese men. As each encounter is situated within specific historical configurations, these women's lives certainly cannot be reduced to one homogeneous paradigm.

Yet, taken together, these and other encounters have established a precedent—certainly a varied and ambiguous precedent, but a precedent nonetheless—for women to be thought of and to think of themselves as claiming a special experience with, and intimacy with, the broadly conceived entity called "the West," and the United States in particular. The result has been the emergence of a women's discourse about the West/United States as a site of salvation from what they characterize as a feudalistic and oppressive patriarchal Japanese family system. This discourse posits an alliance between Japanese women and Westerners/Americans against both that system and the Japanese men who they suggest created it and benefit most from it. In part because of the sexual nature of the earliest contacts, this alliance between Japanese women and Westerners/Americans has had an enduring erotic tone. In turn, this perceived alliance has brought about an ambivalent response from Japanese men to the specter of the West as a threat to "traditional" Japanese gender relations and the purity of the Japanese woman/nation.

This chapter looks at each of these outcomes in the context of four different moments of encounter between Japanese women and the United States: Tsuda Umeko as Japan's first female study-abroad student; wartime female internationalism in the work of writer Mishima Sumie; the gendered politics of the U.S. Occupation period (1945–1952); and what Johnson (1988) has called the "sexual nexus" of the United States and Japan during and after the Occupation. At each point I trace women's narrativization of the United States, and by extension the West at large, as "promised land" and agent of their rescue from the oppressiveness of Japanese tradition. I will juxtapose these texts with men's writings of the time to highlight the gendered conventions of internationalism that have come to be so influential in the present day. My purpose is not to provide an exhaustive historical survey of these encounters, but to sketch a genealogy of contemporary akogare: the vocabulary of desire for the United States and the West as site of women's escape and redemption in fact and in fantasy.

Tsuda Umeko and Women's Study Abroad In December 1871, Tsuda Umeko (1864–1929), the seven-year-old daughter of former samurai and government interpreter Tsuda Sen, was sent abroad with four other girls ages eight to fifteen to be educated in America.[3] They made this journey only eleven years after the first official Japanese embassy visited the United States in 1860. They were the first—and for a long time the last—Japanese women to receive an education abroad. This extraordinary venture was the result of an initiative by a coalition of early Meiji male reformers who, anxious to appear civilized in the eyes of the rapidly encroaching Western imperialist nations, particularly the United States, felt it imperative to "raise up" Japanese womanhood in education, refinement, and social status to the level of American women. Only when Japanese women had been lifted from their condition of feudal servitude, it was widely believed, could they begin to function as wise mothers, true guardians of the home, and, thus, caretakers of the nation's future. As Rose writes, "Like many people on both sides of the globe, [progressive men] assumed that one key to Western success was its 'home life,' and that Japan's lack of progress could thus be explained in part by its low estimation of women" (1992, 8).

Tsuda and her compatriots set sail for America charged by their government and empress to acquire the attainments of American women and return to Japan prepared to serve their countrywomen as models of female achievement.[4] Two of the girls fell ill and returned home almost immediately, but Tsuda and two others remained in the United States for over ten years. Because the other two, on their return to Japan, married and became relatively cloistered wives of the aristocracy, in the end it fell to Tsuda almost single-handedly to carry out the lonely, difficult, and by then unpopular task of raising the educational standards for women in Japan. As one of her students was to write of her later, "If Miss Tsuda had wished to lead a life of ease, she could have done so. She was a beautiful young girl, and among a certain group of the upper-class Japanese there was a great tendency to admire Western things. She could have made a shining figure in their society. The two other girls who had been educated in the United States had married great military officers, one eventually becoming a princess and the other a baroness. . . . But [Tsuda] could not close her eyes to the millions and millions of Japanese women suffering because of their helplessness" (Mishima S. 1941, 65).

In the United States Tsuda was taken in to the household of Charles Lanman, the Secretary of the Japanese High Commission in Washington, D.C., and his wife Adeline. With no children of their own, the Lanmans raised Tsuda as their own daughter, and the bonds among the three were exceedingly deep, lasting until their deaths. Tsuda completed elementary, junior high, and high school in the United States and was so thoroughly absorbed into American life during the eleven years that she spent with the Lanmans (from age seven to eighteen) that she entirely lost her Japanese language ability and a large portion of her cultural knowledge of Japan. In one of her first letters to Mrs. Lanman on her return, she wrote, "Still I feel so strange, like a tree that is transplanted. . . . How much to keep of American ways, and how much to go back, and so often I wonder how I am going to do any good to my country-women, and how I must begin. The way is dark and dreary" (November 23, 1882; in Furuki et al. 1991, 18–19).

Indeed, Tsuda was to spend the seven years from her return to Japan in 1882 until her second departure for university study at Bryn Mawr in 1889 in a frustrating and nearly fruitless search for employment. The spirit of reform had died during her absence from Japan, and by the time of her return, support for women's education was scant, despite the efforts of reformers such as Fukuzawa Yukichi, inspired by the writings of J. S. Mill, to raise Japanese women's status (see Kiyooka 1988; Hoshino 1929). Retreating to a renewed emphasis on female domesticity and obedience, the government had no use for Tsuda's educational attainments, although it did not hesitate to produce her "as a convenient example of Japan's progressive attitude toward women in speeches and articles intended for Western consumption" (Sievers 1983, 13). The Ministry of Education consistently ignored her letters announcing her return (Rose 1992, 49), and she was reduced to caring for her numerous younger siblings at her family's run-down farmhouse in the countryside. Far from being encouraged to mobilize on women's behalf, she was increasingly pressured by family and friends to marry and conform to traditional expectations of womanly duties. This she opposed with all her might: "Just think how absurd it does seem," she wrote to the Lanmans, her lifelong correspondents. "It is too dreadful, but as I feel now I would not marry . . . nothing would induce me to make a regular Japanese marriage where anything but love is regarded" (January 16, 1883; in Furuki et al. 1991, 33–34). Later, harassed from all sides, she insisted in a letter to Mrs. Lanman, "Please don't write marriage to me again, not once. I am so sick of the subject, sick of hearing about it, and discussing it. *I am not going to marry unless I want to. I will* not let circumstances or anybody force me into it." Poignantly, though, she follows this with, "It is so *hard,* so very *hard,* to get along alone. Oh it is so hard to feel yourself as different from others, and be looked on with contempt" (June 6, 1883; 75).

Tsuda abhorred the social position of Japanese women, particularly married women, who could not hold property in their own name and were considered "incompetents" under the law. The prevailing views on women that she confronted were summarized by Hoshino Ai, one of her students, and the second president of Tsuda College:

> It is better for women that they should not be educated, because their lot throughout life must be in perfect obedience; and the way to salvation is only through the path of three obediences—obedience to a father when yet unmarried, to a husband when married, and to a son when widowed. What is the use of developing the mind of a woman or training the power of her judgment, when her life is to be guided at every step by a man? Yet it is highly important that she should be morally trained, so that she be always gentle and chaste, never giving way to passion inconvenient to others, nor questioning the authority of her elders. For her no religion is necessary, because her husband is her sole heaven, and in serving him and his lies her whole duty. (1929, 215)

"My heart goes out to Japanese women," Tsuda wrote to Adeline Lanman only a few months after arriving, "and I burn with indignation at their position, while I blame them too. . . . Oh, Mrs. Lanman, you can not know how I feel!! No one can understand, either in America or here. . . . Change seems so utterly impossible. It is so rooted and ground into them" (May 23, 1883; in Furuki et al. 1991, 69).

As a result of these disillusionments, Tsuda became more than ever convinced of the superiority of women's status in the United States. She wrote within a few months to the Lanmans, "If every woman in America is not thankful for her lot, she is ungrateful to God. Thankful for her strong mind, ideas, strength of decision, and the kindnesses she receives, and her position, socially" (May 23, 1883; in Furuki et al. 1991, 70). She began to dream of opening a women's college in Japan modeled after American women's schools. Her prospects, however, were dim given her lack of financial resources and official Japan's intensifying hostility toward higher education for women. Finally she received a prestigious post as teacher at the Peeress's School, the highest-ranked girls' school in Japan, established to educate the daughters of the imperial family and the nobility. But after a time she became disillusioned with the aristocratic girls, who were trained at the school, as one former student later recalled, only to "become obedient wives, good mothers, and loyal guardians of the family system" (Ishimoto 1984, 53). When Tsuda, after four years at the Peeress's School, was given the opportunity to pursue advanced study at Bryn Mawr, she gladly departed.

This period in the United States was, by her own account, the most joyful period of Tsuda's life, surrounded as she was by serious, intellectually passionate women in a young college (founded only four years earlier) run entirely by women. Furuki writes, "It was the Americans who finally recognized and promoted Tsuda's natural talents" (1992, 124). However, when she was offered the opportunity to remain at Bryn Mawr permanently as a researcher in her newly chosen field of biology, she declined, devoting her third and final year in the United States to fundraising among American donors for her planned American-style women's college in Japan (Yamazaki Takako 1989, 39–40). This was not because a life of research in this congenial environment held no allure for her; rather, precisely because her American experience had proven so liberating, she returned determined, in the words of Hoshino Ai, "to have a college of her own where she could share with Japanese girls what she had been given so abundantly in America" (1929, 14).

After her return and resumption of teaching duties at the Peeress's School in 1892, Tsuda increasingly addressed her pleas on behalf of Japanese women to foreign audiences, convinced that both moral and financial support for her educational vision was to be forthcoming only from foreign sources. Western women and men were to be her allies in challenging the recalcitrant men of the government. There was precedence for this view, in that it had been foreign advisors such as David Murray, as early as 1872, who had first encouraged Meiji leaders to improve women's education. For decades Christian mission schools, run primarily by American missionaries and funded by donations from the United States, offered the only higher educational opportunities open to ambitious young women in Japan.[5]

In 1900, in what was a scandalous decision at the time, Tsuda finally quit the Peeress's School to open her own Girls' School of English (Joshi Eigaku Juku). Funded almost entirely from abroad, the Girls' School had fourteen students and operated from a rented house in Tokyo (Furuki 1992, 150–51). Its main aim was to prepare women to pass the government examinations for the public school English teacher's license, which Tsuda felt would accord its possessor the means to earn a living should she find herself unexpectedly widowed or abandoned. Despite inadequate facilities and a chronic lack of funds, the school prospered, and within three years it boasted an enrollment of over one hundred students (Rose 1992, 135). Ultimately, Tsuda's school was officially recognized as a *senmon gakkō* (vocational school), the highest rank open to a women's private school. Renamed Tsuda Juku (Tsuda School) in Tsuda Umeko's honor after her death in 1929, it was finally granted university status and renamed Tsuda Daigaku (Tsuda College) after the Second World War.

In the last ten years of her life, Tsuda was beset with illness that left her an invalid; she suffered as well from family and money worries. Increasingly isolated from her students and their turbulent Taishō-era political activism (several of her students became leaders in the radical Seitōsha [Bluestockings] and women's suffrage movements and in the newly revitalized women's movements after World War II), she died perhaps without realizing the true impact that her Meiji-era vision of women's education was to have on the course of Japanese women's history. It is true that Tsuda's vision for women was entirely domestic. In her writings of this period, including *Japanese Girls and Women* (1902) (cowritten with Alice Bacon in 1891),[6] she always insisted that the home must remain woman's "paramount sphere" (Tsuda 1984, 150). Closely modeled on the nineteenth-century European and American concept of the "angel of the hearth," Tsuda's vision for women's education was above all to make a woman an intelligent helpmeet to her husband, wise mother to her children, and authority within the home:[7] "Can it be said that our women are capable of meeting the problems of the day; that they have the power to restrain the men as the American women do in keeping up the standards of morality and purity; that they can make the home the restful heaven it should be away from the world's temptations? Can they give that influence for good, that broad sympathy and help that a man has a right to demand from his wife, a help so much higher than the mere supplying of his physical needs?" (73). Tsuda viewed with dismay the emerging activist feminist groups such as the Seitōsha, and to the end of her life stressed the "ladylike" concerns of social reform and philanthropic good works as the proper sphere of the educated woman. As Rose writes, her position "was not a call for women to act; rather the plea was directed at men to provide an adequate education for their daughters. Women were simply to await this change, and after they had proved themselves fit for intellectual work, social and legal reforms would fall into place" (1992, 104).

And yet, eschewing feminist activism, Tsuda Umeko changed Japanese women's history. She did this first and foremost by introducing the "foreign path" as an alternative to a life of total dependence on men, and the foundational idea, still fervently accepted by women today, that Japanese women's independence and advancement lie in the command of the English language. Similarly, Bennett et al. argue that Tsuda was almost single-handedly responsible for the image of America as home of women's emancipation subsequently held by generations of Japanese women: "In this rosy image America was in a sense the antithesis of everything the modern Japanese woman disliked in her own country: it was the land where women have equal rights and opportunities; where marriage is based on love and free choice; where wives have an equal voice in family decisions . . . ; where women are respected" (1958, 157). In addition, Tsuda also provided one of the most important early means for women's departure from Japan. Through World War II, Tsuda Juku was one of only two major sources of Japanese women students in America, sending out fully 25 percent of all such students before 1953 (160). Tsuda students were also among the few women to receive the prestigious Japanese Ministry of Education scholarships, which numbered only one per year prior to World War II (339 n. 13).

Countless women used their Tsuda Daigaku education as a stepping stone to active participation in international circles. These included Yamakawa Kikue, a pioneering socialist feminist and first director of the Ministry of Labor Women's and Minors' Bureau; Fujita Taki, the second Bureau director; Nakane Chie, the renowned anthropologist; and Ōba Minako, one of Japan's most important postwar writers (see Ōba 1990, 245). As Ōba writes in the conclusion to her biography of Tsuda, "Each of these Tsuda graduates, as Tsuda Umeko's descendent [kōshin], has carried on the will of the

Founder and has led women into the sunlight. . . . [But] how many un-known Tsuda students branched out from the seed Tsuda Umeko planted, and secretly flowered forth, planting seeds of their own?" (245–46).

Tsuda herself was the model for subsequent generations of Japanese female study-abroad students, and her life exemplified with remarkable precision the themes that emerge again and again in the writings of Japanese women who turn to the West in their rebellion against "feudal" traditions in Japan. Although Tsuda did not choose her original encounter with the United States (and in this differs importantly from all of the women to follow), she quickly embraced it as the standard against which Japan must be judged. She returned from her Western sojourn only to discover her newfound expertise unwanted and unvalued by her countrymen, who instead pressured her incessantly to marry and chastised her "foreign" and "un-Japanese" ways. Lonely and despondent much of the time, she eventually succeeded in finding an outlet for her skills and ambition, but only at an enormous emotional and physical cost. To the end she rejected feminism and any kind of "unfeminine" competition against men, but she was committed to women's individual development and personhood. As we shall see, the defense of individualism and women's personhood, paired with a rejection of feminist activism, has remained the most persistent characteristic of women's internationalism since Tsuda's day.

Tsuda's vision of the United States as women's ally and haven was revolutionary too in the degree to which it flew against prevailing male views of her time. Japanese men who traveled to the West in the late Tokugawa and early Meiji periods did not view the position of Western women with favor. Indeed, as we can see in the candid diary writings of the samurai members of the first Japanese embassy to the United States in 1860, some men were dismayed at what they saw as the forwardness and "shamelessness" of American women. Many responded with nothing short of horror to the spectacle of bare-shouldered upper-class wives and daughters cavorting with men at official balls held in the embassy's honor. "Stupid gullible women!" one spat out in his diary (in Miyoshi 1979, 74); others described them as "unattractive," "noisy," and "indecent." American chivalrous customs toward women were the object of the greatest bewilderment and contempt. As Miyoshi summarizes, "Why women, being frail-bodied and frailer-headed, should assert themselves and men concede to their superior air is a question that the Japanese men could not at all comprehend then" (76).[8] Sharon Sievers concludes that "no Japanese in 1860 suggested that Japan had something to gain by 'elevating' the status of women after the American model" (1983, 2).

In contrast, Tsuda's vision of an emancipatory America, accessible through the means of study abroad, had enormous and enduring appeal for educated women of the middle and upper classes in Japan and soon came to encompass Western countries as a whole. Perhaps inspired by Tsuda's example and her early writings, seventeen-year-old writer Kimura Akebono published in 1889 a best-selling novella, serialized in the *Yomiuri Shimbun*, entitled *Mirror of Womanhood* (Fujo no kagami). It told the tale of a brilliant and beautiful young Japanese woman who, denied educational opportunities in Japan, graduates from Newnham College for women at Cambridge University, travels to New York, where she alleviates poverty through the introduction of silk production, and "returns triumphantly to Japan, where she establishes a textile factory that employs impoverished women" (Rose 1992, 98; see also Kimura 1966, 1988a, 1988b). Rose observes that this "preposterous" yet phenomenally popular plot "tapped a profound desire," confirming to women readers that "only outside Japan . . . could [a woman] claim freedom of action and thereby fulfill her innate excellence" (98). It seems *Mirror of Womanhood* was the vicarious fulfillment of its author's own thwarted ambition to study abroad, for although Kimura apparently excelled in foreign languages, her entrepreneur father forced her to work as a cashier in one of his chain of restaurants (Fukutani 1966, 440).[9] As we shall see, *Mirror of Womanhood* is a fictional precursor to the sustained genre of women's internationalist writing that, in both English and Japanese, has continued unabated to the present.

The Luminous World: America in Wartime Female Internationalism
Tsuda Umeko's practice of challenging intensifying nationalist and militarist repression of women through appeals in English to an overseas readership flourished among internationalist women activists and writers through the end of World War II. Christian author Sugimoto Etsu (*A Daughter of the Samurai*, 1926), birth control activist and politician Katō Shizue (*Facing Two Ways: The Story of My Life*, 1935, published under her former married name, Ishimoto), Christian educator Kawai Michi (*My

Lantern, 1939), novelist and pacifist Ishigaki Ayako (*Restless Wave*, 1940, writing under the pen name Haru Matsu), and journalist Mishima Sumie (*My Narrow Isle*, 1941) all wrote autobiographies in English to both gain a hearing with overseas audiences and in some cases raise money for their causes. They used their writings to contrast the freedom the authors had experienced studying and working in the United States with the repression and misery suffered by Japanese women under feudalistic, and increasingly militaristic, Japanese family structures.

In this section I turn my attention to *My Narrow Isle: The Story of a Modern Woman in Japan* (1941), a book of memoirs in English by Mishima Sumie, a former student of Tsuda Umeko. Mishima had been born in the early 1890s to an American-educated university professor and a Christian mission school–educated mother. When her fortunes declined in later life she turned to writing in English for sale in the United States to earn money in American currency. In her condition of educated poverty, Mishima consciously sought to represent the voices and yearnings of "ordinary" Japanese women under the conditions of Japanese militarism and patriarchy. In *My Narrow Isle* she reveals both the continuing influence of Tsuda on subsequent generations of internationalist women and the increasingly fantasylike image of America and the West as a whole (they are described in various places as "a luminous world," "a land of romance," "a fairyland," and "heaven on earth")—as well as their fetishization in the figure of the white man—that prevailed among internationalist women with overseas experience now struggling against the shrinking horizons (for women) of wartime Japan.

Until the death of her father, Mishima was raised in a liberal atmosphere of Christian humanism and reform that extended to the position of women and education of daughters. She writes in her memoirs, "As long as father lived and mother and children could live their own new way under his protection with no fetters of the old customs forced on their life, ours was one of the happiest homes on earth" (1941, 19). Mishima's father died young, however, and his wife and children were reduced to poverty and dependence on the beneficence of the wealthy but traditional "main house," whose members quickly imposed on them the expectations of a feudal family. As Mishima wrote of the eldest aunt with whom they lived for a period, "Her outlook on the world was thoroughly feudal, in which there was no such idea as individual worth, family honor being all important" (21). Forced to eat only cold rice (the fresh warm rice being reserved for the male family members only, regardless of the family's wealth) and to cook, clean, and sew for the household, Mishima, against her will, was trained for a traditional marriage: "I had been a very social and talkative child, but now I became thoughtful, timid, and extremely nervous." She began to rebel inwardly against these expectations, coming to believe that a profession and economic independence were "the key to my liberation from that sort of 'humiliating life.'" She writes, "I would build a life for myself where I had neither to eat smelly cold rice nor wait on boring guests for hours on end" (49). Mishima determined to become a teacher.

Mishima's mother quietly prevailed on unwilling elder relatives to allow Mishima to pursue further schooling, and with her own family money sent her to Tsuda College. When her mother died, however, and Mishima neared the completion of her studies, the relatives began pressuring Mishima to marry. In revolt, Mishima determined to study in America. Having heard constantly of the kindness and generosity of American teachers from her parents (86), she was convinced that the West was "a land of romance, a land of all good things to be desired on earth" (86). She writes, "To me, as to most of the Japanese people of the time, the West was a luminous world where we could hardly distinguish Europe from America and the different nations in them" (87). Even lacking the money to support her planned studies, to Mishima going to America seemed "almost like going to a fairyland," and she determined to work her way through university if necessary: "It was far better to be a factory girl or even a housemaid in America than a slave-wife in Japan!" (89). Regarding an arranged marriage proposal, she responded, "Being fed on Western romances and new Japanese stories of idealized personal freedom, that sort of matter-of-fact marriage was repugnant to me. . . . This was what happened in Japan, I thought angrily, while in America no girl was forced to marry a man whom she could not love!" (88). Finally her family provided just enough money to allow her, with a scholarship, to study at Wellesley for five years. This was not an altruistic decision; the relatives determined that with Mishima rapidly proving herself "unmarriageable," at least a foreign education would yield tangible returns on their investment in the form of income after her return to Japan.

Once at Wellesley, Mishima's idealization of America intensified: "Wellesley seemed to me then a veritable heaven on earth . . . [and] the social life around me seemed a succession of gorgeous apparitions which I beheld wonder-struck" (104). It is true that she became disillusioned with what she considered the excessive rationalism of Western education, based on distrust of authority and tradition. She observed that "many Orientals have their high ideal of the Occident shattered by the very intellectualism of the education they received in the West . . . [and] baffled by the rationalism of the West, come home downright nationalists and demagogues for 'Orientalism'" (117–18). Mishima argued that Japanese men abroad were particularly prone to this "reorientalization." Especially when it came to the question of women's status, she wrote, "Many Japanese, particularly Japanese men, come home covered with hard shells of reactionism and extoll the 'superior spiritual civilization' of their country and in particular the 'peerless self-sacrificing spirit' of their women" (118). Mishima, however, took a different path, responding to her disappointment with a renewed belief in "Western humanism": "I had at last learned to see the best and noblest side of the West—a wide vision of humanism possible only to a race who had conquered the world with their moral courage, science, and material resources" (119).

Like Tsuda Umeko before her, Mishima was struck by American women: "Nothing was more marvelous than these educated women of America, for they assured me of great possibilities for women's intellect and spiritual power" (126). But she was frankly in thrall to American men. Practically her first comment on her arrival was about the chivalrousness of American men she encountered in the street: "In a distracted state of mind, I dropped all sorts of things in the street—handbag, gloves, hat, umbrella . . .—but there was always some American gentleman appearing and picking them up for me. . . . [My fellow students and I] were overwhelmed by the masculine courtesy shown in this country" (100). Later, Mishima's romantic attraction to American men intensified, as she reveals in the following account of a dance at Wellesley:

I was completely flustered and was very grateful to these courteous and handsome Albany boys who so kindly led me in spite of my clumsy following in cumbrous kimono and heavy silk and felt sandals. What a lovely thing, I thought, that boys and girls came to know each other this way, instead of as in Japan men and women stealthily looking at each other and girls being taught that it was the most unwomanly and irredeemable crime to fall in love with a man. I was charmed by the courtesy of American boys and particularly by their beautiful table manners. In Japan, men's eating was a sheer conviviality which was thought to be the better expressed when one made a noise in the mouth and threw bones on the table. Japanese women dislike such bad masculine manners, but feminine thought was completely ignored in the social life of Japan, where women had no choice of men.

"It was entirely natural," Mishima concluded, "that I was more attracted by American than Japanese boys" (128–29).

Finally, however, the day came when Mishima had to return to Japan. Dismayed at the prospect of leaving her friends and the life she delighted in, she was nevertheless optimistic: "I was going home as a grand 'returner from the West,' to do a great deal for my country and for better international understanding!" (140). As she poignantly wrote later, she was convinced that "my money, youth, relatives' kind care—the loss of all these seemed nothing compared with the wonderful social and economic advantages that would be awaiting me" (155). However, forty years after Tsuda Umeko returned from her epochal study abroad in the United States, her student Mishima was to find, in the late 1920s, little changed for women returning from overseas: "I was bitterly disappointed when I saw that the world around me paid not a thought to my precious experience abroad, and that there was no work at all for me" (155). Her desolation was complete:

> I was literally penniless, and on whatever condition I had to get a job. . . . But no gilt carriage stopped at my door to announce my appointment to an office of honor. Neither did any college come to beg me to be its honorable professor. It was entirely out of the question that I should get a position that would requite me and my benefactors for the enormous sum of money expended on my education abroad. Now I began to realize what had been taking place at home during the five years of my absence. The postwar [WWI] depression had ended [Japan's] prosperity. Moreover, a sharp reaction had set in after more than half a century of

posthaste Westernization of the country. . . . It was time for all returners to surrender their privileges and live buried among the multitude. (156)

In the end, Mishima was only offered part-time teaching work at her own former girls' high school and at her alma mater, Tsuda College.

Like Tsuda Umeko, Mishima rejected involvement in a feminist movement. She wanted not to protest for legal or political change, but "to challenge Japanese men in an intellectual field" as a college professor. However, university classes were closed to her—as to all women—and in the meantime, more and more isolated from family and friends, she was incessantly pressured to marry. Her desperation deepened: "I was now intellectually and emotionally famished, and the vital experience of my American years, where there was so much for me to see and learn and enjoy that I had continually to gasp both with joy and pain of growing, made me feel the more lonely and restless" (165). Eventually succumbing to the pressure, Mishima reluctantly accepted an offer of marriage from a young university professor whose wife had left him with four children. Although prior to the marriage the professor had promised that Mishima would be permitted to continue her work outside the home, after the wedding Mishima found herself in the midst of a "feudal matriarchy," ruled over by the professor's tyrannical mother, with whom they lived. Almost immediately the man and his mother began insisting that she perform all of the tasks of a traditional daughter-in-law (*yome*), even submitting to the detested diet of cold rice from which she had rebelled as a young girl (174).

In dire financial straits (her husband's salary was inadequate for the household of seven, and her own income a mere pittance), Mishima was forced to petition American friends for money: "Only the 'fairy money' of America would save me," she wrote (212). Finally, at the end of a long descent into illness and poverty, Mishima stumbled in the mid-1930s on the idea of writing in English for publication in the United States, in order to earn income in dollars: "Possible or impossible, I had to stand on an international plane economically as well as mentally" (246). It is this decision that explains the peculiar book of memoirs, *My Narrow Isle*, from which the preceding account of Mishima's life has been drawn, which trails off in the last chapters to desultory accounts of different Japanese customs, the author's own unending financial struggles, and comparisons with the "fairy-tale" conditions of America: "When I am filling our huge bathtub by pumping water, while pondering on how I can collect the next few yen to buy a little bale of charcoal to keep our children's finger tips warm for the coming month, sometimes I am attacked by a dark thought that my struggles are futile; that my past life in the steam-heated American homes, where hot water hissed and fat logs burned in beautiful fireplaces, was a mere dream" (248).

Mishima's desperation, and her effort to appeal to an American audience, permeate the latter half of the book, which, although written in 1941 scarcely mentions the war. Only in the last two pages does she express an opinion on Japan's imperialist advances in China and Korea, first calling them "inevitable," but later predicting that "for the destruction that we have committed in China, we shall be called upon to bear the consequences for many generations to come" (279–80). She closes the book with a paean to internationalism, which to the end she makes dependent on the destruction of the traditional Japanese family: "When I pray for the disintegration of our feudal families into a modern nation, I naturally extend my prayer for the coming of a time when this group of contending nations shall be superseded by a greater society where new laws of humanity will be discovered and made to work" (280).

Certainly, *My Narrow Isle* should not be read as a disinterested account; it is an open appeal to American readers for sympathy and money. Yet there is no mistaking the passion with which Mishima advocates the thoroughgoing reform of the Japanese family and marital relationship along Western lines. Resolutely refusing any recognition of the intermixed histories of Western and Japanese imperialism that brought the fat logs to the beautiful fireplaces of American homes while reducing herself and other Japanese to penury, Mishima determinedly reduces the scope of her international gaze to the figure of the white man as liberatory agent—that is, the white man as husband. For in her view, if American women have opportunities for self-fulfillment, it is because they are permitted these by "understanding" American men. "I wondered who ever trained these American gentlemen instinctively to run to help a woman with a burden," she writes, "[and] to feel uneasy to see women toiling." "I rather discontentedly remembered Japanese gentlemen who left the greater part of menial labor to women and let them work patiently like beasts of burden" (133). If fantasy expresses what is socially denied or repressed, then in Mishima's fantastic representations of American "gentlemen," there is a repressed discourse of rage ("I rather discontentedly remembered") against Japanese patriarchy and Japanese men.

That Mishima's vision for social change is a specifically gendered one emerging from a quasi-feminist agenda becomes apparent when *My Narrow Isle* is contrasted with prewar writings by Japanese men. It is worth noting that there were few equivalent English texts by Japanese male writers, as men had little cause to publish in English. The few texts that do exist however, which are, not surprisingly, from earlier dates, even if adulatory of the West, can hardly be said to be seeking the remaking of the Japanese woman or family along Western lines. To give only one example, in his 1910 book, *Life of Japan,* Miyakawa Masuji expresses abject "gratitude" to the United States for setting Japan on the course to modernization, but in his chapter on the Japanese woman, he writes, "It is part of the wife's grace to be obedient to her husband in all things right and reasonable" (45).

While Japanese women abroad closely observed foreign women and men as actors in larger gender systems that encompassed marriage, family, politics, economics, and education, Japanese men abroad tended to isolate American women as sexual objects of observation and evaluation.[10] As Mitziko Sawada points out in her study of early Japanese emigrants to the United States, there is much ambivalence in men's accounts of Western women (1996, 165). Poet Noguchi Yone's memoirs, *The Story of Yone Noguchi, Told by Himself* (1914), for example, are permeated by this sexualized ambivalence (undoubtedly colored by the author's bisexuality). The following description of "San Francisco girls" is illustrative: "The San Francisco girls sting you often as a wasp; they have the grace and small waist of the wasp. Their golden hair is dyed in the everlasting sunshine and the freshest air; their eyes are fallen stars of dreamy summer night . . . they are so glad to show their well-shaped shoes and slender ankles by raising daintily their skirts. How happy I felt mingling among them! I was perfectly intoxicated with their beautiful faces as with wine. Their sharp, melodious voice was a queen's command to me. I became tired with them all; I needed change. I left the Pacific coast" (88–89). Precisely those qualities of American women that were so attractive to Japanese women are described by Noguchi and other male writers (see also Makino 1912a, 1912b) with dismay. American women's talkativeness, for example, is described by Noguchi thus: "These [Chicago women], I observe curiously, have, it would appear, no perfect balance. How is it possible to grow wise, or gentle, or serene, when they are talking loud all day, raising their voices in competition with the roar of the city's thousand strident voices? If two are together, always they are talking—never silent. They make such a mad noise in meeting as do morning sparrows hunting a breakfast" (86).[11]

Perhaps the greatest difference between women's and men's accounts of sojourns abroad from this period, however, is the evident ease with which male writers seem to adapt to life in Japan after their return. No amount of praise of American women's "intellect," "developed personalities," or "education" (see Sawada 1996, 165) alters the well-established and entirely conventional marital and family relations in which such male writers appear contentedly to settle. Noguchi, for example, ends the memoirs of his journeys in America and England with a rapturous account of a new life in Japan with his second wife (a Japanese woman he married after divorcing his American wife, Leonie Gilmour) and three new children (born after his half-American child by Gilmour, Noguchi Isamu, who grew up to become the famous sculptor). Of his son Isamu's efforts to adapt to life in Japan during a visit he writes, "Isamu noticed that I clapped my hands to call my servant girls, and they would answer my clapping with 'Hai!'—that is the way of a Japanese house. And he thought to himself, of course to my delight, that it was proper for him to answer 'Hai' to my handclapping, and he began to run toward me before the girls, and kneel before me as they did, and wait for my words. . . . And he even attempted to call me 'Danna Sama' (Mr. Lord), catching the word which the servants respectfully addressed to me. . . . I could not help smiling delightedly at it" (1914, 192–93). What complacency is expressed in the short phrase, "that is the way of a Japanese house"—a complacency entirely unavailable to foreign-returned women.

It is worth noting briefly that the same conventions hold true—indeed, are intensified—in the numerous prewar autobiographical accounts written by men about their sojourns abroad in Japanese. To take only one example, Harada Tōichirō's memoirs from 1912, *Nyūyōku* (New York) treat American women as the objects of a kind of sexual rage: "Because their society has indiscriminately raised them up far too high, all American women are arrogant and full of themselves. . . . The greatest faults of New York's women are their rudeness [*fugyōgi*] and their bad manners [*busahō*]. A woman came to New York who said she had previously acted as tutor to the British royal family, but I was so disgusted with her display of these faults that walking down the street with her I lost my patience again and again and wanted to grab her and give her a piece of my mind" (282–83). This text too is permeated by ambivalence, as when Harada remarks of suffragettes that they are "cheerful and intelligent, and quite astonishingly skillful in their ability to charm a man" (284). He shortly follows this by opining that all New York women are like "geisha in training" (*oshaku*), who "view every man as either a manservant or a customer" (284). So "paradoxical" does Harada find New York women and so "troublesome the problem of understanding them" (282), that he turns the matter over to a Swedish female journalist, translating an essay in which she writes, among other things, that "New York women have no sparkle of interest, no high aspirations, no dreams of love, no old-fashioned beauty; in short they are lacking in the display of all the unique essentially womanly qualities such as grace and poetics" (285–86).[12]

In this way, in the prewar and wartime years we see the emergence of distinct men and women's discourses vis-à-vis the United States, and the West more broadly, which narrated akogare on the part of women, sexual ambivalence on the part of men. Women's fantasy of the West as "luminous world" and "land of romance" expressed a repressed rage against Japan and found a focus in the figure of the white Western man. This fantasy built on Tsuda Umeko's more pragmatic harnessing of English-language study and study abroad as women's economic device to form a potent image of escape and opportunity in the minds of women discontented with their place in Japanese society. When women brought this image to bear on their encounter with the thousands of American G.I.s who actually arrived in Japan during the U.S. Occupation, and who almost immediately on arrival proceeded to legally obliterate the "feudal" family system that women had so resented, the results were nothing short of incendiary.

The U.S. Occupation and Women's "Liberation" In 1945, with Japan's unconditional surrender and occupation by Allied (in practice, American) forces, Japanese women's legal status altered virtually overnight. One of the first acts of the Supreme Commander of the Allied Powers (SCAP), under the direction of General Douglas MacArthur, was the revision of the Election Law, granting Japanese women suffrage and the right to participate in politics at all levels. Seventy-five women ran for office in that first election of 1946, and an astonishing thirty-nine were elected. When the new Japanese Constitution, which had been virtually written by Occupation authorities, was promulgated in 1947 over heated Japanese male opposition, Japanese women's legal status changed still more: The Constitution abolished the feudal family system and instituted extensive equality under the law in many matters pertaining to marriage, choice of spouse, property rights, inheritance, choice of domicile, divorce, and more (see Pharr 1987, 224–25). Ironically, as Susan Pharr has pointed out, the rights guaranteed to women under Japan's American-written postwar Constitution of 1947 surpass anything available to American women to the present day (225). Kyoko Hirano has written, "In the eyes of the American[s] . . . , Japanese women had been consistently and without exception victimized under the traditional social system, and required liberation. The Occupation's role was to assist in this process" (1992, 72).

Katō (Ishimoto) Shizue, an aristocratic Occupation advisor and elected official in Japan's House of Representatives from 1949, was to say later, "General MacArthur was really very nice to Japanese women. The first thing he said in 1945 was to give them equal rights" (in Chapman 1993, 20). Whether women's political and legal rights should accurately be considered a "gift" from Douglas MacArthur or the result of Japanese activists' own long years of effort before and immediately following the war has been a topic of debate among Japanese historians almost since the day these rights were granted. On the one hand, Pharr has maintained that Japanese women leaders' efforts played a very minor role in policymaking processes early in the Occupation (1987, 233), as these leaders had lobbied almost exclusively for women's suffrage and not for the more radical and far-reaching reforms enshrined in the new Constitution (277). Yamazaki Tomoko, in her introductory essay to a recent reader in Japanese feminism, remarks that women were "liberated" by the American victory because "the rights they had been fruitlessly fighting for since the Meiji Restoration were granted in a single gesture" (1997, 18). As the spokeswoman at a meeting of thirty-one new female Diet members with General MacArthur in 1946, Katō Shizue read a formal statement to MacArthur that began, "We, the women members of the Japanese [D]iet . . . thank you very much for granting us suffrage and educating us as to the use of it to establish democracy in Japan" (in Beard 1953, 178).[13]

However, many other feminists disagree. Marxist historian Itō Yasuko writes, with some asperity:

> Too many people in Japan accept the prevailing view that Western feminism or American democracy was responsible for [Japanese] women's liberation, as evidenced by the common description of suffrage as a gift [*purezento sanseiken*]. But the results that Japanese women achieved after the war were not a "gift." As I have tried to show, while they were indeed an outgrowth of global democracy, involving antifascist, labor, and self-determination movements, they were ultimately the result of women fighting to make their own demands known. (1974, 90; see also Tanaka S. 1984, 59)

Historian Inoue Kiyoshi argues that "even without GHQ's orders, women's suffrage would have been achieved anyway within a short time" (1967, 305).

What is clear in this debate, however, is that virtually all Japanese historians of women mark the U.S. Occupation as a watershed. What is also clear, as numerous feminist historians and scholars have been at pains to point out, is that for some women at least, Japan's defeat and Occupation by the Allies were experienced as a "liberation."[14] Certainly, men and women both struggled with food shortages, joblessness, exhaustion, and despair in the first years after Japan's surrender. Dower has written of the *kyodatsu* effect, in which practically the entire population of Japan fell prey to a condition of such intense collapse and prostration (kyodatsu) after the surrender that it required the adoption of a previously little-used clinical term to describe (1999, 89). However, a number of Japanese historians have made a point of distinguishing between kyodatsu as a specifically male postwar experience and a sense of *kaihō* (liberation) as a characteristically female one. Feminist Tanaka Sumiko writes, "While men were still in a state of collapse [kyodatsu] over the ashes of defeat and unable to mentally respond to their new circumstances, women turned the calamity of defeat into an opportunity [*chansu*] for women's liberation" (1984, 60). Certainly, this women's adaptability was a class-bound phenomenon, for only those women who had a minimum supply of food, shelter, and clothing could begin to participate in the "liberatory" potential of the Occupation. And yet, as Michael Molasky has observed, even lower-class women, denied recognition as full-fledged imperial subjects in the first place, did not experience the defeat "as a threat to their identity as women or as Japanese." He remarks that women "tended to associate their loss with the war and rarely attributed it to the Occupation *per se*" (1999, 132; see also Itō 1990, 15; 1987, 274–77). Ōhori Sueo observed, "[After the defeat] many of those who could only be called Japan's finest sons shut themselves up in frustration [*zasetsu*], doubt [*kaigi*], and remorse [*kaikon*], and not a few of them degenerated from there into collapse [kyodatsu], violence, and then to crime. . . . [But] in this period when despair and hope were intermingled, the quickest to respond to the new conditions were those who for so many years had been kept down in a lowly status, without political rights, as legal incompetents—women. Women instinctively knew that in these changes they had more to gain than to lose" (1984, 296).

Katō Shizue, the Occupation advisor on women's issues, was certainly one such woman. In her memoirs she recalls her delight at the arrival of U.S. troops, calling the U.S. planes that flew overhead dropping propaganda leaflets immediately before Japan's surrender "gods of salvation" (1997, 122) and referring to Occupation reforms as "the country's dawning" (130). Her optimism derived, as she explained later in her Japanese autobiography, from her faith in the "gentlemanly" nature of American men, a faith derived from several years spent studying in the United States: "[Before the surrender] I strangely felt no worry about our imminent defeat. America is the land of democracy, and even if it were to occupy us, it would never permit the kind of atrocities practiced by the Japanese Army in Nanjing" (118–19). Mishima Sumie, not surprisingly, was of the same mind. For her the Occupation constituted a liberation in which she exulted. In her second book, *The Broader Way: A Woman's Life in New Japan* (a kind of companion piece to *My Narrow Isle,* their respective agendas apparent from the titles), she concludes, "Deepest gratitude is due the Occupation from all Japanese women for giving them complete legal equality with their men, and showing Japanese men good manners toward women. It would have taken ages of hard battling if Japanese women had had to fight for these rights by themselves. 'What would have been our status,' Japanese women say thoughtfully to each other, 'if our militarists had won the war and continued to rule the country with their brutal force?' This is a candid confession of Japanese women's sincere appreciation of the Occupation" (1953, 238–39). As in her previous book, global political issues do not intervene in her day-to-day account of the difficult yet rewarding conditions in the Occupation economy. She does not mention the bombing of Hiroshima and Nagasaki until almost the last page of the book, and then only in passing.

Yet even Mishima, with her rose-colored view of America, was forced to struggle with the contradiction of a "democracy" imposed by military force—a contradiction compounded by the openly discriminatory practices maintained by the U.S. Occupation Army toward the Japanese populace (see 1953, 227–39). Of this contradiction Mishima gamely writes:

> The Allied Occupation of Japan must have been the most liberal and kindly of military occupations recorded in history. . . . We shall never forget the days when we beheld for the first time the magnificent Occupation setup in the midst of our war devastation. We were a nation of desperate people, hungry, ragged, and filth-covered. . . . Planting itself in the midst of the hordes of such people, the Occupation Army had naturally to draw a definite "off limits" line around it for the sake of defending its security and efficiency. That line had to be determined necessarily by a very technical, discriminatory mechanism where nationality was all-important and individuals did not count. And that line was to mark the sharp boundary between abundance and hunger, rainbow-colored cleanliness and gray sordidness, privileged victors and a nation in bondage. (228–29)

In this characteristically dramatic prose we see the first fault lines emerge in the internationalist narrative, marking its confrontation with American geopolitical power and the entrenched hierarchies of race, ethnicity, and nation that girded even the most "liberal and kindly" of international encounters. In the rest of Mishima's book, however, this fleeting recognition is again repressed in a discourse of adulation.

I return to these contradictions later. Before doing so, however, I wish to turn away from English texts and consider material written during this time in Japanese for a Japanese audience. Whereas English texts were essential in women's early efforts to establish alliances with a sympathetic foreign readership,[15] the U.S. Occupation marks the beginning of a far more prolific and sustained female genre of exhortatory writing directed exclusively at Japanese women themselves. These works were written increasingly by ordinary Japanese women from middle-class families who had benefited from Japanese or, more commonly, U.S. government scholarships for study in the United States (see Yamamuro 1947). Study abroad, funded by foreign sources, continued to be the primary means by which Japanese women acquired meaningful university education of any kind. As socialist feminist activist Yamakawa Kikue was to write bitterly, "Japan's higher education for women depended on American charity" (1984, 180). Claiming no special privilege but the knowledge gained through lengthy sojourns abroad, these authors bypassed foreign readers entirely to exhort other "ordinary" women to seek overseas experience and establish foreign connections on their own.

This section turns to the text *The American Woman* [Amerika no josei], written in 1946 (reissued in 1950) by the postwar liberal intellectual Sakanishi Shiho. This text, a best-seller of the time, is perhaps the first of this new type of writing for the ordinary Japanese woman reader. In it, Sakanishi depicts the Japanese woman as the object of American scrutiny under the Occupation and sets forth a program of relentless self-reform based on the daily life of American girls and women in the 1940s, which she proposes as the model of correct behavior and example of "the standards by which Japanese women are being judged" (138).

In her accomplishments Sakanishi Shiho herself was anything but ordinary.[16] Born to a Christian farming family in Hokkaido in 1896, she was by all accounts a prodigy. Taught English from childhood onward, first by her father, later at school, and later still at college in Tokyo, she obtained in 1922, through the influence of American friends, a scholarship to study at Wheaton College. She planned to stay for only one year, but the Great

Kantō Earthquake of 1923 intervened, and she stayed on to graduate from Wheaton in 1925. She immediately enrolled in graduate school at the University of Michigan, finishing her M.A. in English one year later, at the age of 30. In 1930 Sakanishi began working at the U.S. Library of Congress Oriental Division, charged with the task of building a Japanese collection. She continued in this post for twelve years, associating with some of the most important American intellectuals and writers of that era. At the same time, she commenced a career in translation, rendering some of the most important works of modern Japanese poetry and literature into English for the first time.

In 1942, however, Sakanishi, under suspicion by the U.S. government, was incarcerated in one of the newly formed relocation camps for Japanese Americans (Kitayama 1997a, 23–24). Forcibly repatriated to Japan on a prisoner exchange ship, she subsequently lent her skills to the Japanese war effort as a translator and propagandist until Japan's defeat.[17] After the war's end, however, she emerged as one of the leading liberal, pro-American public intellectuals in Japan, serving on countless government committees for reform, and publishing prolifically and to enormous acclaim on social issues under the new Americanized regime (see Sakanishi 1946, 1947, 1953, 1956). During this time she also helped to found the Japan Writers Union and the *Japan Quarterly* journal, and translated the immensely popular "Blondie" comic strip for the *Asahi Shimbun* (for which she gained perhaps her greatest fame among mass audiences). In 1963 Sakanishi was awarded an honorary doctorate from the University of Michigan. She continued publishing practically until her death in 1976, at the age of seventy-nine.

In *The American Woman,* her most popular book, Sakanishi states that her purpose is not simply to sketch American women's history but to explain the meaning of true democracy and its implications for women's status. Insisting that American democracy does not mean "doing whatever you want," but rather "believing in human dignity, and respecting the values and beliefs of all people, regardless of their religion, profession, wealth, or class" (1950, 141), she goes on to demonstrate the ways that this democratic attitude is allegedly present in American practices and lacking in Japanese. She makes a special point of defending the American custom of "ladies first," asserting that it is neither insulting to women nor based

on assumptions of women's weakness, but "among the working intellectual class today at least, does not affect the relationship of men and women
as one of virtual equality" (143).

Sakanishi insists that proper behavior is the same the world over, arguing that for women, this behavior includes "not wearing thick makeup,
baring skin before others, having dirty fingernails or clothes, or being late
for appointments" (144). To be truly "international" (*kokusaiteki*), she goes
on to claim, is not to slavishly imitate the practices and values of other
countries, but to represent the best of one's own. However, the bulk of her
own argument contradicts this claim, as she proceeds to lambaste her
fellow Japanese for failing to adhere to the American model in such matters as expressing independent opinions, using scientific knowledge to
better the quality of daily life, employing the talents of women to improve
the domestic sphere, and fostering an inventive, "can-do" spirit (146–52).
Warming to her theme, she warns the reader that Occupation officers
newly arrived in the country see Japanese women as beleaguered "slaves"
and "workhorses," and "cannot understand why women who contribute at
least fifty percent to the common labor of the household should themselves continue to adopt a 'slave-like mentality' " (152–53).[18] "It is a mystery
to foreigners," she continues, "why Japanese men view education in
women as a handicap. That is natural, for foreign men seek wives who are
not only beautiful, but as educated and refined as themselves" (153).[19] She
relates an incident in which she met a high-ranking Japanese official at
a diplomatic reception in Washington, D.C., who greeted her with the
words, "Oh, so you are Dr. Sakanishi [*dokutā Sakanishi*]? I despise educated women." Sakanishi tells us she responded pithily, "Oh, I'm so sorry,
I despise uneducated men." But her outrage at this incident is clear: "Democracy can never flourish in a society in which man's personhood [*jin-
kaku*] is respected while woman's is denied" (154).

Stating flatly that the Japanese practice of "going along with the crowd"
is "wrong," Sakanishi (somewhat contradictorily) exhorts women to remake their lives according to the model of American women:

> The women of a democratic country on the one hand fulfill their own
> responsibilities, and on the other, make demands that would cause a
> Japanese woman to flinch—equality of the sexes, respect for the individ-

ual, the abolition of the sexual double standard. There are many American men who forgive their wives' adultery, but American women nearly always take unfaithful husbands to court and divorce them. A husband can be sued for insulting his wife in public. The wife does not become intimidated, or cry, or simply accept it, nor does she have to. Because she can work and somehow survive on her own, a woman who respects herself and loves her independence never settles for a life of degradation. She will never have to tolerate virtual enslavement for the sake of financial security. (157)

Anticipating an outcry that such a wife "has no gentleness nor affection for her family," Sakanishi hastens to disagree:

I know many couples so courteous to one another, so caring, that they seem to be newlyweds. The wife leans on her husband and the husband depends on his wife. When the time comes to greet her husband as he returns from his day at work, the wife freshens herself up, fixes her makeup, and prepares in her mind the event of the day that might most interest her husband to hear. The husband, meanwhile, never forgets family birthdays and the anniversaries of their engagement and wedding, and hastens home on these days with beautiful flowers or chocolates in hand. (158)

In the epilogue Sakanishi reassures her female readers that foreigners see them as Japan's best hope for the future, mustering as evidence the testimony of a series of unnamed high-ranking foreign men: "A captain in the American navy, the executive director of America's largest broadcasting company, businessmen, educators, politicians, and an English diplomat have all insisted to me, since Japan's defeat, that 'women are the future of Japan.' When I demand to know why they believe this, they tell me that as Japanese men sink into a pit of despair in the face of the total failure of all of their endeavors, they will eventually remember that among their women there is still human beauty, kindness, and profound courage, and they will be revitalized" (160).

The 1940s vision of the Feminine Mystique that Sakanishi unabashedly advocates for the Japanese woman—even to the point of "freshening up" her makeup to greet her husband returning home from the office—can only be considered bizarre given the harsh, hand-to-mouth economic conditions prevailing in Japan in 1946 (this may be a reason for the book's reissue in 1950). Her vision is indeed willfully indifferent to the actual conditions of women's lives during the Occupation; her book is an application of a pure idealism, based on a wholesale appropriation of the tropes of "America" and the "American Woman" for her own reformist ideological principles. That Sakanishi, incarcerated by the American government during the war simply for her Japanese nationality, could reemerge as one of Japan's leading celebrants of American "democracy" in the postwar period reveals the degree to which internationalist women like her required, and remained loyal to, the "idea" of a democratic America as liberatory ideal and foundation of both their gender project and their very self-identity, despite any and all evidence to the contrary. Like Mishima before her, Sakanishi's own experiences of racism and exclusion at the hands of the U.S. government could not be permitted to shake her faith in the power of American "equality," so essential to her program of domestic gendered reform in Japan. In *The American Woman*, Sakanishi allows no hint of ambivalence to enter her account. In a relentless project of self-criticism, she projects on the Japanese (female) self the disavowed recognition of exclusion: if Japanese (women) are excluded from the democratic realm, it is because they have not yet earned the right to participate in it.

And yet the popularity of Sakanishi's book suggests that its tone of aggrieved idealism struck a chord with its readers. It certainly ran counter to broad masculine sentiment of the time. It is revealing to juxtapose *The American Woman* with a 1953 volume of study-abroad memoirs, *Husband-Wife Study Abroad* [Meoto ryūgaku], by journalist Kurata Yasuo. Kurata and his wife spent one year studying at the University of Oregon in 1952 on the Government Appropriation for Relief in Occupied Areas (GARIOA) scholarship, the predecessor to the Fulbright. Although this book's appeal seems to have derived mainly from the novelty (considerable for the time) of a husband and wife studying abroad together, Kurata's wife never speaks in the book; indeed, we are never told her given name. Nevertheless, the silent presence of Kurata's wife permeates the text, for she permits the ironic distance on American women and men that constitutes its apparent appeal to its most likely male audience.

The primary advantage for Kurata of having his wife accompany him abroad seems to have been, as he describes it in the introduction, that he could save money on food and laundry and remain aloof from the sordid "blood-letting" that in his view constituted gender relations in the United States (1953, 8):

> What was good about studying abroad with my wife was that I didn't have to worry about finding a date for dance parties and such occasions. If you're alone, first you have to find a date, and if you manage that, first it's dinner, then it's drinks. And if it's an American girl, then this being the country of "ladies first," you've got to follow her around waiting on her like an orderly waits on his commanding officer. For an Oriental accustomed to the practice of male supremacy [*dansonjohi*], this is no ordinary task. . . . Now if you've got your wife along, then you eat at home, she's your date, and you don't have to drop anything on drinks. No worries, and very convenient. (7)

A page later Kurata has returned to the problem of American women, which clearly irritates him. The custom of "ladies first" comes in for particular criticism:

> I tell you, that country, the U.S., was literally made for women. In fact it's downright strange that there hasn't been a female president there yet. During that one year of study we were not "man and wife" [*fūfu*] but "woman and husband" [*fufū*]. The practice of "ladies first" is taken to such an extreme there that frankly you wonder why American women's hands and feet don't atrophy. They say when you're in Rome do as the Romans do, so I went along with the basics of ladies first for what it was worth, but I didn't follow it to the degree that my wife would wind up not getting enough exercise! Anyhow, she hated it too. Maybe the Oriental male despotism isn't great, but as far as I'm concerned the American style of female despotism is just going too far. (8)

Throughout the book Kurata seems to feel a special glee in showing American women and men at their humiliating worst, describing with relish the marital spats of his neighbors in the apartment next door, which always ended with the husband sleeping in the car. His chapter "Sketches of American Women" opines that American men "have only themselves to blame" for the state of American women, commenting elsewhere that American women age quickly and tend to obesity. Echoing earlier male texts Kurata focuses particular disdain on American women's speech: "As a Japanese, the thing I liked least about coming into contact with American women was their lack of a softer women's language [such as women use in Japan]" (47). Criticizing various women's usages he encountered at the university, he writes, "If you tell me that since everything is 'equal' in America there shouldn't be words that only men can use, well, I don't have an answer. But still, as far as I am concerned, they sounded unpleasant to the ear, and I for one was not impressed" (48).

Kurata really hits his stride in his chapter "American Husbands," which opens with the line, "Coming from Japan, the land of male chauvinism [*teishu kanpaku*], American men, every last one of them, look to be cases of henpecking [*kyōsaibyō*] beyond curing" (27). In this chapter Kurata compiles a parodic "Ten Commandments of the American Husband," which read as follows:

1. Thou shalt love thy wife, and bear all things with determination;
2. Thou shalt help thy wife, and wash the dishes;
3. Thou shalt never forget thy wife's birthday, nor thy wedding anniversary;
4. On Sundays thou shalt awake before thy wife and make breakfast for her;
5. While driving in the car thou shalt listen quietly to thy wife's backseat driving and take care to preserve her and thy own safety;
6. Thou shalt speedily hand over thy monthly paycheck to thy wife;
7. Should a repair be required in the house thou shalt attend to it with haste;
8. Thou shalt put the children to bed, and if a child cries during the night, thou shalt arise from bed and make the best of it;
9. All hedge-trimming, lawn-watering, and automobile-repair tasks shall be thine;
10. If thou shouldst go out drinking at night, be thou well-prepared for the terror of thy wife's wielding of the broom upon thy return. (30)

To a remarkable degree, Kurata and Sakanishi seize on the same aspects of American marriage as evidence for their opposite perspectives. The sharing of chores that Sakanishi views as idyllic partnership Kurata ridicules as the worse example of "henpecking." The legal recourses that Sakanishi praises as enabling American women to defend their rights, Kurata abhors, relating with a combination of disgust and contempt American court decisions forbidding men to divorce their wives for poor cooking or drunkenness, and others permitting women to throw an unemployed husband out of the house. "Can men possibly be content under these conditions?" Kurata wonders in amazement, and concludes that American men must simply be "resigned," unable to think of a way to alter them. He ends the chapter, however, on a bright note, with an account of a man who, disgusted with "spoiled" American women, "imported" a mail-order bride from Germany: "See," he writes, "even in America there are a few fellows who've got balls!" (36).

In the end, Kurata's year at an American university led him to conclude that under no circumstances should Japan imitate the United States, least of all in regard to the relations of men and women. That Kurata's experience was not atypical is suggested by an exhaustive 1958 anthropological study of Japanese students in America by John W. Bennett, Herbert Passin, and Robert K. McKnight, *In Search of Identity*. The authors relate the "general judgment" among their male subjects that "American women are *kowai* [frightening]" (1958, 122), and suggest that the American experience has the effect of confirming for Japanese men the superiority of the gender status quo in Japan, regardless of their ideological sympathies otherwise. The authors elaborate:

> The experience with American women . . . often confirmed that the traditional passive and obedient Japanese woman was much better— even though one remained a militant pro-democrat and socialist at the same time. (Many "modern" Japanese women complain loudly about this "contradiction.") One engineer in his late thirties . . . who said that what he most admired in the United States was its "equality," listed as what he "most disliked" "equality between men and women." "How dry and dull a country becomes when women dominate!" he complained. . . . "American women are awful, so unfeminine. . . . They show no affection, no grace." (142–43)

Predictably, Bennett et al. found the opposite view among their Japanese female informants, who revealed a "romantic conception of the emancipated Western woman" (1958, 158). "Freed from the restraints of her life in Japan," they wrote, "the woman student surrendered herself to America, to its brightness and luxury, in a way that the men never could" (163). They found that such women returned home "not with gladness but with resignation," "torn" between their American-acquired "independence" and the subservience expected of them in Japan (169). Among women's most immediate problems, they suggested, was an inability to find a husband. Sakanishi herself (who never married) observed dryly that "there would seem to be some kind of relation between higher education and non-marriage among women" (in Bennett et al. 1958, 170).

However, all was not completely bleak for study-abroad returnees in the early postwar years. Noting that the majority of postwar female U.S.-returned students ended up single and employed in the "fringe area" of American business or army offices, UNESCO in Japan, or teaching English, Bennett et al. observed that women had at the same time established a niche for themselves as contact points or bridges between Japan and "the many academic and business visitors from America" (175). In a 1956 article, McKnight and Bennett noted that returning women had a much stronger tendency than returning men to view themselves as "links" between Japan and America, "indicating a greater concern for furthering Western social patterns in Japan" (46). Bennett et al. elaborate: "They represent Japanese culture to the Americans and can once again find that their feminine grace is received with curiosity and respect—yet at the same time they can avoid the restrictive aspects of a 'normal' woman's role in Japanese society" (1958, 175). They quote one young returnee woman active in the foreign community: "We are a new sort of professional woman—a kind of geisha maybe—only we don't resent being called that now" (175).

This woman's invocation of the geisha image is suggestive in its linkage of new opportunities for women with a sexual or sexualized access to foreign men. As in previous eras, postwar Japanese women could successfully seek potential alliances with sympathetic Westerners in their quest for "liberation" only insofar as there were many foreigners sympathetic to Japanese women's struggles. Fed by a stream of journalistic reports in *Life* (see Busch 1947) and the *New York Times Magazine* (see Parrott 1945, 1946), a steady interest was growing in the States about the conditions of Japanese women under their new postwar status. Americans were eager to see Japanese women "free themselves" from the shackles of the past, and were prepared to help. Thus, in 1949 a group of female Occupation officers and Occupation wives joined together with some overseas-returned Japanese women, all with degrees from Mount Holyoke College, to form the Mount Holyoke Club, whose purpose was to raise funds to send Japanese women to America to study (Katō M. 1984, 277).

Yet more and more after World War II, those whose sympathies were most aroused on behalf of Japanese women were not so much American women as American men. Caroline Sue Simpson's and others' work shows us that from the Occupation onward (and indeed before), Japanese women became the objects of widespread American male curiosity, attraction, and sympathy, both in Japan and at home. It was men who increasingly imagined themselves, as Simpson writes, not only as generous father figures to young Japanese children but "loving, supportive 'democratic husbands' to Japanese women whom they had freed from a medieval patriarchal system" (1994, 188–89).

There were many reasons for women's popularity. In Japan, as I show below, women were not only desired as exotic Madame Butterflies (although that image, of course, played a role); they were also quickly rehabilitated as the "good" Japanese who, in contrast to duplicitous and violent men, were imagined to be malleable to and eager for democratic reform. Red Cross officer Lucy Herndon Crockett wrote in her Occupation memoirs, *Popcorn on the Ginza:* "Next to the bright-eyed, burheaded children, Japan's often-called 'better half' has formed the biggest sympathetic group helping to bridge the gap between conqueror and ex-enemy. Downtrodden Mama-san tottering along the roads beneath enormous burdens, standing in streetcars and trains while her husband sits, makes a strong appeal to G.I. sympathy. Winsome little 'Baby-san'—as the cutest among the waitresses, room girls, and typists in Allied-occupied buildings throughout Japan is usually known—is completely appealing" (1949, 132). Meanwhile, the rapidly shifting postwar gender relations of the

United States also worked to foster this attraction. During the war years American women had entered the workforce in vast numbers, taking over men's jobs and posing a threat to male authority in the home. It was not a sight war-fatigued returning soldiers were happy to see, and those who found themselves in Japan after the war were, by and large, frankly enthralled with the women they found there, apparent paragons of domesticity, shrinking fragility, and an alluring femininity.[20] In turn, American women, particularly those who came over as Occupation staff (many came in search of husbands), were dismayed to find so many of their men under Japanese women's spell. As American men, in their eager attentiveness, threw their weight on the side of Japanese women (against both American women and Japanese men), the Occupation quickly took on an openly erotic aspect. As Crockett observed, Occupation solders' "countless little acts of consideration toward women make a terrific impression on Japanese wives and mothers. Perhaps for the first time they are beginning to realize that possibly they *are* the 'unhappiest women in the world' " (142).

The Sexual Nexus of the Occupation In this way, an explicit erotic politics shaped the nature of postwar Japanese women's and men's encounters with the United States, and the West more broadly, an erotic politics that originated from a single broad equation: Japanese women were desired by American men, while Japanese men were rebuffed by both American men and women. Of course, there were numerous exceptions to this "rule," and one can find examples of American women dating and marrying Japanese men and American men hostile or indifferent to the attractions of Japanese women. Nevertheless, the sexual economy of the U.S.-Japan postwar encounter was primarily an extension of a system that had been in place since imperial Europe's encounter with a feminized and exoticized Orient from the eighteenth century onward (Said 1978; Kabbani 1986). Long before 1945, Pierre Loti had already written *Madame Chrysantheme* (1916 [1888]), his memoir of a "marriage" to a Japanese "native wife," which in 1906 became fixed in the European and American erotic imagination as Puccini's opera *Madama Butterfly*.

Japanese women exercised a powerful hold on the collective American male imagination, a hold that only grew stronger as the years passed. As Frank Kelley and Cornelius Ryan write in *Star-Spangled Mikado:*

> The G.I. had formed a mental picture of Madame Butterfly long before he reached Japan. He had heard of the charm and dignity of the Japanese woman, her delicacy and graciousness. . . . It was regrettable that the G.I. had been introduced at the beginning to the fake geishas and prostitutes. . . . [However,] in the tiny villages and towns he was also meeting the average Japanese girl and housewife, and unwittingly he was playing a major role in breaking the feudalistic bonds which had held Japanese women for centuries. He found in the Japanese woman a childlike, pleasant, and hospitable person with an avid curiosity. . . . The American soldier and everything he had came from the land of democracy—to the Japanese women, that land and its way of life was [*sic*] to be their pattern for the future. (1947, 146–64)

Despite official Occupation policies against fraternization, the Japanese female–American male romance almost instantly emerged as the symbol of the relationship between a grateful gracious, and feminized Japan in thrall to the American military men who had liberated her (Simpson 1994, 160). Dower writes that the "enjoyment was palpable. . . . Japan—only yesterday a menacing, masculine threat—had been transformed, almost in the blink of an eye, into a compliant, feminine body on which the white victors could impose their will" (1999, 138). The Occupation was called, on the American side, a "love affair" (see Pharr 1987, 288) with "a honeymoon atmosphere" (Mears 1948, 109). "To say that American men and Japanese women got on well together [after the war] is a gross understatement," wrote Fosco Maraini in 1959; "they flung themselves into each other's arms as if they had been waiting for each other all their lives" (90).

Interracial romance caught the public imagination Stateside as well. One novel from 1947, *Tokyo Romance,* became a best-seller in both English and Japanese for its depiction of the struggles of an American G.I. to marry his Japanese actress sweetheart over the opposition of Occupation policy and Japanese social prejudice (Hoberecht 1947). The novel got a splashy four-page review in *Life* ("Japanese Best Seller," 1947), which, despite calling it "possibly the worst novel of modern times" (107), did not fail to treat readers to a dramatic photographic "enactment." Less than a month earlier,

Life had published a well-received photographic essay on "the most popular geisha in Tokyo" (supposedly named "Miss Peach Blossom") who, the author hastened to assure readers, thoroughly appreciated her new American clients (Busch 1947). Japanese men are absent from this *Life* photo-essay, with the exception of a single bowing rickshaw driver.

Indeed, Simpson notes that as Japan became increasingly represented to Americans as a nation of "fawning young women and cheerful school children," Japanese men virtually disappeared from the landscape (1994, 160). In *Popcorn on the Ginza*, Japanese men were scarcely mentioned, and on the few occasions they appear, described in openly racist terms: "Mr. Tsutsui seemed to beam right from his swarthy, charcoal-outlined face down through the crumpled shell of his shabbily suited figure to his toes nestling beneath his weight on the silk floor cushion" (Crockett 1949, 226).[21] Crockett quotes one young Japanese man asking rather plaintively, "Why is it . . . that Americans blame us—the men—for everything, yet seem to think our women are wonderful?" (131). The disparity is graphically illustrated in two full-page photographs printed side by side in Maraini's *Meeting with Japan*. On the left, in a photo titled "Victors," a tall uniformed American G.I. strides through a nightclub district in the company of two young women; on the right, a photo titled "Vanquished" shows a single maimed Japanese soldier, dressed in rags and holding an accordion, reduced to begging on the street (1959, 152–53; see figures 5 and 6).[22]

Much has been written of the shock and rage of Japanese soldiers who, on returning from the war, found the women they had been fighting for walking arm in arm with the former enemy. As Dower remarks, "The *panpan* [Occupation prostitute] arm in arm with her G.I. companion, or riding gaily in his jeep, constituted a piercing wound to national pride in general and masculine pride in particular" (1999, 135). One woman recalled that Japanese men scowled at the soldiers' red-manicured girlfriends (only such women had access to American nail polish and cosmetics) and cursed them as tramps who "walked with blood dripping from their fingers" (Miyamoto 1988, 50). Such resentment and jealousy were still fresh in a 1987 letter to *Asahi Shimbun* by an ex-soldier: "Arrogant Japanese women walked onto the trains arm in arm with American soldiers. Abusing the Americans' extraterritoriality under the Occupation,

5. "Victors." Source: Fosco Maraini, *Meeting with Japan*. New York: Viking Press, 1960, 152. Courtesy of Fosco Maraini.

6. "Vanquished." Source: Fosco Maraini, *Meeting with Japan*. New York: Viking Press, 1960, 153. Courtesy of Fosco Maraini.

they assumed they too would be allowed to ride for free" ("Tora no i ni makenai namaiki," 1987, 4).[23]

As a result, for many Japanese men the Occupation was an experience of sexual humiliation. As Molasky writes, "For men, the simultaneous loss of Japan's empire and the commencement of foreign occupation signified a loss of control over both national and bodily boundaries" (1999, 132). The right-wing novelist Mishima Yukio, in his 1967 polemic, *The Way of the Samurai*, deplored that Japanese men had become "feminized" as the inevitable result of "the influence of American democracy, 'ladies first,' and so forth" (1977, 18).[24] This rhetoric of sexual betrayal found expression in several best-selling books written by former military men. The best known of these was *Chastity of Japan* (Nihon no teisō; Mizuno 1953; see also Gotō 1953, 1965), a book by one male author which purports to recount the tragic stories of four women raped by American servicemen.[25] Throughout *Chastity of Japan* the author claims to speak on behalf of the victimized women, urging understanding and compassion on the part of the Japanese people toward all those innocent women whose innate "purity" had been stolen through the depredations of marauding and bestial foreigners. In the final passage of the book, however, a different agenda emerges, one more concerned with men's honor than women's rehabilitation: "Half-breed children [konketsuji] will continue to come into this world. That is, as long as the present conditions continue in which *our* wives, daughters, and sisters cannot walk in the streets, day or night, without facing violation, unprotected and unrevenged. One after another these women will slip away from us [watashitachi no moto o hanaresatteiku] to drop out [datsuraku shite] and swell the ranks of the panpan girls. How long must we stand by with arms folded watching this tragic procession? Is this not a situation whose weight is on our shoulders as Japanese, to be decided by our will?" (286–87; emphasis added).

Within days of Japan's defeat, the Japanese government established a system of official government brothels to serve the Occupying forces. Conceived as a lower-class "female floodwall" (onna no bohatei) protecting the chastity of "good" middle-class women, thousands of Japanese women—most not professional prostitutes but homeless, destitute, orphaned, and desperate teenagers—were hired as "Occupation comfort women" (senryō-gun ianfu) to work in these brothels.[26] When this official prostitution system was abolished by MacArthur only one year after its inception (due to skyrocketing rates of venereal disease and growing outrage among women's and Christian groups stateside), the young women by and large found themselves even worse off, having lost such official protections as they had been accorded and reduced to walking the streets as panpan girls. The sad fate of these Occupation comfort women has been the subject of sustained critical interest in Japan and elsewhere.[27] Yet it is interesting to note that in the prolific recent Japanese feminist revisionist writing on the topic, the authors' condemnation is primarily directed not at "marauding foreign soldiers," but at the Japanese men of the government and police force who conceived of and created this exploitative system and who abducted young women from their homes to serve in it (see Inoue S. 1995; Tanaka Sumiko 1984, 60). Women writers are also at pains to point out, with some bitterness, that it was the Americans who in the end finally abolished the system. Inoue Setsuko writes in the conclusion of her book-length study of the Occupation comfort women, "When I reflect that a major reason for the abolition of the Occupation comfort stations [had to come from] opposition from American women's and Christian groups directed at GHQ, I for one, as a Japanese, am ashamed" (231).

The obsessive recent critical and literary focus on lower-class Occupation comfort women and panpan girls, however, has deflected attention from the fact that this was not the only form of sexual or romantic contact between Japanese women and G.I.s at the time. As Paul Spickard observed, some women explicitly sought to marry American G.I.s, women who were "united in their interest in pursuing life beyond the restrictions that bound their more traditional sisters" (1989, 129). If the most vulnerable women experienced the Occupation as a new form of increasingly sexualized oppression, women whose class standing in the prewar and wartime periods had provided them with skills (such as English, accounting, or first aid) that they could market in the Occupation labor economy also had the opportunity to exercise a sexualized agency toward American G.I.s in an agenda of their own to change their status. The Occupation offered such women a space for the potent conflation of fantasy and opportunity.[28]

Not surprisingly, Mishima Sumie was one of the most flamboyant in her praise of the G.I.s and their treatment of women: "The courteous or gallant manners of Occupation men, and the breath-takingly marvelous things they possess have become absolutely irresistible to many Japanese girls" (1953, 170). Elsewhere she writes, "The American ladies-first custom is followed everywhere by foreign men, and for the first time Japanese men have come to understand that to be courteous and friendly toward women is neither a detriment to masculine dignity or to feminine chastity" (166). However, Mishima was far from the only woman so impressed. One woman wrote in a letter to the women's magazine *Fujin Gahō* in the first year of the Occupation, " 'I find [the Occupation soldiers] courteous, friendly, carefree and perfectly at ease. What a sharp and painful contrast to the haughty, mean, and discourteous Japanese soldiers who used to live in the barracks near my home' " (in LaCerda 1946, 54). It was a mark of distinction to be seen in the company of a Western man and treated with "ladies first" gallantry. Spickard cites the example of Nobuko "Cherry" Sakuramoto, who married an Australian soldier in the Occupation, quoting from her biography: "She felt it strange but exciting to be walking in step with the Goshujin [Australian], he so tall, she barely up to his shoulder, a man who walked on the outside of the pavement and helped her over ditches and gutters. She intercepted sidelong glances from other Japanese and she was proud of the way they stared at the barbarian's height and fairness" (Carter 1965, 31, in Spickard 1989, 129).

The pleasure that some middle-class Japanese women took in their encounters, however brief, with American soldiers is evident in an extraordinary dialogue (*taidan*) entitled "Daily Life in Defeat" ("Haisenka no seikatsu") that was published in the journal *Shinseikatsu* in November 1945, only two months after the Occupation began. This dialogue among seven apparently single working women (identified as two department store clerks, two dancers, a radio announcer, a movie company employee, and a *Shinseikatsu* journalist) and an unnamed male *Shinseikatsu* interviewer breaks down repeatedly along gender lines whenever the topic of G.I.s comes up, as it does regularly, regardless of the ostensible topic under discussion.[29]

The male interviewer attempts to set a tone of injured masculine nationalism from the beginning: "Everyone has undoubtedly walked down the Ginza recently. Now that it is filled with American soldiers somehow it doesn't even seem like Japan anymore, and one gets the profound sense that this is the landscape of a defeated nation. However, there is an Oriental saying that 'the defeated soldier never speaks,' so today talk of the war is forbidden, and instead I would like to speak with you all of postwar daily life" ("Haisenka no seikatsu," 1984, 220). He proceeds almost immediately to introduce the question of women's safety in the streets, and from there asks leadingly, "The G.I.s carry around with them chocolate and all sorts of candy. Don't you want some of it?" (To which one of the women replied, "Not really"; 222). He insinuatingly inquires into their impressions of foreign men. The following is an abridged version of the ensuing dialogue:

SECOND DEPARTMENT STORE CLERK: On the trains, they give up their seat [to women].
MALE INTERVIEWER: Do you accept it?
DEPARTMENT STORE CLERK: Yes I do.
MALE INTERVIEWER: Without saying anything?
DEPARTMENT STORE CLERK: I say "thank you" [sankyū]. . . .
RADIO ANNOUNCER: Foreigners are nice to all women, not just to young ones.
FIRST DANCER: One day I was holding a [large] package [on the train]. The men around me were empty-handed, but not one of them offered to help me to lift it to the rack. But two American soldiers came and picked it up for me. I was so happy then. I thought, wouldn't it be nice if Japanese men would do this kind of thing occasionally?
MALE INTERVIEWER: Well, sorry. (laughter)
DEPARTMENT STORE CLERK: Japanese men might want to do it but feel too embarrassed.
MALE INTERVIEWER: I'd like to hold packages [for women] but I think the people around me might think I was strange, so I don't.
FEMALE JOURNALIST: Do you think you can reform?
MALE INTERVIEWER: No! Please! I have a weak heart! . . .
SECOND DANCER: American men truly are kind to women. And not just to women but to women and children and anyone weak. . . . Of course, Japanese men aren't all unkind.
MALE INTERVIEWER: Absolutely not. (laughter)

As the interview goes on, the women continually shift the tone of the conversation away from the teasingly half-defensive, half-risqué themes introduced by the male interviewer to gentle but pointed praise of American (and criticism of Japanese) men. Later, the interviewer introduces the topic of returning Japanese soldiers, then flooding back into Japan from China, Manchuria, Korea, and elsewhere in enormous numbers. When he asks suggestively, "Don't you all feel some compassion toward these returning demobilized soldiers [and want to marry them]?" the women evade answering, turning the conversation to a sympathetic discussion of the suffering of Occupation comfort women and the common sight of Japanese women walking with American soldiers. When the interviewer hastily attempts to return the conversation to the topic of heroic Japanese men, asking more pointedly, "Don't you want to quickly marry the returned soldiers and comfort them and repay them for their long years of suffering?" (229), the women proceed to express nothing but contempt for Japan's military and pity for its ex-soldiers:

> FEMALE JOURNALIST: I think the "military spirit" [*gunjin seishin*] might be [Japan's] biggest problem.
> RADIO ANNOUNCER: Yes. Some people say that there is nothing more corrupt [*fuhai*] than the Japanese military. Of course we haven't seen it personally so we might not know, but the military certainly isn't all good. I used to believe that there was nothing more upright and fine than the Japanese military, but I've heard that the reality is quite different, and that with each succeeding day in the military life, a man only degenerates further.
> SECOND DEPARTMENT STORE CLERK: Yes, I once used to believe that the military was truly fine too.
> MALE INTERVIEWER: For heaven's sake [*mattaku ne*]! (230)

In desperation, the interviewer attempts to introduce the bland topic of recent books. Yet this too leads the women directly to a critique of the Japanese family.

> SECOND DEPARTMENT STORE CLERK: Women need more time to read books. Women who have families have almost no time at all for reading. In foreign countries, even if you have a family you still have time to read books.

FIRST DANCER: And some Japanese men even say that they hate "book-reading women."

FEMALE JOURNALIST: Those kind are hopeless!

Echoing Sakanishi Shiho's *The American Woman*, the women use the gender roles of 1940s America as the basis for a pointed critique of women's position in Japan:

FIRST DEPARTMENT STORE CLERK: I checked into the situation in America, and I learned that a good wife over there will read the day's newspaper from front to back, and when her husband comes home from work, she will tell him what was in it. Since the husband is busy he has only the time to glance at the headlines on the train, but after dinner, he hears the rest from his wife. I want time like that for us too.

MALE INTERVIEWER: You don't have it?

FIRST DEPARTMENT STORE CLERK: Perhaps I wasn't clear. No, we don't. (laughter). . . .

MOVIE COMPANY EMPLOYEE: I recently read Arishima Takeo's collection *To Those I Love* [*Ai suru hitobito e*]. It's a collection of impressions from the United States. I think he sees America very clearly indeed. I suppose there are those who live frivolous, unbalanced lives in places like New York, but I realized that there are many things we need to learn from upright American homes. (231–32)

In *Dear General MacArthur* [Haikei makkāsā gensuisama], a provocative book analyzing letters written to Douglas MacArthur by Japanese people during the Occupation, political historian Sodei Rinjirō argues that Japanese women "adored" MacArthur, even to the point of writing him love letters. This adoration, he argues, was paradigmatic of "the true nature of the Japanese Occupation" (1985, 142), which, he insists, should be seen not as a "rape," but a "seduction":

Since beginning research on the Occupation, I have often said that the Japanese of the time "slept with" the Occupiers. This has earned me the displeasure of more serious individuals. Nevertheless, I still hold to that belief. . . . Japanese during the Occupation were not forced to reform by the Occupying forces under MacArthur. Didn't we actually want to be raped? The Americans were rich and attractive, and the offspring—"democracy"—wasn't bad. To raise the half-breed [konketsuji] thus born—"democratic Japan"—was certainly the responsibility of "the father." But was it not even more the responsibility of the members of the nation themselves, as its "mothers"? (142–43)

Sodei here (ironically?) deploys a troubling metaphor of sexual violation in a passage that foregrounds the larger gendered relations of power between Japan and the United States after World War II. In historian Igarashi Yoshikuni's words, "The drama [of postwar U.S.-Japan relations] casts the United States as a male and Hirohito and Japan as a docile female who unconditionally accepts the United States' desire for self-assurance" (1998, 273). In Sodei's passage, Japan after its defeat and Occupation was not even the "wife" in an ostensibly harmonious postwar "marriage" to the United States, but the temptress who couldn't say no, burdened, after her rape, with the illegitimate child of democracy.

This eroticization of national power relations is reflective of the larger erotic politics of Orientalism, which, as Said (1978) pointed out, is not limited to the actual sexual encounters of a small number of actors, but becomes paradigmatic of the larger relations between the East and the West. Said and others (particularly Frantz Fanon, 1967) have shown that white men's power in the world is manifested in their sexual access to the women of other races, rendering white and nonwhite women competitors for their patronage. Nonwhite men, meanwhile, are the perpetually excluded other; in the case of Asian men, they are rendered emasculated and abject, incapable of controlling their own women, let alone gaining access to white women. Japanese men in the postwar period attempted to resist the sexual power relations of the Occupation and its legacy by deflecting these sexualized humiliations onto the bodies of treacherous Japanese women. In a 1957 dialogue with writers Nakaya Ken'ichi and Takagi Takeo in the pages of the prestigious journal *Chūō Kōron,* writer Ōya Sōichi proposes using Japanese "girls" as reparations payment to the United States. Takagi responds, "It might take care of the population problem! We could just send the leftovers, the ones over thirty" (175). Lurking beneath this misogynistic fantasy is the writers' fear and resentment of Japanese women who, in Ōya's words, can "pass" anywhere. Ōya remarks that Japanese girls "don't seem to want to marry Japanese men," prompting Nakaya to deride the "spoiled Japanese girls" he encountered in the United States:

> There aren't very many Japanese girls in the States, but since it's too much trouble for Japanese [male] students to try and date American girls, and the dating customs are so different, the men all try to find Japanese girls. The result is that the Japanese girl students get extremely spoiled. On top of that, when these girls go out with Americans, they fall completely head over heels. Meanwhile, the Japanese American [*nisei*] girls all marry [white] Americans, so the Japanese American boys all look for the girls from Japan. The upshot is that with Japanese female study-abroad students, to put it bluntly, half of them don't come back. My thinking is, we should let top-class Japanese girls go to study abroad only *after* they've become engaged to a man in Japan.

Ōya wraps up the dialogue by opining sarcastically, "For ages [Japanese] men have enjoyed special male chauvinistic privileges, so when they go abroad, they can't adapt. In other words, Japanese males are just too awful; I guess what it amounts to is this: any man is better than a Japanese" (175).

Such male resentment against the internationally mobile Japanese woman reemerges in the findings of Bennett, Passin, and McKnight in the context of male students in the United States. They write, "One of the big complaints against American soldiers in Japan has been that they take away 'our girls,' as if by right of conquest" (1958, 122). "In the etiquette of race relations," they continue, "the 'superior' males always have access to the 'inferior' females, but the 'inferior' males cannot approach the 'superior' females. Was not something of this kind involved? This was the question lurking in many minds" (122). In this melodramatic description of the real-life effects of Orientalist erotics, Bennett et al. reveal the contours of the white male magnetism derived from American geopolitical might in the postwar period.

I return to this in subsequent chapters. For now I wish to explore some of the ways these erotic power relations found expression in one piece of women's writing that, while treating the Occupation period, stages Occupation history for women's consumption in the internationalist Zeitgeist of the late 1980s, moving our discussion into the present era. Written by contemporary internationalist author Miyamoto Michiko in 1988, this text, entitled *American Lover* (Amerika no koibito), is the biography of Ishihara Yuriko, a young woman from the countryside who, during the Occupation, had several G.I. lovers. Later in life, Yuriko became the long-term mistress of one of these men, who set her up in an apartment in New York City, where she lived the rest of her life, becoming a well-known figure in the local Japanese community. Her significance for Miyamoto (and her readership), it seems, lies in her ability to candidly articulate the precise terms of the erotic hierarchy of the Occupation through the eyes of a young Japanese woman of the time. As a text, *American Lover* celebrates the power of intimacy with white men to render Japanese women independent of "tyrannical" Japanese men, finally brought low at the hands of the Americans. In its gleeful enunciation of the ensuing power reversal, the text exhibits Yuriko's story as a model and an inspiration for discontented women of the contemporary era.

Miyamoto quotes Yuriko on her first impression of an American G.I. arriving in her small Nagano town in 1945: "How slim he is, how tall and proud, and handsome!" (1988, 23): "The giant G.I.s in their Jeeps, who at that time began to appear in her quiet little temple town, caught everyone's eye and were indeed a thrilling sight. . . . And in an era when Japanese girls wore *geta* [wooden sandals] and *monpe* [baggy, rough cotton trousers], with not a stitch of makeup and their hair in bowl cuts or braids, only the women who dated Americans could dress up in high heels and red lipstick and nail polish. . . . [And the Americans] smelled so good, like fresh soap and Suave shampoo! Yuriko loved the way Americans smelled" (26–27).

Yuriko's friend Mitsuko found a job as a housemaid in an American official's home and regaled Yuriko with tales of her employers' elegant table manners and delicious cooking: "Yuriko sighed when she thought of all the Japanese women standing in their cold dark kitchens, suffering from frostbite because they had only freezing cold water to use. She compared them in her mind to the smiling American women she'd seen in movies, wearing pink aprons and moving lightly about their bright, white, sparkling kitchens" (28). Mitsuko told her happily how the man of the house behaved toward even her, the housemaid, with ladies-first courtesy treating her as a "human being and an individual." In response, Yuriko "thought of her ex-fiancé Nakamura in his military uniform. Nakamura, and her father too, like all Japanese men, saw women as one step below them, and examples of their tyrannical behavior sprang to her mind. She was so enchanted with the world that Mitsuko described that it seemed as though she was swept further and further inside it" (28). Attending her first dance party with the American soldiers, she felt a "tiny liberation" (*chiisana kaihōkan*) as her cares melted away (29).

Even her rape by an American soldier, which led to her surreptitious departure for Tokyo in the middle of the night, did not change Yuriko's views. Rather, in Tokyo she became the "only" (*onrii*, i.e., steady girl) of a G.I. named John. Of this relationship she recalled later, "Never in her life had she been treated this gently and equally by a man, and without a feeling of oppression" (44). The first time they made love, Yuriko recalled, "She was for a moment frozen with fear of large men [because of the rape], but John didn't rush, and slowly, slowly, as if gently soothing a child to sleep, guided her to feelings of reassurance and pleasure" (46).

Thus it was, according to Yuriko,

That all the women of Japan had nothing but akogare [longing] for America; meanwhile Japanese men, undernourished and pale, were frail and thin. The fact that the men dressed their weakly bodies in loose, baggy trousers that flapped around them as they walked made them appear even seedier. They may have been her countrymen, but even so, Yuriko would unthinkingly avert her eyes. On top of the wretchedness of their clothes, Japanese men constantly had a pinched and angry look. . . . Japanese men had witnessed the hell of war, and the humiliation of defeat. Silently, with bitter faces reflecting the bitterness of their lives, Japanese men reproached the "American pretentions" [*amerika kabure*] of Japanese women. (51–52)

In Yuriko's Occupation, we see the process by which the white man is fetishized as the object of a helpless akogare, the inevitable result of American military victory and world dominance. That the book's title is "American lover" renders the identity of the lover ultimately meaningless, for that he is American and white is what accords him his power and allure. It is this power, or some part of it, that passes to the woman who aligns herself with him. By contrast, the Japanese man, abject, pathetic, and rejected, is the disavowed reminder of Japan's failure and defeat, before whom Yuriko "would unthinkingly avert her eyes." Better that she turn her eyes away than be reminded of the lack (of status, money, power) that she sought the favor of the white man to conceal or forget.

Miyamoto, a popular writer of the late 1980s, transforms this story into a parable for the internationalist longings of the newly mobile young Japanese female population of the "bubble" era, then seeking an avenue for gendered resistance and escape. As we shall see, although the "American lover" is not the sole condition of women's internationalist movements in the late twentieth century, he continues to figure in persistent dreams of escape and redemption.

2 ≋ Internationalism as Resistance

Women's recent moratorium on marriage has struck complacent Japanese men . . . like the arrival of Commodore Perry's black ships in Tokugawa Japan, forcing them from their peaceful slumbers.—ECONOMIST ŌHASHI TERUE, *Mikonka no shakaigaku* (Sociology of nonmarriage)

In a noisy American city, I feel safe from the oppressive silence of my past.—KYOKO MORI, *Polite Lies: On Being a Woman Caught between Cultures*

The turn to the West that was primarily the privilege of a small number of elite, highly educated women in the Meiji and Taishō eras, while expanding in scope in the years following World War II, only emerged as a widespread and popular option for middle-class women with the growth of the Japanese bubble economy in the 1980s. From this point on, young unmarried women in the cities began to command a high level of expendable income, derived from their secretarial "office lady" (OL) positions in Japan's corporations, combined with often company-mandated residence in their parents' home. Despite their relatively low wage level compared to male workers, this rate of expendable income left them, in terms of personal consumer spending, by far the "wealthiest" sector of Japan's mainstream population, and one of the wealthiest groups in the world. Using the money generated by the Japanese economy to embark on a program of intensive consumption of foreign goods, food, and travel, young single women soon emerged as the most thoroughly "cosmopolitan" population in Japan. In the process, some of these women, particularly urban office workers with a degree of professional ambition who were frustrated by the unapologetic gender discrimination of the Japanese corporate structure, began to pursue more serious involvement with the foreign through language study, study abroad, employment in foreign-affiliate firms, and other means. Appropriating the narratives of internationalism popularized by their predecessors in the Meiji, Taishō, and mid-Shōwa eras, these "internationalist" women began to speak anew of the West as a site of deliverance from Japanese gendered structures of family and work.

Examples of internationalist narratives abound in a genre of Japanese women's writing about the West by authors such as Mori Yōko (1988), Marks Toshiko (1986, 1992, 1993, 1999), Yamamoto Michiko (1993a, 1993b), and Miyamoto Michiko (1985, 1988). An approximate English equivalent of these texts exists in the oeuvre of U.S.-based writer Kyoko Mori, particularly her 1997 memoir, *Polite Lies: On Being a Woman Caught between Cultures*. These are accompanied by a popular genre of informal, minimally edited autobiographical accounts by ordinary young women, who have no other literary qualification than their personal experience of quitting an ol job in Japan to study, work, or reside abroad. These texts, which follow distinct formulaic conventions, and which have appeared with remarkable regularity each year since the mid 1980s, narrate an allegiance to a "global democratic humanism" that makes the modern West the universal model against which the backward particularities of Japanese tradition must be judged, rejected, or reformed. I discuss many examples of this genre of writing in this chapter. However, women's narratives are not limited to published texts, but are widely spoken, and acted, by a stratum of young, urban, middle-class Japanese women who are discontented with the options open to them in Japan and who use internationalist opportunities to circumvent them.

It should be noted at the outset that, as in previous periods, such internationally active women constitute a minority of Japanese women; as Ogasawara observes in her recent book, the majority of young women in Japan still hold marriage and full-time motherhood as their primary life goals (1998, 62–63). For those women, however, who are enabled by their age, marital status, economic resources, and familial flexibility (among other factors) to explore the cosmopolitan possibilities of internationalization, the foreign option can lead to opportunities for travel, study, and work abroad and for the discovery of a female niche in the international job market as translators, interpreters, consultants, bilingual secretaries, entrepreneurs, international aid workers, and United Nations employees, among other possibilities. It also leads to a profound questioning of domestic Japanese expectations concerning the female life course, culminating in many cases in the assertion of a "new self" (atarashii jibun) that is based on a broad and deep shift of allegiance from what women describe as insular and outdated Japanese values to what they characterize as an expansive, liberating international space of free and unfettered self-expression, personal discovery, and romantic freedom.

However, women's own stories, spoken in personal conversation, were not unqualifiedly celebratory, but tentative, shifting, contradictory, and contingent. Women aligned themselves with internationalism at different points in their lives, only to reject it later, and did not at any time unproblematically accept all of its claims. My project was to observe what happened when they sought to exploit transnationally circulating public images and narratives of the West to open a much needed and effective space for oppositional female praxis, and to trace the steps by which they moved in and out of cosmopolitan associations as active subjects who were yet constituted by the limits of late capitalist and postcolonial regimes of power.

In this chapter I examine debates about women's consciousness (ishiki) and lifestyle (ikikata) as these were expressed in popular media accounts from the late 1980s and 1990s and in my conversations with internationalist women in Tokyo. I relate these to women's frustrations about the corporate dynamic that has simultaneously bound Japanese men and expelled professionally ambitious Japanese women, and discuss the complexities of gender and privilege that push women and men into different choices regarding foreign language study, study abroad, and employment in international organizations and foreign-affiliate firms. Finally, I consider women's dependence on tropes of female flexibility and the "new self" to explain and justify their turn to the foreign, and reflect on the workings of akogare and eroticized desire for the white man as emblem of Western modernity in women's larger imaginary of the emancipatory West.

I note at the outset that the post-1990 recession in Japan has not sig-

nificantly altered women's narration and practice of oppositional internationalism; indeed, if anything, it has intensified it. Although women have
recently been joined by a stratum of young men responding to a diminished job market by seeking foreign opportunities, women continue to
claim a natural intimacy with the West as a specifically female prerogative.

Consciousness Gap In the mid-1980s Japanese women began to complain about an *ishiki no gyappu,* or a "consciousness gap," between Japanese men who were said to want a stay-at-home wife to fulfill "traditional"
duties of childrearing, cooking, and housework, and women who wanted
an "equal partner" who would share housework, interests, and values,
accommodate his wife's career, and put the couple's relationship before
family and work responsibilities. As in previous eras, women were again
raising the question of individual "personhood" in their relations with
men (Kashima 1993, 102–16). Writer Ebisaka Takeshi commented on this
quest in 1988: "In coffeeshops where I do much of my writing, I often
overhear women complaining about their husbands. . . . The word *human
being* crops up frequently in the speech of these unhappy wives. . . . Underlying its use is the married woman's fervent plea that she be treated not
simply as a wife, not as a live-in prostitute, not as a maid, not as a mother,
not even as a woman, but as an independent human being. It reflects the
belief that the relationship between a married couple is first and foremost a
relationship between two human beings" (46; emphasis in original). "The
majority of men, however," Ebisaka concludes, "see a wife as someone
who takes care of their personal needs and does the housework. . . . As a
consequence, the husband is either oblivious to or baffled by his wife's
desperate need to find herself" (46).

This so-called gap undoubtedly has been one important factor behind
Japan's steady trend toward delayed marriage. Japanese women's average
age of first marriage in 1997 was almost twenty-seven (Kōseishō 2000b),
the highest in Japanese history and the highest among industrialized nations. According to the Health and Welfare Ministry, the total proportion of
unmarried Japanese women increased from 41 percent to 49 percent between 1990 and 1995 alone (Nihon Keizai Shimbunsha 1998, 3). Feminist
Ōhashi Terue, investigating the causes of women's "moratorium" on mar-

riage in her 1993 study *The Sociology of Nonmarriage* (Mikonka no shakai-gaku), argues that the phenomenon must be read as a fundamental rejection not only of social norms governing marriage for women, but of the economic division of labor that has legitimated these norms throughout the postwar era. As women's wages have risen, their marriage rates have dropped; currently, she writes, only economic "demerits" accrue to married women, who are not only required to provide unpaid child care labor for the state, but to singlehandedly shoulder, without compensation, the state's burden of care for the elderly. Under these conditions, women's enthusiasm for marriage has apparently cooled. A 1998 survey of unmarried women in their thirties in Tokyo, Kobe, and Osaka found that, although 90 percent of them wished to marry, almost a third of that number hoped to live separately from their husbands. Tanimura Shiho, the author of the popular and controversial book, *The "I May Not Marry" Syndrome* (Kekkon shinai kamoshirenai shōkōgun), argued, "Women want a partner. But men as usual just want a 'wife' [oyomesan]. . . . With partnership consciousness so far apart, who knows how long women will keep postponing marriage?" (1991, 26).[1]

The so-called consciousness gap is certainly one of the reasons behind the drastic fall in the Japanese birthrate as well. The birthrate continued to decline after the "1.57 shock" of 1989, reaching 1.39 in 1997 (Kōseishō 2000a), well below the rate of 2.2 necessary to maintain the Japanese population at its current level. Because of the precipitous decline in the birthrate, the Japanese population is shrinking, and also aging rapidly. The paired trends of delayed marriage and reduced birthrate have inspired intensive public commentary, much of it alluding darkly to the "depravity" of the younger generation, who care, it is argued, for nothing but personal pleasure. Certainly, the high cost of raising children and the inadequacy of child care facilities have discouraged women from having children. Yet, thoughtful observers have pointed to women's changing attitudes as an equally important cause. Sociologist Inamasu Tatsuo has argued that women are engaged in a profound quest for a new *ikikata*, loosely translated as "lifestyle" or "way of life" (1993, 7), that exceeds the current options open to them in the home or the workplace. Young women especially, he and others suggest, are questioning the very foundations of what constitutes a good life. As journalist Yamamoto Michiko writes, "Just earning money is not success. Leading a life that is truly 'alive' is success. . . . Today our goal is to 'find ourselves' " (1993a, 170).

On one level, the question is a gendered one: What is a good life for a woman, a life that is not limited to marriage and family? Journalist Fuke Shigeko observes, "The era has ended when women will be satisfied just with being the section chief's wife [*kachō fujin*]. . . . Today's women, filled with desires and ambition, are no longer satisfied with either of the choices 'company' or 'marriage' " (1990, 281). On another level, however, women's discourse of ikikata constitutes a critique of Japanese men's lives and the values propagated by the patriarchal nation-state. This is the point of social psychologist Iwao Sumiko's controversial 1993 book, *The Japanese Woman: Traditional Image and Changing Reality*, in which she argues that women increasingly see male "corporate warriors" as objects of pity and contempt. "Watching their menfolk over the decades," Iwao writes, "wives see how much of the joy and richness of life can be lost by becoming preoccupied by only one sphere of work; they see the risks and the distortions of the single-occupation life" (83).

These and other Japanese observers have argued that it is toward an intensifying "individualism" (*ko toshite no ikikata*) that women are groping, an individualism that has led them to refuse the demands of family and company in favor of independence and self-sufficiency. This is the argument made in a 1998 book, *Women's Quiet Revolution: The Dawn of the "Individualist" Era* (Onnatachi no shizukana kakumei: "Ko" no jidai ga hajimaru), based on a multiyear study by the *Nihon Keizai Shimbun*, Japan's leading economic newspaper. The authors posit that women have preceded men (whom they claim are bound more deeply by social conventions) in their embrace of individualism in the chaotic conditions of the postbubble era (273). The authors claim that women's individualist ikikata has the potential to radically transform Japanese society. "The outcome of women's 'quiet revolution,' " they state, will be "the rebirth of a new flexible Japan that can accommodate a variety of ikikata" (273). In a reversal of the gender dogma of the high-growth economy, then, women are held to have the power to reform Japan. By virtue of their exclusion from, in Masao Miyoshi's words, the "nearly total male absorption in the production and consumption cycle," women, it is claimed, are poised to "intercede and wrench men from their 'utopian' unintelligence and insularity" (1991, 211–12).

Professional Frustrations Women's quest for a new ikikata is deeply embedded in Japan's economic conditions, for, as Miyoshi notes, it is women's marginality in the economy that has enabled the emergence of their critical discourse of gendered skepticism and complaint. It is not my intention here to rehearse the various forms of discrimination against women in the workplace that have been described so thoroughly elsewhere; yet it is worth briefly sketching women's position in the Japanese economy as the background to internationalist women's resentment against Japan, for it is here that so many women's narratives of desire for the West begin.[2]

Throughout the postwar period women have served as a financial "cushion," a "large, malleable, unskilled labor force that can be controlled according to changing market conditions" (Yamanaka 1993, 1007). They have been systematically denied access to training programs and job rotations based on circular company reasoning that women lack business knowledge and skills, will quit when they marry or have a child, will refuse job rotations to other cities due to family responsibilities, will give higher priority than men to home life, and will be reluctant to spend long hours at work and after-hours socializing (Bando 1991, 18). Indeed, as numerous scholars have pointed out, and Ogasawara's book *Office Ladies, Salaried Men* (1998) has demonstrated, the dominant urban white-collar employment pattern excludes women at every level; young women are nearly always hired for dead-end secretarial positions and are suspect if they continue working past the age of thirty or thirty-five, at which time they are expected to have married and become full-time homemakers. Meanwhile, married women cannot combine family duties, usually entirely the woman's responsibility, with the demands of a full-time job, particularly the required periodic transfers to other cities. Men, in turn, cannot give the devotion to the company required of them without the support of a homemaker wife. Ironically, as Allison (2000) has shown, the smooth functioning of the Japanese economy depends on the central fact of women's exclusion from it as full-time wives and mothers, whereby they devote themselves single-mindedly to the nurturing and education of succeeding generations of workers. Japan is the only industrialized country, Allison notes, "where education has a negative effect on women's employment" (xviii).

Thus, young women in the urban centers by and large are funneled into the position of the office lady, or OL, a clerical post that involves answering phones, copying documents, filing, keeping the office neat, and serving tea to male staff and guests. Yamamoto Michiko (1993b) coined the term "role harassment" (*yakuwari harasumento*) to describe women's incarceration in the OL position. One former OL wrote, "I was invited to try out a management position. I was good at it and I loved it. . . . But then I discovered the reality of male-dominated Japan: that a woman in management is considered an 'uppity girl.' If I offered the smallest opinion I would be dismissed as a woman [*onna no kuse ni*]" ("Ryūgaku taikenki," 1992, 6).

Of course, young, unmarried urban OLs occupy only one position (a position circumscribed by class, age, and place of residence) in a diverse female labor market that also includes blue-collar factory work, farming, fishing, shopkeeping, and service jobs. As Ogasawara notes, however, the relative number of women in white-collar clerical jobs has steadily increased since 1960, whereas the number of women in blue-collar jobs has decreased; in 1995 one-third of all women employed held white-collar clerical positions (1998, 19). Thus, the urban, white-collar, corporate job market by no means exhausts the possibilities of employment in Japan for either men or women, it remains an important one in the public imagination (fueled by the unabashedly Tokyo centric mass media), as well as in the urban middle-class stratum of the population. More importantly, in an economic sense, the OL is central to the functioning of corporate structures in a way that parallels the role of the mothers by virtue of her very marginality. Young women, in turn, accept this marginality because it exempts them from onerous duties within the workplace and frees them to pursue outside interests (Ogasawara 1998; see also Kelsky 1994a). Yet, in the long run, young women's acceptance of their position permits multiple forms of gender discrimination to continue, hindering possibilities for sustained career advancement for women so inclined, and imposing the "motherhood hiatus" at the institutional level.

Women's subordination has been represented by Japanese men as the key to Japan's economic ascendancy. One woman who requested to be allowed to sit in on company meetings and take on greater responsibilities was told by her male superior, "What ruined the American economy was women pushing themselves forward onto the main stage. Countries where women keep themselves behind men are successful" (NHK Shuzaihan 1990, 56). As Kashima and others have observed, Japanese male politicians long resisted the passage of any kind of equal-opportunity law, arguing that such a law could only be the result of Westerners' "colonialism," "invasion," or "intervention," and would lead to the destruction of time-honored Japanese custom (Kashima 1993, 12; see also Molony 1995). Although Japan's Equal Employment Opportunity Law was finally passed in 1986 as Japan's last-ditch attempt to show progress on the status of women before the end of the U.N. Decade for Women, the EEOL codified in law that only insofar as Japanese women conformed to male employment patterns would they attain anything approaching equal standing with men professionally.

The EEOL, such as it was, gave women a choice between comprehensive, career-track positions (sōgōshoku) with responsibility, salary, and promotion opportunity allegedly identical to male employees, and "generalist," clerical positions (ippanshoku) no different from the OL. According to Bando, "The former leads to the top of the corporate ladder but entails long hours of overtime and job transfers. The latter, by contrast, offers less of a future but allows employees to avoid overtime and job rotations" (1991, 19). The EEOL was revised in 1997, with provisions eliminating gender bias in position advertising, hiring, and promotion, strengthening laws against sexual harassment, and lifting restrictions on women's overtime work. However, neither version of the EEOL addressed what many women claimed was the essential problem of the Japanese economy and the fundamental reason that women cannot participate in it equally: the impossibly long hours demanded of workers. Feminist Ueno Chizuko argues, "Rather than abolishing protection [for women], this protection has to be extended to male workers" (1988, 180). That is, the goal must not only be to allow women into the workplace, but to allow men into the home. Because neither version of the EEOL addressed male work practices, the law did not have much effect in attracting women to the demanding managerial track. One author stated that the effort to "make it" in the sōgōshoku career track while maintaining the demands of the home was as punishing as "the conquest of Everest" (Fuke 1991, 280). Thus, even before the economic downturn, a number of journalists and scholars had observed the surprising phenomenon that fewer Japanese women seemed to be pursuing career-track sōgōshoku positions after the passage of the EEOL than did before (Taylor 1994, 217). Lam observes that the cause is their dismay at the personal costs of a career: "It is as if women [are] saying, 'Now that I can have it, I am not sure I want it'" (1992, 209).

One of the specific ways women are marginalized within the Japanese corporate system is age-related pressure. Brinton has written that "Japanese life course transitions are characterized by irreversibility . . . and low variance in timing across individuals" (1993, 100). In other words, individual women (and men) are expected to move, irreversibly, from one life stage to the next at socially determined age intervals. The most important life stage transition for women is the move from the single to the married state within a narrowly defined period of "marriageable years" (*tekireiki*). In concrete terms, this means that women should be married by age thirty or thirty-five, and those who are not are seen as aberrations and "inferior goods." The EEOL has not significantly changed such age-specific expectations nor, ironically, has the rising actual age of marriage. Women's individual acts of resistance through nonmarriage have not as yet translated into widespread change in the expectations of society as a whole.

The women I interviewed in Tokyo complained bitterly of the effects of these gendered expectations regarding age-appropriate behavior and marital status in their lives. "You know why in Japan jobs always specify that women must be twenty-five or younger?" Hori Toshiko, a forty-nine-year-old bilingual secretary at the United Nations University, asked me.[3] "Because young women will take anything. But when they get to be about thirty, they know how to stand up for themselves. Japanese men hate that." Older single women worked in an atmosphere of continual "age surveillance" that rendered them perpetually on the defensive. Odawara Yumiko, a United Nations University programs director in her late thirties, explained:

ODAWARA: If I were to quit this job and enter a Japanese company, the first thing that everyone would want to know is not my name but my age! They won't ask my name, but rather "How old is the new woman?" That's the first thing that Japanese men have to know.
AUTHOR: What does knowing your age tell them?

ODAWARA: I don't know. I personally think that each person's aging is totally different—chronologically, physically, emotionally. . . . But they can't have a clear image of you without knowing it. They base their evaluation on that. They might imagine that you are in your twenties and think you are fun and full of pep, but then hear that you are actually in your thirties, and they revise their whole image of you and see you as middle-aged.

This age-based surveillance encompasses a woman's marital state. Matsumura Minako, an assistant manager in the international division of Daiwa Securities in her early thirties, told me, "It's so hard to be single here. There is pressure all the time. . . . Every day, all day long, pressure, pressure, pressure. It's hell for unmarried women. And Tokyo is still on the good side!"

Women also confront the imposition of a quasi-domestic role in the workplace. The detested task of serving tea was isolated by many women as emblematic of this subservient role. Katō Masumi, a twenty-nine-year-old woman who had worked at a number of *gaishikei,* or foreign-affiliate firms, said indignantly, "You know what you have to do at Japanese companies? You serve tea, right? And you have to remember that division chief likes black tea with two lumps of sugar, and section chief will drink only green tea, and so-and-so takes only coffee. It's ridiculous. But all my friends are doing it." This maternal role does not diminish during extracurricular company activities. Ojima Yukiko, a technical designer for a major computer firm, described the division of labor involved in a company skiing trip:

At the plant I worked at, people had very strict ideas about a woman's proper role. For example, sometimes groups of coworkers would go skiing. The guys would come around in the car, and the women would have to make lunch. Making lunch means you have to get up an hour early and prepare everything, right? All the women. But only one man has to drive, right? So what are all the rest of the men doing? They don't have to do anything, either driving or cooking. But *all* the women have to cook. I think this is unfair, but all the women know this is expected of them, and they know that if you complain you'll put yourself in a very uncomfortable position. Personally, I love to drive, and I would much rather be the driver. But that's not possible.

In this way, women are expected to conform to expectations for their age, rank, and status and move through their stages of life according to a fixed and predetermined manner. Deviations are not welcomed. Women who postpone their job search for a mere two or three months (while they study English in the United States, for example) are rendered unemployable in the postgraduation hiring season. One young woman newly returned from the United States was asked at each company with which she interviewed only three months behind her peers, "Why didn't you look for a job *right after* graduation like everyone else?" It is the expectation, and imposition, of a stately and preordained progress through the stages of life that women with professional ambitions find restrictive, for it is only toward the domestic stage and status of "mother" that women are encouraged to move.

Yamamoto Michiko (1993a) has labeled this system of rigid social expectations the *issei shakai*, or "en masse environment": a form of "managed society" that constitutes, in her view, the greatest obstacle to women's career aspirations and self-expression in Japan. "En masse [*issei ni*] the whole nation faces the 'front lines' of the 'hiring season,' " she writes; "en masse the whole nation holds company entrance ceremonies. People who miss out on these mass events end up as dropouts or losers who fall off the tracks of the managed society from an early age, and who have very little chance of ever reinstating themselves" (6). Whereas the recent recession has certainly destabilized this system, reducing available positions for both male and female new college graduates, raising the incidence of layoffs among even regular male workers, and diminishing workers' sense of loyalty to and security within the company, it has not substantially changed the mass structure of the Japanese job market. As in previous recessions, women have overwhelmingly borne the burden of corporate economic "adjustment," with almost half of new female college graduates unable to find work and jobs remaining ever more closely reserved for men. Thus, as we shall see, women who wish to resist the "tracks of the managed society" increasingly turn to the realm of the foreign to do so. In turn, however, they thereby render themselves the "dropouts" that Yamamoto observed have little chance of reinstatement to the comforts of "home."

The Turn to the West In recent years study abroad has emerged as the most important corporate avoidance strategy (aside from the time-honored

7. The "overseas advance" as a major means of leaving behind a dead-end job. Source: Ishida Yōko, ed., *Marugoto onna no tenki: Itsukara demo yarinaosō* (The complete women's turning point: It's never too late to get your life in order). (Tokyo: Asupekuto, 1997), 4.

path of marriage) for middle-class, white-collar women. One book on women's work abroad opens, "Of the seven OLs at a certain foreign-affiliate firm located in Akasaka . . . three decided to leave for study abroad in their third year. One left for her MBA at Manchester University in England, the second left for her MBA at Harvard, and the third was me. . . . I went to Thunderbird [the American Graduate School of International Studies]" (Noda 1992, 3; see Figure 7). Women who choose this option of flight believe that in or through the West they will discover an individualist ikikata free from the problems of age harassment and gender oppression. "What I like about the United States is that it gives you a second chance," wrote one woman, "the kind of second chance you hardly ever get in Japan" (Gotō K. 1994, 71). This trend has not yet given rise to an identifiable backlash in Japan, but it has undoubtedly shaken the smoothly self-sustaining and self-referential gendered divisions imposed by the corporate structure.[4] Indeed, it has begun to serve as a precedent for marginalized young men who, in the current market conditions, are themselves increasingly required to turn their eyes abroad.

Women express their turn abroad in a newly updated internationalist narrative that posits the West as model and ally in their critique of discriminating corporate practices. A paradigmatic example of the contemporary internationalist narrative is an August 1994 editorial on the status of women in Japan in *Yomiuri Shimbun*, Japan's largest newspaper, by Kawachi Kazuko, a Keiō University professor and feminist scholar. Her piece, which was quickly translated into English for a foreign readership in the

Daily Yomiuri, was an angry critique of the systematic exclusion of women from Japan's corporate structures and a ringing manifesto for women's rights. The essay's rhetorical force derived from a discourse of shaming of Japanese men in an "international" arena. Japanese men, Kawachi's argument went, should be ashamed of themselves for their poor treatment of women, scandalous by European or American standards. She insisted that Japanese men must immediately reform their ways if Japan is to become truly "internationalized"; indeed, Kawachi equates internationalization (*kokusaika*) with the guarantee of women's equal rights by the Japanese government. The editorial concludes, "I look forward to the day when the U.S. administration denounces Japanese firms for having achieved prosperity at the expense of women" (1994, 6).

Space is the recurrent image in these narratives, absent in Japan, abundant in the West. In an autobiography entitled *Shall I Leave Japan?* (Deyōka nippon), the journalist Yamamoto Michiko (who spent five years studying and working in England and the United States and is something of a spokesperson for the internationalist route) insists that Japan is a "pond" that keeps its women stunted in size and forever swimming in circles, whereas the West is a vast lake in which women may finally grow to their full proportions and capabilities (1993b, 167–68). Yamamoto argues for a female "warrior discipline" (*musha shugyō*) in which women reject the constricting bonds of Japanese tradition and school themselves in self-knowledge on the world stage. Tanabe Atsuko, an international business consultant who has lived in Mexico for over thirty years, writes that the solution to women's "limited mental and physical space" in Japan is "salvation" in the "limitless space of the foreign [*kaigai no mugen no supēsu*]" (1993, 170–73).

As in previous eras, the United States reigns as the object of women's most intense internationalist hopes. The copy from a job recruitment pamphlet targeting young women reads, "My American Dream: America is the land of dreams. Just as it did for so many of my predecessors, America gave me hope to turn my dreams into reality" (see Figure 8). In the early 1990s New York City began to stand in as the pinnacle of Japanese women's foreign opportunity. Former OL Fuke Shigeko, in her memoir *Beguiled by New York* (Miserarerete nyū yōku, 1990), claims that compared to the

8. "My American Dream." Source: Selnate Shūshoku Annai (Job search information) brochure, 1990.

"sleepy hick town" of Tokyo, New York is "the big city," holding out the promise of success, fulfillment, and freedom for Japanese women. "Why do [Japanese women] all aim for New York?" she asks. "Because it is filled with everything that Tokyo lacks. On the one hand you have Japan, which emphasizes efficiency, order, and harmony, and which makes no effort to respect ikikata that stray from the norm. Then you have America, a country in which individuality, creativity, and personal expression are the top priorities, and which respects people's right to live as they please" (281–82). Taga Mikiko expands on the theme: "One after another Japanese women flock to New York City seeking opportunities. . . . It is a harshly competitive world, but these courageous women with shining eyes keep at the challenge, believing that if they give it all they've got, they're sure to grasp success" (1991, 157). This belief continues unabated in the postrecession era. In 1999 the respected weekly newsmagazine *AERA* featured an article touting the lures of a New York career for women in language indistinguishable from that of ten years earlier (see Hamada 1999).[5]

The Means of Departure In this section, I briefly sketch some of the methods women use to accomplish their defection into internationalist professional settings: English study, study abroad, work abroad, and employment at nongovernmental organizations (NGOS) such as the United Nations and in foreign-affiliate (*gaishikei*) firms. There are other sectors of the economy that internationalist women have colonized, particularly English-language teaching in Japan and Japanese-language teaching to foreigners in Japan and abroad, but the five I focus on here are the ones that were dominant among the women I met and also within the internationalist literature I read. As I noted above, in the recent recession each of these strategies has been increasingly marketed to Japanese men; in 1998 international recruitment firms were pushing study abroad, work in foreign-affiliate firms, and work abroad to men through seminars, workshops, and publications in unprecedented ways. Representations of the specific attractions of the foreign, however, continued to differ significantly in the cases of women and men.

English as Woman's Weapon. English and other foreign languages are perceived as the single most indispensable "weapon" (*buki*) in women's battle for advancement in the business world. Matsubara Junko, in her 1989 book *Eigo dekimasu* (I can speak English), writes, "For men, business comes first and English only second, but for women English is always first" (76). She goes on, "Essentially, in the case of women, if you cannot speak English, you have no chance of even getting your foot into the business world" (54). English allows women to monopolize the ever growing need for bilingual people to facilitate Japanese economic interactions with the rest of the world. In 1993, for example, over 90 percent of NHK broadcast interpreters were women, and one industry source reported that 90 percent of the interpreters and 60 percent of the bilingual guides she dealt with were female (Seo 1993, 12). Women monopolize the field of interpreting to such an extent that men are now being exhorted not to reject the field as a women-only domain. Although not to the extent of interpreting, translating too is a largely female-dominated field, with more and more women translating foreign books by female authors ("Women Translators Gaining More Clout," 1993, 3). Of the 120 students enrolled in the NHK Bilingual Center interpreting/translating courses in 1994, nearly all were women ("Tōsei 'dōji tsūyaku' jijō," 1994, 14).

Increasingly, as the number of Japanese who can speak English fluently grows, third languages are becoming necessary for women's advancement. Fushida Kazuko, a twenty-three-year-old graduate student in Burmese language and history at the respected Tokyo University of Foreign Studies (Tokyo Gaikokugo Daigaku), believed that her Burmese ability would guarantee her a job after graduation: "The interesting thing is that with Burmese, just by speaking Burmese, suddenly my status is different. It's like 'Please, Your Highness; sit right here, Your Highness . . .' Or, say I need a pen, then the response is, 'Come on, didn't you hear? Her Highness wants a pen!' [laugh] It is quite an advantage!" As she exclaimed gleefully, "As long as I have my Burmese, men serve *me* the tea!"

English and other foreign languages are far more than simply professional tools, however; they are the means by which women enter bodily into alternative systems of thought and value. Matsubara argues that whereas Japanese men may study English with little effect on their ultimate success in a predetermined career path in Japan, women who do so find not only their careers but their marriage prospects, their self-identity, and the very fabric of their lives deeply and irrevocably changed. "English is not just a language," she writes, "it is something that has the power even to transform women's lives" (1989, 172). Japanese, with its highly codified rules of speech hierarchy and masculine and feminine speech, is isolated as one of the fundamental obstacles to women's self-expression. For U.S.-based author Kyoko Mori, Japanese is "a steel net" hauling her into "a galaxy of the past, where I can never say what I feel or ask what I want to know" (1997, 5). English, by contrast, is said to provide women with the means to pure and unmediated expression of their "personhood" beyond gender. As Takahashi Nobuko, the former assistant director of the International Labor Organization (ILO), remarks in her memoirs, English gives Japanese women "a clean sense of liberation [kaihōkan]" (1979, 131).

Matsubara introduces a thirty-one-year-old woman named Miyahara Kyōko who insisted that her very identity was contingent on her command of English: "In my case, if you took away my English, there would be nothing left. I can't even imagine myself existing without English [*eigo nashi no watashi wo kangaeraremasen*]" (in 1989, 103). Takahara Etsuko, a thirty-six-year-old market researcher at an American financial news firm with a BA from UCLA, asserted, "I studied English hard since middle school. I spoke broken English back then, but I didn't care, because I had so many opinions that I wanted to express. I felt like I couldn't possibly say them in Japanese. I wanted to learn this new vocabulary to express myself better. So I worked really hard. The average Japanese doesn't have any opinion! Even in Japanese! But I had loads of opinions, and because of that I learned English fast."

Although the most recent job-hunting publications for men (see Tanaka N. 1998c) have also begun to emphasize English skills for professional advancement, they do not link the language with the promise of free personal "self-expression." Indeed, English-language study was treated very differently in a 1994 men's magazine article entitled "The Stupidity of Japanese Worship of English." Ridiculing Japanese women who "forget their Japanese and think they've become 'international' just by learning to speak English," the article concludes by urging Japan to "take a lesson from France and reject English" (Shiohara 1994, 36).

Study Abroad (Ryūgaku). Study abroad (ryūgaku) is currently the most common means women employ to circumvent the Japanese corporate system. In the past twenty years the nature of Japanese ryūgaku has changed dramatically. From the 1950s through the 1970s, ryūgaku was the privilege of elite, management-track males who were sent by their corporations to earn MBA degrees at high-ranking U.S. business schools. In the 1980s and 1990s however, such men gradually came to be almost entirely eclipsed by independent, self-funded women: in 1998 nearly 70 percent of all Japanese studying abroad were female (ICS 1998). So popular is language study in the United States that classes at many English-language schools since the 1980s have almost entirely comprised Japanese women (Matsubara 1989, 145). Matsubara Junko writes in *I Can Speak English*, "U.S.-Japan trade friction might soon be resolved—right now Japan doesn't export Toyotas and Nissans so much as female study-abroad students" (145).[6]

In *Escape from Affluence*, a study of Japanese study-abroad students in Australia, the authors note that not only are there twice as many female as male students there, but the number of Japanese female travelers to Australia between the ages of twenty and twenty-four increased 350 percent between 1988 and 1990 alone (Andressen and Kumagai 1996, 9). Japanese Ministry of Justice data show that, in total numbers, over 130,000 women travel abroad to study each year (Sōrifu Tōkeika 1999, 70). Although men too have begun to pursue self-funded study abroad in the past few years (1998 data suggest that they currently constitute a little over 30 percent of all Japanese students abroad), Andressen and Kumagai note that male students by and large tend to be "wanderers" who have rejected the Japanese system and have little desire for upward mobility. Female students, by contrast, they characterize as "escapees" from Japanese society, with strong motivation to succeed (84–85).

Almost all women point to discrimination in the workplace as their motivation for study abroad. Kubota Kaori and Ishizaki Reiko, two friends in their mid-twenties who both spent two years studying at Sacramento State University in California, said, "We already could see that there was no future at work [saki ga mieru]. If we wanted to have any kind of real career, we knew we had to study abroad." Kitahara Satoko, a bilingual securities trader in her early thirties, told me of her study-abroad experience at Loyola University, "The reason that I first decided to study in America was that Japanese society is male-dominated. . . . When I thought about how I could get my foot in the door, the first thing that came to mind was to study English in the United States and get qualified abroad."

Women's enthusiasm for study abroad is all the more remarkable given that, unlike the majority of male students, women must fund it on their own. Matsubara notes, "Women must quit their jobs entirely and leave for study abroad not only unemployed, but shouldering the total burden of cost themselves" (1989, 52).[7] Women pay for study abroad by expending tens of thousands of dollars of savings carefully accumulated over years of office work, and when this is exhausted, by loans from parents, despite the fact that for most of their middle-class families this represents a significant financial sacrifice (see Matsui M. 1995, 360). That women are willing to exhaust their savings and inconvenience their families (often facing considerable pressure to desist in their plans) demonstrates the degree to which ryūgaku is perceived as an essential means for women to gain the

English-language ability, professional training, and international expertise that they believe is indispensable to compete against Japanese men in the domestic job market.

There are two types of female ryūgaku: "career-up" ryūgaku for ambitious professional women, and "short-term" or "refresh-type" ryūgaku (previously belittled as *yūgaku* in a pun that incorporates the character *yū*, meaning "play" or "waste time"), in which women go abroad only for a few months of language study (Kashima 1993, 190). The so-called OL ryūgaku boom of the late 1980s reflected a surge in short-term ryūgaku; as this experience became common, more serious professionally oriented women turned to long-term ryūgaku, with the goal of acquiring a graduate degree (Ishida 1997). At the peak of women's study-abroad opportunities is the MBA (Kashima 1993, 188–89). In 1993 women made up over 20 percent of Japanese students in each entering class at major business schools, having risen from nearly zero in 1988 (O'Toole 1993, 20; see also Matsui M. 1995, 358). That number has since risen still further.

Journalist Sasaki Kaoru describes the MBA trajectory in the case of a young woman named Mochizuki Shinobu. Having spent one year in Wisconsin during high school, Mochizuki eventually returned to the United States as an assistant in a small Japanese futures trading firm in Chicago. Four years later she moved to a Japanese brokerage house in New York. When she discovered the Japanese management would not promote her, she quit her job and enrolled in the MBA program at Columbia. After finishing, Mochizuki was hired as a dealer at Merrill Lynch. Sasaki quotes her as saying, "Sometimes it's hard to wake up in the morning, but when I think of how miserable I was at those Japanese companies, I am so grateful for the chance that I have now, that before I know it I am jumping out of bed" (1993, 216–18).

Nevertheless, embarking on a self-funded MBA entails even more than the usual risk and hardship for women. Noda Kaori, who earned an MBA at Thunderbird, recounts that the Japanese men in her class, entirely funded by their companies, drove around in convertibles and sports cars and traveled regularly to California or Central or South America for vacations. "On the other hand," she recalls, "we female students had to shell out $10,000 for just one semester's tuition. Even if we could finally go on a single much-anticipated trip, we had to stay in the cheapest hotels, nibble on bread, and calculate our leftover money at the end of each day" (1992, 146–47). The gendered differences extend to the rank of the institution as well: "For men, who are funded by their companies, it doesn't matter where they take their MBA. Their life will not be any different. . . . But for women, their professional lives will be significantly altered depending on whether they have an MBA from Harvard or Idaho" (Matsubara 1989, 54).

It is thus clear that the support of the company provides many advantages for men. On the other hand, in the long run this same corporate support may have the effect of narrowing men's personal and professional horizons. The demands of the Japanese corporate structure follow Japanese men all the way to their foreign study-abroad locations, constraining their behavior. Men who are sent abroad by their companies are urged not to become too deeply involved with the local community. One woman I interviewed observed of the Japanese men at her university in the United States, "Japanese men must always act 'properly' Japanese. There's peer pressure. If they don't, they'll be left out of company business when they go home." The force of the mechanisms by which these expectations are imposed on males, in ways that exceed mere company pressure, are evident in the case of kikokushijo, or returnee children who have been raised all or in part abroad. As Goodman has shown, while female kikokushijo are generally allowed to stay abroad longer and attend local schools, gaining bilingual and bicultural fluency (but becoming marginalized from school and career paths in Japan), boys are sent home early to attend Japanese schools and assure their smooth transition into an elite university and career path (1990, 152).

Again, however, as in the case of English-language study, it is by no means simply professional qualifications that women seek in choosing study abroad. Rather, it is access to an entirely new realm of value and meaning that will lead to transformative life experiences and self-fulfillment. The distinctiveness of Japanese women's belief in, and akogare for, the liberatory potential of the West becomes apparent when their experiences abroad are contrasted with those of other female students from Asia. In sociologist Matsui Machiko's (1995) comparative study of Japanese and Chinese female study-abroad students at a northeastern U.S. state college, she argues that compared to their Chinese compatriots, Japanese women suffer from a lack of not only economic resources, but also family and societal support for their study-abroad decision. Consequently, because they cannot anticipate professional success on their return to Japan, they have vague and uncertain long-term career goals. The result, she argues, is a much deeper investment in American values and unwillingness to return home. Whereas the Chinese students she interviewed expressed skepticism about American women's status and did not engage in a critique of Chinese patriarchy as a result of their study abroad, Japanese women were "impressed by the relative gender equity in American society" and eager to see Japan change along an American model. Younger Japanese women are more likely to admire American culture, Matsui reports, "and they more often report that American 'individualist' culture has made them more 'self-confident,' 'self-expressive,' and 'self-assertive'" (363–65).

In this way, Japanese women's desire for an individualist ikikata merges with their akogare for the West in a narrative of self-transformation through study abroad. Although the latest material is also urging on men the self-funded BA or MBA as a path to entrepreneurship or employment in foreign-affiliate firms (Tanaka N. 1998c; see also Kosugi 1998), it does not reference this discourse of self-transformation, which remains entirely gendered female. As a former OL wrote of the impact of study abroad in America: "Now, when I draw my life plan, it includes marriage *and* work *and* study. I know from experience how hard it is for women to be this greedy in Japanese society. But if I were to lack even one of these things, I know that I cannot live as myself [*jibun rashiku ikirarenai*]. Once the child has wakened, you cannot put her back to sleep" ("Ryūgaku taikenki," 1992, 6).

Work Abroad. A more demanding path by which women explore the foreign option is through work abroad. There are two standard trajectories for female work abroad: women in Japan may seek work opportunities overseas, or women already studying abroad may postpone their return home by taking jobs locally.[8] In either case, however, women define work abroad as the ultimate female opportunity to both explore the "limitless space of the foreign" and to test and temper new priorities, talents, and ikikata. As a *Nihon Keizai Shimbun* article entitled "Working Women's Overseas Advance" summarizes, "The number of women seeking a workplace overseas is increasing. . . . Frustrated with the Japanese working environment in which women are not treated equally with men, their goals seem to be to 'test themselves,' 'develop language skills,' and cross the ocean in search of new meaning in life [*ikigai*]" ("Hataraku josei kaigai shinshutsu," 1993, 15).

The degree to which work abroad has become a "feminized" realm is revealed in one woman's account of her Japanese firm's vain search for Japanese male employees to work in its New York office. She remarks that "no matter what, Japanese men will avoid an American company where there is no lifetime employment system and no standard pay scale. . . . Even the ones that joined usually quit within a year, because they didn't like working under so many women" (Noda 1992, 140–49). She concluded her account: "The company was becoming more and more a woman's domain" (149).[9]

Japanese women seeking the work-abroad option concentrate their efforts on the United States. Women's accounts of American work experience constitute latter-day Horatio Alger tales of success and self-knowledge through perseverance, talent, ambition, and luck, real-life testimonies of faith in the American Dream. The following is just one example:

> Ms. T works at a Los Angeles architectural firm . . . as part of management, the team leader of a group of bright young architects. These up-and-coming architects all have graduate degrees from Harvard and MIT. . . . Meanwhile she is Japanese, and has graduated from no architectural school. . . . What did she do during the ten years it took her to get here? She arrived each day before anyone else; she did any chores that she saw needed to be done, even when it was not her job; when she made coffee for herself, she made a cup for everyone. And of course, she took on any job, no matter how unpleasant. . . . Gradually, she gained the affection and trust of her superiors, and eventually became a management member of a famous architectural firm. (Inage 1989, 197–200)

It is ironic, to say the least, that doing chores and making coffee for the office in order to gain the "affection of her superiors" are held up as Ms. T's route to success abroad. This is especially so since America is nearly always represented as a completely "meritocratic" environment (*jitsuryoku shakai*) in which gender, age, and racial discrimination have been eliminated. One woman interviewed for a 1990 NHK television program and book on the exodus of Japanese working women abroad expressed her amazement that on American résumés "you don't have to write one single thing about your sex, age, marital status or family situation!" (NHK Shuzaihan 1990, 127). Another claimed that in America, "your education and results speak for themselves regardless of whether you are male or female . . . if a secretary wants to move up to a professional position, she can go back to college or graduate school at any time . . . and if you quit work to have a baby, you can always come back and find a job at the same level!" (157). She concludes, "America is a society in which you can always start over, no matter how old you are." Yamamoto Michiko (1993b) reports that she exclaimed upon arriving in America, "I feel like youth has come again!"

This view has only intensified with the worsening recession. A 1999 article in the journal *AERA* once again praised the U.S. "meritocratic" environment and noted that the number of Japanese women who choose to work in U.S. companies in order to "develop their full potential as professionals" is growing. One woman working as a software designer in Silicon Valley is quoted in the article as saying, "If you're talented, you get respect, regardless of your gender or your age." She goes on, "More and more of Japan's most talented young people are going to end up overseas" (Hamada 1999).

Work abroad of course carries its share of difficulties for Japanese women. Author Noda Kaori, in her book *Employment Report from New York: The Real Working Woman's Story* [Nyū yōku kara no saiyō tsūchi: sugao no wākingu uōman sutōrī, 1992), cautions her readers:

> Sure it's fun to commute in white sneakers to your office in the skyscraper forest of Manhattan, and get a good deal on a beautiful leather briefcase. You have a nice apartment with a bathroom decorated all in blue, and shape up at your aerobics class on the way home from work. But all this is not really the point. When you actually work in New York City, you find out how demanding it really is. Women who decide to settle [*eijū suru*] here have to make hard choices: Do they want a career people will be envious of? The security of marriage? A wonderful lover? The thrills of New York? A spacious apartment and a comfortable life? A full savings account? Education? To be an "internationalist" fluent in

foreign languages? Each of us has to prove ourselves in our own way. (229–30)

Women I met in Japan who had worked abroad confirmed the sacrifices they had made, and constantly drew contrasts between themselves and other Japanese women who, they claimed, were interested only in "taking it easy" (*raku o suru*). Iizuka Miki, who left an OL position at Mazda to work overseas, said, "All I can say about the women at my old company in Japan is that nobody expected anything of them professionally, and they didn't expect anything of themselves."

In nearly all cases, the work abroad option also entails a significant decline in economic status.[10] Women working abroad frequently note that their standard of living, in terms of salary, expendable income, and housing, is far lower than they enjoyed in Japan. Yet there is agreement that they have chosen " 'a good *life*' over 'the *good* life' " (Yamamoto 1993a, 115). This is particularly so in the case of women working in the arts. The number of Japanese female artists and musicians who have forged their careers in the West is remarkable, and includes avant-garde painter Kusama Yayoi (who left Japan in 1957 claiming "Japan killed my mind"; Milne 1994, 11), actress Mori Naoko, violinists Kimura Mari and Nishizaki Takako, ballerina Kobayashi Hikaru, jazz pianist Ōnishi Junko, and filmmakers Satō Shimako and Ibi Keiko (who won the Academy Award for Best Documentary in 1999), to name just a few. Well-known concert violinist and avant-garde musician Kimura Mari has often been quoted as saying that the single greatest influence on her music is the "freedom and dynamism" of New York City, so different from "distant" and "insular" Japan: "When I was living in Japan, I knew that there were other people in the world, but it's so self-contained. We import, we export, everything works, or at least seems to work, but as a society that is so tremendously organized . . . and so prosperous, you get a feeling that you really don't relate to the other world. . . . [Now] my eyes are not focusing on my own kind. I feel closer to the other world than I did before leaving Japan" (in W. Roberts 1993, 64–65).

In the past few years Hong Kong and Singapore have emerged as major new locations for women's work abroad. The number of Japanese women seeking jobs in Hong Kong increased 50 percent between 1993 and 1994 alone ("H.K. Job Seminars Lure Women," 1994, 3; see also "Honkon mezasu kyaria josei," 1994; Ebi 1994; JAC Shingapōru and Parutī 1998). Hong Kong and Singapore differ from Western nations in their chronic labor shortages and critical need for local Japanese staff, but the reason for women's interest in these countries is strikingly similar: the belief that they are merit-based societies without gender- or age-based discrimination. It is frequently their "Western" features, such as the large white population and English-speaking workplaces, that many women point to as their primary attraction. Ebi Naomi, a journalist residing in Hong Kong, writes in her 1994 *Career Girls Who Fell In Love with Hong Kong* (Hon kon ni koi shita kyaria gāru) that Hong Kong's appeal lies in "its mixture of Chinese and British culture, its being the closest English-speaking country to Japan, and the freedom it provides for self-expression" (25). Another journalist writes of Hong Kong, "With so many people of different nationalities living and working there, it is like living in New York or London, if only on a much smaller scale" ("Young Workers Flocking Abroad to Find More Challenging Jobs," 1994, 9).

As in the case of ryūgaku students, Japanese male expatriates (*chūzaiin*) employed by overseas branches of large and powerful Japanese firms enjoy far greater financial stability than independent women, who have to scramble to find jobs and procure work visas. Yet for some of them, at least, the foreign work practices that women find so liberating may be seen as an unpleasant experience of lost privilege. Anthropologist Nakane Chie wrote a well-known description of the masculine experience abroad in her 1970 text *Japanese Society*: "There is no alienation, loneliness, or irritability comparable to that of the Japanese whose work takes him to a foreign country. . . . Most Japanese men abroad are quite homesick. . . . It is not surprising, then, that the Japanese does not like to leave his own community for very long periods" (1973, 141–42). Almost twenty years later, Merry White reached a similar conclusion in her study *The Japanese Abroad: Can They Go Home Again?*: "The Japanese overseas employee is . . . a ferryboat-man, rowing the stuff of international exchange back and forth across otherwise uncrossable waters . . . a stigmatized deviant" (1988, 122).

The degree to which such descriptions are valid today, when men's position vis-à-vis the foreign is in such flux, is not clear. Certainly, however, and I return to this again in chapter 3, such images of the abject Japanese male abroad are vital landmarks in Japanese women's own narration of assimilation and desire. Anglophile writer and editor Igata Keiko perpetuates the image of the "stigmatized deviant" in her account of Japanese male chūzaiin whom she encountered at a party in London:

> "What is it you like so much about England?" one of the men asked me. He went on, "I want to go home so bad I can't stand it. Those people (the English) are crazy. The local Japanese staff women are crazy too." Dissatisfaction toward England spewed out of his weakly mouth. Another thin, pale-faced man standing beside him muttered, "I think I'm turning neurotic. How could they send me to a place like this?"

Igata's disappointment was great. "I had been so interested in meeting these men," she wrote, and continued,

> They were the same age as I, and I was thrilled that here they were working and living in the England of my dreams [akogare no igirisu]. It was terribly disturbing for me to hear them complain, half-neurotically and with glazed eyes, that all they wanted to do was go home. I felt that the "vision" [bijon] of England that I had nurtured in my heart for so long was threatened. No matter what I said to them, the answer was the same, "Japan is number one." (1993, 167–69, abridged)

Running counter to such characterizations, the latest information is now touting work abroad as a vital outlet for creative young men in search of both professional and personal "freedom." In an article in a 1998 job-hunting magazine entitled "No Freedom, No Life," author Tanaka Nobuhiko chronicles eight young Japanese men who have "pioneered" careers overseas to accommodate artistic creativity, hobbies such as surfing, individual entrepreneurship, and other qualities that they claim were stifled in Japan (1998b, 94–135). Nevertheless, Japanese men as a whole, by virtue of their continued categorical privilege in Japan, undoubtedly still have potentially more to lose than women do in a relocation abroad.

International Organizations. Since the late 1980s, the majority of Japanese active in the United Nations have been women. In 1991, for example, 80 percent of the Japanese who passed the competitive exam given to candidates at the U.N. Secretariat's New York headquarters and other branch offices worldwide were female. The year before, thirteen out of the sixteen selected were women (Satō 1993, 3). Currently, there are forty-four females out of a total of ninety-two Japanese employed by the u.n., a rate of female participation far higher than the total u.n. average. Furthermore, many of the males currently there are elderly first-generation Japanese members nearing retirement age; they are not being replaced by younger males, but by young women. Japanese women's high rate of participation in the u.n. is so conspicuous that by 1993 the organization was sending out special recruiting missions to Japan to attract more female recruits (Ozaki 1993, 21); 80 percent of the eight hundred participants who showed up for one information seminar were female (Akimoto 1994, 14). Similarly, although the number of successful Japanese applicants for the associate expert training program offered by the u.n. has remained steady at fifty since 1989, the proportion of women in this number has risen from approximately 40 percent to approximately 70 percent in 1999 (15; Nagamine 1999). Japan now has a higher relative rate of female participation in the United Nations than Britain, France, Germany, and the United States (Satō 1993, 3). This level of participation dwarfs women's participation in domestic governmental positions, which currently stands at approximately 11 percent for the Diet and 4 percent for regional assemblies.

Ise Momoyo, officer in charge of the u.n. Administration and Training Division, observes that talented Japanese women come to work for the u.n., even when they have been promised positions with leading Japanese companies, "because they don't want to waste their energies in coping with sexual discrimination" (in Ozaki 1993, 21). Meanwhile, Ikeda Akira, chief of the Foreign Ministry's recruitment center for international organizations, remarks that Japanese men are reluctant to join such organizations because "the language requirement is hard to meet, and many Japanese corporations pay higher salaries" (in Satō 1993, 3). Because big corporations will not hire someone after a stint at the u.n., life at international organizations may appear "insecure," according to Ikeda.

The attraction of international organizations for women exceeds mere professional gain, however. Women have responded in a visceral, personal way to the call for a greater Japanese "international contribution" (*kokusai kōken*) to the world community. This spirit of voluntarism has led to a sharp surge in the popularity of the Japan Overseas Cooperation Volunteers organization, the Japan International Cooperation Association

(JICA), the Overseas Economic Cooperation Fund, and the Japan Youth Volunteer Association (JYVA) among female college students ("Kaigai kyōryoku no dantai ni ninki," 1993, 14). This trend has continued well into the postrecession era (see Sasaki I. 1998, 58–71). In most cases, the salaries at these organizations are only half those offered to OLS at major corporations; their appeal lies in lifestyle and values they represent.

Among the women I interviewed, one woman, Odawara Yumiko, exemplified the spirit of those who choose to devote themselves to the United Nations and other such organizations. When I met her, Odawara, then in her mid-forties had been employed for seven years as Fellowships Program director in the United Nations University in Shibuya. After graduation from Sophia University she worked in a number of gaishikei, but joined the U.N. University out of commitment to its internationalist ideals. "When I first entered here I was so excited about the U.N. Charter," she told me. "I never asked about salary. I was so idealistic!" Although she came to regret her initial naïveté, Odawara remained convinced of the United Nations' value as a force for social justice worldwide. After the interview was over and the tape recorder turned off, Odawara began speaking of her involvement in a variety of social causes, including antiwar demonstrations (it was during the time of the Gulf War) and reform of the Japanese prison system. Angrily she recounted tales of human rights violations of prisoners awaiting trial in Japanese prisons and urged on me a variety of publications describing prisoners' plights. The last I spoke with Odawara, she was considering taking a volunteer position in New York at Ramsey Clark's International Action Center. She had worked there for two weeks during the war crimes trials and had been offered a position on the volunteer staff. However, she was hesitant. Although the chance to work in a grassroots activist organization was appealing, the financial sacrifice involved would be great.

Nagata Hiroko was another woman I met (I return to her story later) who quit her well-paid position at a foreign-affiliate securities firm at the age of thirty-seven to join the Japan International Volunteer Center at starvation wages. At that time she sent out announcements to her friends and acquaintances:

For the past eight years I have watched the dynamism of the world economy in such things as the official discount rate, money supply, and the unemployment rate . . . but I was not more than an irresponsible observer. Then in July I spent a week in a small farming village in Ethiopia. Despite the harsh conditions in which they live (with a per capita GNP of only $120!), Grandpa, Grandma, Dad, Mom, and kids were all full of vitality. I decided to move a step beyond my four years of after-five volunteer activities. . . . In November this year I started looking for human dreams and [the] power to live with nature and share its wealth with many different people.

"My salary is less than half what it was," she told me, "but like the people in Ethiopia who are working so hard each day, I as a single individual need to keep my eyes on the ground and do everything I can to improve the world's conditions."

Foreign-Affiliate Firms (Gaishikei). The majority of women who master English or complete a period of study or work abroad return to Japan hoping to work at a foreign-affiliate firm, or gaishikei (Kashima 1993, 189). It is widely believed in Japan that gaishikei bring with them the allegedly nondiscriminatory hiring policies of their home companies in the West, and that Japanese women who work in them will be treated as well as men (*danjosabetsu ga nai*). Matsubara describes gaishikei as "the Messiah" of overseas educated Japanese women (1989, 14; see Figure 9).[11]

Although many gaishikei in Japan have ironically come in recent years to more closely resemble Japanese firms in their gender breakdown, there are still many that seem to be Japanese female domains. At the securities firm Lehmann Brothers, for example, in the mid-1990s, 70 percent of the Japanese staff was female (Hayami 1993, 63). At McCann Eriksson Haku-hōdo, a foreign-affiliate advertising agency, there were 106 Japanese female employees compared to only 4 Japanese males. At the foreign law firm in which one woman I met was employed, 100 percent of the Japanese staff was female. Other women working in gaishikei reported that between 40 and 60 percent of their companies' Japanese staff were women. More to the point, the women employed at these companies generally occupied higher positions of authority than in most Japanese firms. This has intensified in the recent so-called "gaishikei-fication" (*gaishikeika*) of many long-established Japanese firms, in which major Japanese companies have come to be majority-owned by foreign interests. The growing

9. Japanese women workers headhunted by foreign businessmen in Japan. Source: *AERA*, 6 August 1991:65.

level of foreign investment in Japanese companies in Japan's reeling economy has brought a new ethos of "meritocratism," often linked to English-language ability, in which women are felt to have benefited most. At Nissan, owned since 1999 in part by the French company Renault, and Mazda, a subsidiary of Ford, English-speaking women are being promoted to management in large numbers (Takahashi Y. 2000).

Until recently, Japanese men tended to stay away from gaishikei, leaving avenues for promotion relatively open for women. A foreign general manager with thirty years of experience in Japan remarked, "What incentive is there for a Japanese [male] to risk an unknown future in a place where people speak a foreign language and put their feet on the desk? A person who does join is odd and most likely a dropout." By contrast, he argues, "for many foreign companies . . . women will comprise the majority of their employees . . . [and are] probably a foreign company's only access to first class education" (Huddleston 1990, 30, 42). Given that gaishikei are increasingly becoming the target of young men unsuccessful (or uninterested) in mainstream Japanese corporations, however, conditions in the gaishikei are in flux. The most recent job-hunting advice

increasingly valorizes the gaishikei as a site for male professional fulfillment and improved ikikata. This rhetoric is colored, however, by a tone of
competitiveness lacking in women's accounts. "You want to test your own
possibilities, you want to find your own ikikata," begins one essay. "For
people who feel that way, the doors to the stimulating and attractive world
of the 'gaishikei' are now opening wide. You only live once; it's never too
early to test yourself. Let's fly into a world where you compete based on
your abilities [*jitsuryokushōbu*]" (Tanaka N. 1998a, 11). By contrast, in wom-
en's narratives of the gaishikei, competition takes a back seat to images of
international "cooperation" and mutual respect.

The gaishikei are essential to Japanese women and men who have
studied abroad not only because they provide opportunities to utilize the
English ability, technical skills, and qualifications acquired abroad, but
also because, in general, only there can individuals be hired in midcareer.
As I described earlier, Japanese companies hire almost exclusively among
brand-new college graduates. Kitahara Satoko told me, "After my period of
study abroad I had no choice but to work at a gaishikei. Japanese companies will hire girls only if they are just out of college." This is especially so because it is widely accepted that once a Japanese (particularly
a woman) has worked in a gaishikei, she can never again be hired by
a Japanese corporation, having been allegedly "spoiled" by the individualism and equal treatment. Nagata Hiroko told me, "I could never work
at a Japanese company at this point. In fact, I would probably be fired.
I'm too assertive now. They would be mad at me all the time. Both sides
would be unhappy." For this reason, there are headhunting agencies
in Tokyo devoted solely to moving women from Japanese companies to
gaishikei, and from one gaishikei to another. Mack International, one such
agency, reported that these moves made up 100 percent of its business in
the 1980s; during that time, it handled not even one case in which a
woman sought a transfer from a gaishikei to a Japanese company (Hoyano
1991, 65).

The gaishikei itself becomes an object of akogare in the sense that
working for and with Westerners is seen as a way to materialize a new
ikikata. As one article on gaishikei observes, " 'To work at a gaishikei' is a
symbol of a Western lifestyle for women . . . [and] an ikikata like [former]
American First Lady Hillary Clinton" (Hayami 1993, 61). Western men, as

bosses and coworkers, add to the allure. Kitahara Satoko reported her observations on beginning work at her gaishikei:

> It was the first time I had really seen for myself the akogare of Japanese girls who work among foreigners, that is, the "gaishikei liberation of the Japanese female heart" [gaishikei ni hataraku kaihō sareta nihonjin no onnagokoro]! I was shocked.
>
> The branch manager was foreign, my boss was foreign, and there were lots of foreigners in the office. The girls dressed in bright clothes, and would fly off to foreign countries on their vacation. It was still the bubble economy back then, and the foreigners would have big parties at their houses and invite all the girls. There were a lot of girls there who wanted a foreign boyfriend, and the foreigners who worked in that company all had Japanese wives. Japanese women's defenses were so weak. I'm not talking about yellow cabs here, but average girls.

In chapter 4 I return to the erotic politics of the gaishikei working environment. In order to examine the larger politics of race, gender, and sexuality that constrain women's position in the gaishikei corporate structure and in internationalist venues more broadly.

Women's Flexibility As we have seen, women who turn to the foreign not only express an almost religious faith in a redemptive West (the gaishikei as Messiah), but insist that the very marks of gender discrimination—cultural marginality and professional exclusion—instantiate a "natural" female flexibility that frees Japanese women from oppressive and outdated laws of nation and race. Japanese women, it is claimed, can instinctively negotiate the demands of global society because they "are not hemmed in by the rules of Japanese male society, and haven't been subjected to the same social discipline as men, based in a [traditional] Japanese social environment" (Katō K. and Berger 1990, 272). As fifty-three-year-old housewife and amateur poet Nakagaki Sachiko expresses it in a poem, "Women Have No Need of Borders," published in *Yomiuri Shimbun* in 1993:

Women have no need of borders
We need only bear the child of the man we love
Race, nationality, religion—none matter

Men war to make women theirs
They make boundaries, they make nations
But women have no need of borders
We need only to love.

The poetry editor remarks of this poem that "women are internationalists by birth."

Morita Tokiko, who worked as a bilingual secretary at the United Nations, told me that "women are more internationalized because they have adaptability. Women are like chameleons; in a green place they turn green." Different women located the origins of women's adaptability in the corporate structure or the patrilocal patrilineal family system. In the words of Ojima Yukiko, the thirty-one-year-old technical designer in a major Japanese computer firm, "Japanese society has always been male-dominated, so there are a lot of expectations about how a man must behave, much more than for women." She went on, "Women have had only to obey men. But men have responsibility, heavy responsibility, so even if they have an interest in Western things, they can't pursue them, because parents have strong expectations of them to join a company and conform because they are boys." As Mori Mayumi, an international volunteer nurse, described her husband, "He sometimes tells me he's jealous of me for being able to travel abroad so much. He plays rugby, and has always wanted to go to New Zealand for a year to play. But the company would never permit it; if he went, he would lose his job and all the benefits he gets as a male in Japanese society—good salary, status, company perks. When push comes to shove, he won't leave. He might be envious of me, but he's not going to give it up." She concluded, "The merits for men of living within Japanese society are just too sweet [*oishisugiru*]."

Women's internationalist narratives thus hinge on a reversal of gender privilege: men's very power, they claim, has bound them and rendered them immobile. Women construct the Japanese national economy as not only narrowly confining, but marginal to the "world." Men's lonely privilege within it, they argue, has cut them off from the possibilities of the "genuine" privilege that is mediated by the West. As Morimoto Tomomi, a graduate student at the University of Texas, told me, "With the lifetime employment system in Japan, even if men have akogare, they cannot make it a reality."

In this way, women's internationalism challenges hierarchies of the native over the foreign, of male over female, of the nation over the world, constructing an alternative reality under which all that had been maligned is now revered, all that had been revered now rejected. Ironically, invocation of female international "adaptability" has also become almost talismanic in the mainstream, male-dominated Japanese media. FOCUS magazine, wondering why Japanese female athletes are so successful in international sporting events, opines, "Women are blessed with adaptability, so that even abroad, no matter how many times they're knocked down, they just keep coming back for more. Japanese males, on the other hand, give up easily" ("Heroine: nihon no josei wa tsuyoi nē," 1993, 8). A male writer in the *Nihon Keizai Shimbun* observes of "internationally married" Japanese women writers, "Women's high level of adaptability and emotional flexibility is uniquely effective in serving as a bridge between different cultures" (in Ishikawa 1992, 30). Such male invocations of female adaptability appear to be contemporary attempts to deflect onto women the distasteful imperative of internationalization (reminiscent of the 1957 Ōya-Nakaya-Takagi dialogue introduced in chapter 1). They exemplify what Ivy has identified as the masculine effort to expel the "duplicitous feminine" from the realm of the masculine native (1995, 41–42): backhanded compliments that serve to valorize men's own native "authenticity" manifested in a stubborn inability to adapt to the West.

However, as I have shown, women's own assertions of the same adaptability serve as a defense of their command of and monopoly over the international realm against intrusion by men. As Hannerz writes, the enunciation of a cosmopolitan consciousness can be an enactment of autonomy vis-à-vis the native, and the more starkly the cosmopolitan and native are contrasted, the more conspicuously "surrender" to the foreign becomes "a form of mastery at home" (1996, 104). In women's narratives, mastery of the "rules" of the West is the crucial means for the insertion of women into the elite class of the global cosmopolitan community. In the narratives' most utopic form, women call on each other to break out of their "prison of culture" and the inward-looking obsolescence of Japanese particularity and clear a path for the bright light of the universal West. One "primer" on internationalism targeting young women tells them that "international rules [*rūru*] are Western rules, and . . . [Western rules] are universal" (Takahashi E. 1995, 20).

It is an Enlightenment vision of modernity, based on liberal democratic humanism, individualism, and verbal self-expression, which becomes the foundation for a critique of the "group conformity" and unspoken communication of Japanese tradition (what Ivy has called "the notion of a volkisch unity defined by a near-telepathic, transparent, harmonious communication"; 1995, 18). The editorial collective of *Women Love the Earth* (Onna wa chikyū o aishiteru) insist that "Japanese women active on the world stage are all individuals who have crossed borders, and embody a practical humanism in the midst of 'global democratic society'" (*UPDATE* 1990, 1–2). To be modern is to speak out in the international marketplace of ideas: the primary signifier of maturity on the personal and national levels is command of an assertive individual speaking voice. "Japanese are poor at speaking, withdrawn, and antisocial," Takata Kiyoko claims in her book *Little Bridge across the Pacific: Living in America I Came to See Japan* (Little bridge across the Pacific: Amerika de kurashite nihon ga mieta), "and must learn to speak for themselves like Americans if they want to be seen as 'adults' on the global stage" (1995, 244–46). Words take on an almost talismanic power, especially those English words that are held to exemplify Enlightenment truths. Takahara Etsuko, with five years study abroad experience and a BA from UCLA, exclaimed, "The first time I heard the word 'egalitarianism' in English I loved it! Americans value equality and fairness. They are always fair. . . . They have another good word: 'a balanced person.' I love it! There's nothing like that in Japan! But by hearing it over and over in America, I finally learned that it is true. I have hope in America! Japanese men may say America is going downhill, but I know that America is still a symbol of justice!"

The metaphorical linkage of women with the West against an exclusionary male system has led many women to turn to metaphors of *emigrant* (Tanabe 1993), *alien* (Iizuka 1993), *gaijin* (Tajima 1993), and *refugee* (Yamamoto M. 1993b) to describe their status betwixt and between Japan and the foreign, their aligning of their gendered position in Japan with the claims of internationalization in the world. In the words of Nakajima

Midori, a former OL who studied in the United States and went on to found her own international consulting firm, "the isolationist [sakokushugi] Japanese corporate structure relegates women, old people, and foreigners to a single category, jorōgai [literally, 'women-old-foreign'], which it treats as 'alien' to itself" (1996, 16). Yet, within the rubric of internationalism, women embrace their "alienation" as a mark of identity. In the words of literary scholar Mizuta (Lippett) Noriko, the reason contemporary female Japanese authors so often set their stories and novels in foreign countries with foreign main characters is that women are themselves foreigners (ikokujin) within Japan, and thus find their characters' foreignness "deeply intertwined as metaphor for the strangeness and exclusion of women's lives" (1993, 31). She continues, "no matter where women live, they write from the strangeness and isolation of a foreign country" (31). Outspoken feminist media icon Tajima Yōko has insisted that if women are simply gaijin (foreigners) in the eyes of Japanese men, then "only when Japanese men have learned to deal with women as 'gaijins' successfully, will they be able to say they have achieved the qualifications of a true 'internationalist'" (1993, 19).

The critical point about such rhetorical strategies is that they expand the possibilities of the internationalist narrative to include the longings of women who never study abroad or work for a gaishikei. That is, by insisting that women as a gender are marginalized in Japan but liberated abroad ("in America our abilities are evaluated just as they are"), the imagined other and the possible (Western) alternatives, even if left untaken, still serve to intervene in domestic gender relations for any woman inclined to rely on them. The foreign alternative becomes not simply an external site of professional opportunity, but an internalized marker of transformed identity.

The New Self Narratives of internationalism owe a great deal to what Bruce Robbins has called "the American dream of self-invention from nothing" (1994, 139). In women's narratives interactions with the Other become the opportunity to examine (mitsumeru) the (Japanese) self and, usually, to find it lacking—cramped and stunted from the pressures of "Japanese society"—while discovering a new, confident, and expansive self (atarashii jibun) in the atmosphere of "freedom" of the foreign/West.

Yamamoto Michiko writes of her own journey, "The foreign country becomes a mirror that reflects back your own country to you. To look at your own country is, to put it another way, to look at yourself" (1993b, 280). One of Matsui's informants exclaimed of life in the United States, "What a great therapy to be here!" (in Matsui M. 1995, 364).

This new self is less a new entity constructed from scratch than it is said to be a woman's natural abilities and desires "freed" from or discovered under layers of oppressive tradition. The finding of the new self is on the order of a revelation, a vindication of values that had been ridiculed and suppressed in Japan. Nagata Hiroko spoke of this transformation in her life: "When I was in Japan I had no confidence in myself at all. I had no idea what I wanted to do, what I could do, what I was suited for. But after I went to America I experienced [eyes twinkling] *freedom!* For the first time I discovered my own opinions about things. In Japan when you say things or think things that are different from others, people say you are strange. But in America it's expected. It's actually *better* to be different. By being in America I became confident. I finally realized that being different is not inferior, but superior!" Takahara Etsuko told me, "People always made fun of me when I was growing up in Japan. I would always try to say my opinion, and people would call me strange [*kawatteru*]. Then I went to America and found out that it is okay to state your opinion. I had gradually begun to lose confidence in Japan, but in America, I recovered it."

At the same time, a woman does not necessarily have to go abroad to find this new self. Kida Megumi describes how merely studying English changed her life: "Around the time I started studying English conversation, I was . . . a very willful person who couldn't trust others. . . . But in the process of learning English, I learned about the cultures, customs, and ways of thinking of many countries. . . . From the bottom of my heart I want to thank my American teacher for showing me that the greatest happiness can be found in everyday things . . . and heart to heart communication between people" (1994, 46).

According to this internationalist rhetoric, then, the foreign strips away the "false consciousness" of the requirements of Japanese womanhood, leaving the Japanese woman, for the first time, truly "free." This is a freedom that transcends mere "equality," or, as I discuss later, any economic or political gains that might be achieved through feminist activism;

rather, it is an exhilarating freedom of the spirit that leaves Japanese men and their exclusive, insular games of company and status far behind.

That the journey to the West may be read, as Robbins (1994) argues, as a parable of "upward mobility" becomes evident in the discourses of class and race anxiety that pervade internationalist discourse. For some writers in the internationalist genre, identification with the West goes beyond *akogare*, or the belief in European Enlightenment notions of democracy or individualism, to encompass a messianic faith in the racial and cultural superiority of the West, a true *seiyō sūhai*, or Western "worship." For them the West is lodestar, standard, and judge, and they construct their identity around a mastery of Western practices, which, although sometimes distinguished by country of origin, are nevertheless posited as uniformly bearing the aura of transnational elite class status.

One of the most idiosyncratic was a personality of the early 1990s who went by the name (in Japanese) of "Miss Minako Saitoh" (*misu minako saitō*). Based on a claimed ten years as a doyenne of European aristocratic circles, Saitoh (who advertised herself as a "modern goddess with supermodel looks, the brains to speak five languages, and a man's vitality") urged Japanese women to follow her philosophy of "super top-classism," which entailed an unabashedly elitist rethinking of lifestyle, beauty, and values based on a supposedly European aristocratic mold. In her 1993 book *Super Top-Classism* (chōichiryūshugi; Saitō 1993), Saitoh divides the world into "upper" and "lower" halves, in which "lower" people gulp their beer, dab perfume behind their ears, wear little makeup, and "let themselves go," while the upper half wear heavy eye makeup, lift weights, and delicately sip their drinks. "Any woman who doesn't beautify her own face," Saitoh claimed in a book-signing talk in Tokyo, "has no place demanding the beautification of the environment." Saitoh's book became an instant best-seller among young women in 1993, and she became a fixture on the motivational speaking circuit for her theory of "positive thinking." When, shortly thereafter, several men's weeklies began accusing her of fabricating her aristocratic past (an exposé appeared in *Shūkan Bunshun* titled "Tearing the 'Thick Makeup' off Saitō Minako," 1993), Saitoh (who wears heavy makeup) retorted that "Japanese men are just jealous of me."

Igata Keiko, the author of *Someday I Shall Live In England* (Itsuka igirisu ni kurasu watashi, 1993) and editor of a personal ad magazine, is another, if less flamboyant, example. At the time of her first trip to England, Igata was searching for new values on which to base her life, which had ground to a halt as an unwed mother in Japan. What she found was revelation. "I was not shocked or shaken by any of the things I discovered in London," she writes. "On the contrary, to each new thing I learned I would respond with clapping and cheers, feeling 'yes, this is it! This is what I've always wanted to know!' My life there was like a catalogue of those 'somethings' I had always yearned for since the time I first gained consciousness as a child" (54). "England," she concludes, "became my ultimate value, my ultimate goal" (219). Unable, however, to gain permanent residency status in England after a failed romance with an Englishman she had desperately hoped to marry, Igata blames herself for not "having the capacity" to live up to the standards of England and an Englishman: "The more I learn to see English life from the inside, the more I know that I am not ready to reside within it. . . . *I am not yet worthy to live in England*" (248; emphasis added).

The conflation of class and race in this narrative of cosmopolitan upward mobility (and denigration of the self) emerges most clearly in a fixation on the trope of "good manners." Mastery of the manners of the elite (read British) upper class is considered by writers such as Igata or Saitoh the essential capital investment for women in their achievement of inclusion into "world society." Thus, Takahashi Eiko's *Primer for Internationalists* (*Kokusaijin nyūmon*, 1995) bears the subtitle *Manners and Lifestyles Accepted by the World* (Sekai ni tsūjiru kurashi to manā), and includes instructions on minutiae of social life from the proper acceptance of party invitations to the choosing of conversational topics and the acceptable way of having one's door opened by a man.

Takahashi admonishes her readers that in international society an appealing woman (*ii onna*) is an "adult" woman who grasps the three fundamental rules of adult society: "partnership," "ladies first," and "privacy" (99–136), all, in her view, the distinguishing features of upper-class life in cosmopolitan circles. In this book and elsewhere, "international society" is "adult society," and the relations of Japanese to its inhabitants are figured as the relations of children to their adults. This trope is made explicit in Toshiko Marks's book *England, Country of Adults; Japan, Country of Children* (Otona no kuni igirisu to kodomo no kuni nippon, 1992), which features on its cover a diminutive, knock-kneed young Japanese woman pertly gesticulating to a distinguished older English gentleman, who scratches his chin in consternation (see Figure 10). In this book—as in her others, including *Japan, Country of Ridiculous Mothers and Pathetic Men* (Tondemo nai hahaoya to nasakenai otoko no kuni nippon, 1999), *England the Rich, Japan the Nouveau Riche* (Yutori no kuni igirisu to narikin no kuni nippon, 1993), and *I Became a British Aristocrat* (Eikoku kizoku ni natta watakushi, 1986; she was previously married to Lord Marks of the Marks and Spencer chain of grocery stores)—Marks heaps scorn on a Japan that fails to conform to refined British manners, especially the code of "ladies first." She reserves her purest vitriol, however, for the recent "pollution" of the hallowed English girls finishing school caused by an influx of Japanese and Arab students: "There are no more real English girls at the English girls finishing schools. Instead . . . they are full of Arabs and Japanese. In such an atmosphere, can anyone learn true manners? To put it bluntly, can anyone even learn to speak proper English?" (1992, 139–45). She goes on, "All the Japanese girls come out of akogare, but they make no effort to understand or master true English manners. Therefore, no matter how long they attend, the finishing schools make no dent in their deplorable manners" (144–45).

Marks's hatred of the Japanese presence in the England she idealizes is echoed by another internationalist writer, Mori Yōko, also writing of the British girls school: "Japanese and Arabs are scavenging up the hotels of the world, and now they've even stretched out their greasy fingers to the English girls finishing school. . . . What kind of finishing school is it where you only hear Arabic and Japanese spoken?!" (1988, 198–99). For these writers, the presence of "Arabs," another nonwhite population, inhibits the fantasy of Japanese women's transparent absorption into the "raceless" world of proper manners. The presence of another Other is intolerable; it makes embarrassingly evident Japanese women's nonwhite subject position, aligning them with the faceless mass of Others to the British upper class.

If there is a phantasmatic self in these hyperbolic discourses of West worship, women's narratives of internationalism also produce their phantasmatic other: the Japanese male, for whom the possibilities of internationalist transformation and elite sophistication are foreclosed. Japanese

大人の国イギリスと
子どもの国日本

マークス寿子

10. Cover of *England, Country of Adults; Japan, Country of Children*. Source: Marks Toshiko, *Otona no kuni igirisu to kodomo no kuni nippon* (Tokyo: Sōshisha, 1992). Reprinted with permission.

men in women's accounts are characterized (when they are mentioned at all) as the backward (*okureteru*), static, and dehistoricized emblems of Japanese marginality and particularity. Fuke Shigeko scoffs, "How different from [Japanese women] are those expressionless middle-aged men we're all familiar with. They won't tell you 'yes' or 'no,' and all they know how to do is grovel to their superiors, network among themselves [*nemawashi suru*], and have 'unspoken understandings' [*haragei*]" (1990, 287). They stand accused of being intransigent defenders of "feudal" Japanese tradition, incapable of change. *Asahi Shimbun* journalist Shimomura Mitsuko argued in 1990 that although Japan may have appeared on the surface to become a global economic superpower, it was in fact a "rotten, pus-oozing" system created by men, which was paralyzed in the face of globalizing forces, and literally putrefying from the inside out from its pathological insularity (*UPDATE* 1990, 90). Japanese men are portrayed in women's accounts as hating and fearing the West and working actively to prevent its influence on Japan. I was told by Maeda Seiko, a thirty-six-year-old housewife who had made nine trips to Western countries, had been employed in two foreign-affiliate firms, and had spent one year studying abroad in the United States, "We cannot look forward to significant internationalization in Japan. The problem is Japanese men. They think Japan is number one in the world, and refer to white people as *ketō* [hairy barbarians]. Men hate foreigners. As long as Japanese men's attitudes don't change, true internationalization is out of the question."

It is true that sources such as the young men's magazines *SPA!* and *Popeye*, there is scant discussion of the West compared to equivalent women's media, and what little there is frequently takes an ambivalent or negative tone. Whereas women's magazines each year come out with Christmas special issues full of breathless descriptions of "authentic" Christmas celebrations from Europe and the United States (and instructions on how to recreate these at home), an article in the December 1993 issue of *SPA!* grumbles, "Aren't you people Buddhist? You're not even Christian! What is this 'Merī kurisumasu'?? Get serious! If you want a holiday, have one on April eighth—the 'Flower Festival,' when Buddhists the world over celebrate the birth of the Buddha in a Himalayan flower garden" ("Sonzai riyūnaki monotachi," 1993, 58). In contrast to the women's magazines' promotion of the latest foreign imports, *SPA!* editors

11. Japanese woman surrounded by foreign coworkers. Source: Fuke Shigeko, "Kazari janainoyo: Eigo ryūgaku wa" (It's not a decoration: English study abroad). *CREA* (February 1991): 141.

ridicule both Americans and their products. Describing an imported chopping device, they write, "A big hit among clumsy American housewives. Just roll it and you get minced vegetables. How American to invent a new product instead of attempting to improve their own skills" (*SPA!* "Ura gudoo dezain taishō," 1994, 49).[12]

In the context of the rapidly shifting position of Japanese men vis-à-vis the foreign, however, the point is not that contemporary Japanese men necessarily reject the West, but that Japanese women find it necessary to continue to insist that they do. For within women's narrative universe, the community of the West, to be effective as an escape, *must* exclude Japanese males. To this end, Japanese men are literally "eradicated" from the non-Japanese world in women's accounts. An ex–Japan Air Lines stewardess writes in a book entitled *Hello Alien* (Konnichiwa eirian): "The farther men travel from Japan, the more slippery and formless they become. They slither between people like jellyfish, and even try to make themselves transparent so that no one will notice them" (Fujikawa 1992, 64). Illustrations that accompany internationalist texts show a Japanese woman alone in a crowd of foreigners or speaking fluently to foreigners in English. Japanese men are either absent or depicted as tongue-tied outcasts, incapable of blending in (see Figures 11 and 12).

This is the point at which the West becomes gendered, for it is the Western male who is made to embody Western modernity and to stand in contrast to the "backwardness" of Japanese men. As I describe again in chapter 3, the white Western man stands in Japanese public culture as adjudicator of racial upward mobility in the world. In women's narratives it is the white Western man who most often appears in the role of teacher, mentor, or guide. In a lengthy essay published in the economic newspaper *Nihon Keizai Shimbun,* one of my informants, the founder and president of her own consulting and translation firm, wrote of a volunteer social program in which she participated and the inability of the Japanese members to function without the enlightened leadership of Reed, the American male director. "We Japanese spend all our time and energy on preserving harmony and maintaining relationships," she wrote; "if Reed hadn't opened the door for us, we Japanese would still be stuck in one place" (Nakajima A. 1994, 40). Author Kawataki Kaori writes of her first American boyfriend, "Until the day I met him, what I had thought of as 'the world' was no more than a narrow, narrow well. It was from listening to him that day that I first caught the briefest glimpse of the great wide world beyond. . . . On that day, he was my 'black ship' " (1992, 15).

Women's shift of loyalty to the West is fraught with erotic nuance, and narratives of foreign encounter are filled with sexual metaphors: *Embraced by Australia* (Ōsutoraria ni dakarete) one book is titled (Blair 1991), and another, *Falling in Love with Foreign Cultures* (Ibunka ni koi shite, Akizawa

12. Illustration from an article entitled "Are Girls Better at English Than Boys?" Source: Brian Powle, "Test Your Word Power 196: Are Girls Better at English Than Boys?" *English Journal* 1 (1994): 57.

1995). In the distilled utopianism of some of the published autobiographical accounts, the Western man provides the seed in the birth of both a new Japan and a "new self." "For me," wrote Fuke Shigeko, "New York City is a lover [*koibito*]. But not a lover who gently holds me, no, but one who pushes me ever harder to 'live more, live harder, live the life you want.' *He* [*kare*] knocks hard at the doors of my heart, to where my desires are hidden deep inside. He is a wild, thrilling lover" (1990, 290; emphasis in original; see Figure 13). Nearly every published autobiographical account culminated in the author's sexual, romantic, or marital union with a white man. Kurihara Nanako, the maker of the film *Looking for Fumiko* (Rukkingu foa fumiko; in English, *Ripples of Change*), a paradigmatic text in the female internationalist genre, features a photograph of herself and her American partner Scott Twinkler as the frontispiece of her autobiography *Finding Myself in New York: Angry Women Are Beautiful!* (Nyū yōku jibun sagashi monogatari, 1994), and in the text describes her union with him as the turning point in her quest to become a filmmaker. Author Takahashi Toshie writes in her book *No Demons on the Road to America* (Wataru amerika, oni wa nashi, 1989), "Through [Herbie] I encountered a world more exciting than any I had ever known; in truth, he taught me how to enjoy life" (196). Igata Keiko, in her text *Someday I Shall Live in England* (Itsuka igirisu ni kurasu watashi, 1993), writes of her lover Rick, "Through [him], the first true Englishman I encountered, I greedily imbibed the values and culture of England. The new world that I had longed to see spread out before me, and I was filled with a deep happiness" (119).[13]

These eroticized discourses of new selfhood resonate suggestively with the 1970s Japan National Railway "Discover Japan" advertising campaigns described by Marilyn Ivy in *Discourses of the Vanishing* (1995). As Ivy relates, the JNR advertising team led by male advertising executive Fujioka Wakao targeted young women as travelers/consumers, manipulable markers of cultural inauthenticity for whom travel promises a new self through the means of erotic possibility (39). Revealingly is the fact that one internationalist writer, Kokuni Aiko, appropriates Fujioka's formulation in her book *The London You Don't Know* (Anata no shiranai rondon, 1990). After devoting her final chapter to a series of stories about Japanese women with charming English lovers, she writes, "A while back everyone was talking about 'Discover Japan' [*disukabā japan*]. But when you come to

異文化に恋して
JUNKOの世界ウォッチング

秋沢淳子
TBSアナウンサー

廣済堂出版

13. The West as phallic male. Cover of *Falling in Love with Foreign Cultures*. Source: Akizawa Junko, *Ibunka ni koi shite* (Tokyo: Kōsaidō Shuppan, 1995).

London, you find the chance to 'discover yourself' [*disukabā jibun*]. You can meet the self that you had never known was there, and have the chance to contemplate the self that you are going to become. . . . Here you can believe in your talents that have been hidden up until now; here you can dream" (234–35).

Akogare thus encompasses the desire for the Western lifestyle and the white man as lover/husband, or, put differently, the lifestyle as it is mediated by the man. As Nagaki Mitsuko, a freelance journalist in her early thirties, said candidly, "The reason that intelligent women have akogare for white men is that they know, well, to be perfectly honest, that Euro-American society is much more mature in terms of human relations than Japan. And they want to get inside that mature society. If you can find a white husband, you can get into that society so easily. They have a desire to climb up in society, to rise up in the world [*jōshō shikō*]. They have a 'success dream' [in English]. You know, the 'American Dream'!"

Erotic desire cannot be separated from women's desire for escape from Japan and akogare for a foreign-inflected ikikata. What does it mean that women "fall in love" with foreign cultures, that so often the "new self" is associated with a romance with a white Western man, or that the white man as lover is figured as transformative agent ("black ship") on an epic scale? It is necessary to attend more closely to the relationship between women's narratives of Western rescue and the eroticization of the Western man. I argue in the next chapter that the white man is packaged and sold as a romantic hero in Japan and globally, by both domestic and multinational corporations, in ways that make him "imaginable" as the agent of women's professional, romantic, and sexual liberation.

3 ≋ Capital and the Fetish of the White Man

My opinion is that international marriage is a "circle of the weak" [*ja-kusha no wa*]. The weak of the world always look for women outside their country—weaker women. So weak white men marry Japanese women, who have lower status. Then weak Japanese men marry Thais or Filipinas. Chinese women try to marry Japanese men. Middle-aged, divorced Japanese women pick up Middle Eastern men in Japan. The Middle Eastern guys want young, sexy Japanese women but can't have them. The middle-aged Japanese women want Japanese men but can't have them. Meanwhile, white men have a racial prejudice against "Japs" [in English]. They feel that if they're going to accept a "Jap" as a wife, she had better be young and beautiful. They feel they have that right. So I've got all these middle-aged white guys, balding, whatever, who won't consider any woman over the age of twenty-three.—YOSHIMURA FUMIHARU, president of international dating and marriage service in Tokyo, in a 1993 interview

The Yellow Cabs Revisited In this chapter I pause in my discussion of the lived experiences of cosmopolitanism among internationally inclined Japanese women to inquire into mythic images of the white West/white man that circulate globally and that constitute the iconography available for women's enactment of internationalist desire, as this is both enabled and recuperated by the workings of global capital. I begin by revisiting the "yellow cab" phenomenon of ten years ago, when a population of young

Japanese women became notorious for their pursuit of white and black male lovers abroad. I move on, however, to show that the white man has been "sold," both to and by women, as object of desire and agent of change in ways that exceed the yellow cab moment. Indeed, the white man in his ubiquitous normativity and his hegemonic (in)visibility, is impossible to ignore in the Japanese popular imagination. Just as in the West, Japan is embodied in the Japanese woman, he is the West, and all roads lead to him. I examine, then, the mutuality of attraction that is increasingly enabled in deterritorialized spaces, as Western men's long-standing fetishization of the Japanese/Oriental woman is met and mediated by Japanese women's desires for the white man and the Western lifestyle he represents.

I begin with the yellow cabs. In the late 1980s and early 1990s, small groups of young, single Japanese women began appearing in places like Hawai'i, New York City, Bali, the U.S. military bases in Japan, and the Roppongi nightclub district of Tokyo, seeking out white, black, Balinese, and other gaijin (foreign) men for short-term sexual affairs. The young women paid for the expenses associated with these affairs using sizable sums of money saved up from their dead-end OL jobs in Japan's corporations. These women quickly gained a kind of notoriety and were branded with the label "yellow cabs," a name alleged to have been invented by American men who supposedly saw these Japanese women as "yellow" and as easy to "ride" as taxis. The term was actually brought to Japan, however, and perhaps entirely fabricated, by a Japanese female journalist, Ieda Shōko. Ieda claimed that she heard the term used by white and black men in New York City and Hawai'i to refer to their Japanese female conquests, but her goal in exposing it in her lurid best-selling "nonfiction" books, *Yellow Cabs: The Women Who Took Off from Narita Airport* (Ierō kyabu: Narita o tobitatta onnatachi, 1991a) and *The Women Who Flocked to My Skin* (Ore no hada ni muragatta onnatachi, 1991b), was most likely to capitalize on the Japanese popular obsession with the specter of Japanese women copulating with foreign men, black men in particular. The male-dominated Japanese media took Ieda's bait, and in articles in low-brow men's weekly magazines quickly elevated the yellow cab phenomenon to scandal of the year, salaciously excoriating the women as sexually insatiable sluts in thrall to the black phallus—a threat, to say the least, to Japan's racial and national purity. Anthropologist John Russell writes, "The result of all this media attention was to popularize these relationships while at the same time condemning them. Ironically, media coverage of these so-called black groupies may have contributed to the apparent growth of the phenomenon, as what started out as a trend among a small number of Japanese women was sensationalized and promoted as the latest fashion, complete with features on trendy night spots and on-air testimonials by satisfied consumers" (1998, 125–26). Russell concludes, "If indeed Japanese women were seeking a way to upset the status quo, the media itself had provided the women with the weapons of resistance and, in so doing, created more fodder for additional 'investigative' reporting" (126).

The yellow cabs shocked because they defied standard understandings—on both sides of the Pacific—of the Asian–Western sexual encounter: here it was wealthy and leisured young Japanese women who had the resources to travel to exotic locations and to "hire" the sexual services of foreign men there, as well as to publish accounts of their experiences. Indeed, the yellow cabs came in large part from the ranks of OLS who, as I noted in chapter 2, enjoyed a larger expendable income through the strategy of living with their parents than almost any other group of people in Japan. The OL lifestyle and subculture of the 1980s revolved around increasingly complicated and sophisticated patterns of consumption. As Tobin claims, it was a "carnivalesque" consumption that "transcend[ed] our conventional notions of extravagance" (1992, 21). It demanded a single-minded commitment to commodity ethics and aesthetics that went beyond mere shopping and entered the realm of connoisseurship. This connoisseurship which quickly exhausted the resources of "native" or Japanese products, and by the late 1980s encompassed the goods, services, and opportunities of the entire globe, and of the West in particular. Things Western were not merely coveted, however; that was the case for a previous generation for whom imported goods were still exotic. Now, Western goods were entirely contained as signifiers within a largely self-sufficient OL universe of style and status, and the exotic had to be sought in ever more esoteric, ever more unconventional realms. Tobin noted that Japan in the 1980s had "the desire, wealth and power to import and consume passion in many forms from the West" (11). Thus, it is perhaps not surprising that a few of these cosmopolitan young women—these "connoisseurs of the West" and citizens of the (late capitalist) world—should cross Japan's

135 ≈ Fetish of the White Man

borders in search of the "gaijin lover," the exotic sexual experience that represented the final frontier of the foreign left to consume.

Each of the locations in which yellow cabs sought out gaijin men was geopolitically ambiguous, caught within the post/neocolonialist regimes of U.S. military presence abroad, Japanese investment, mass tourism, international labor flows, and commodification of the native. The foreign men in these locations were often wanderers from Europe and the mainland United States who gravitated to the borderlands of Asia and the West in search of the Oriental erotic.[1] In Hawai'i these men were known locally as "playboys" and formed a conspicuous population that roamed the streets of Waikiki daily, seeking out and accosting Japanese female tourists for money and sex. At the American military bases of Yokosuka and Yokota, Western men were admitted free to some local bars and discos in the knowledge that they would attract Japanese female customers. The clubs of Roppongi overflowed, as they still do, with foreign men and Japanese women seeking one another's company.

Once in these locations, young women purchased the company of foreign men, not through a system of institutionalized prostitution, but through individual short-term affairs, the cost of which were covered entirely by the women. *Mitsugu,* an old Japanese word meaning "to keep a mistress," was the term my yellow cab informants in Waikiki employed to describe their support of foreign men through payment of the costs of the affairs, cash gifts, loans that were rarely repaid, payment of the foreign male's rent, upkeep, outstanding debts, and finally, material gifts of designer goods, watches, jewelry, and in a few cases, cars. It was understood by both parties that both inside and outside Japan, Japanese women, as possessors of the strong yen of the bubble economy, were in the financially superior position. As one playboy in Waikiki told me, "They know if they want us they have to pay."

Indeed, foreign men in Japan, Hawai'i, and the mainland United States quickly jumped on the yellow cab bandwagon (so to speak), making themselves available for pursuit and publishing smug exposés in the Japanese and American press, often disguised as injured condemnations of yellow cabs' "dehumanizing" exploitation of hapless, innocent foreign males (see Harton 1989). These Western male accounts, however, for all their moral outrage, remained oddly wedded to a Madame Butterfly trope, depicting yellow cabs as naïve souls at heart, desperate for rescue from despotic yet sexless Japanese men in the arms of the sensitive (and better endowed) foreign male. These Western male writers appeared oblivious to the yellow cabs' cheerful efficiency not only in traveling to the encounters and financing the affairs, but also in regaling their friends at home with stories of their conquests, and even publishing books and articles about them.

Although the number of yellow cabs was small, the intensity of the public outcry surrounding them shows that they struck a nerve. As I wrote above, the mainstream Japanese media responded hysterically, in a hyper-sexualized, hostile, and prurient male discourse that depended on long-standing imagery of oversexed foreign men and duplicitous Japanese women. The men's weekly *Shūkan Gendai* wrote, "It's the Japanese girls who can be found dancing on the tables at discos, with their underpants showing for all to see. . . . They live in Waikiki hi-rises . . . that their daddies pay for" (*Shūkan Gendai* 1989, 151). The similarly low-brow *Shūkan Hōseki* maintained, "The temperature of Narita Airport goes up each time a plane-load of girls returns from their trips overseas . . . and on outbound flights, they all may pretend to be little ladies, but actually, in their hearts, each one wants to be the first to get a gaijin to bed" ("OL, joshidaisei kaigairyokō no seika hōkoku," 1988, 218).

Writers such as Yamada Eimi and Ieda Shōko cannily fed this hypersex-ualized hysteria by dwelling ostentatiously and obsessively in their novels on themes of black male sexual appetites and genital size. The works themselves are little more than soft-core pornographic novels that capital-ize on the hoariest racist notions of black male sexuality. In the work of Yamada, the black male is primarily a "stand-in" for his penis. A passage in *Bedtime Eyes* (Beddotaimu aizu) reads: "[Spoon's] dick was not at all similar to the reddish, disgusting cocks of white guys. It was also different from the sad and pathetic organs of Japanese men. . . . Spoon's dick shone before my eyes like a living thing. It reminded me of the sweet chocolate candy bars I love" (1985, 15). Meanwhile, Ieda wrote in *The Women Who Flocked to My Skin*, "Jean stood over me as I lay naked on the bed, holding his heavy dick in his left hand and swinging it back and forth. I'm not usually so eager, but all I could think about was being wrapped in Jean's powerful body . . . I was crazy with lust. . . . While he toyed with it, his copper-colored 'thing,' which had been dangling in his left hand, swelled.

It seemed as if it reached to his navel. I can only say, it was a wonderful sight" (1991b, 14). These representations appealed to Japanese audiences (both mass and scholarly): *Bedtime Eyes* was not only a best-seller, selling some 260,000 copies, but was also awarded the prestigious Naoki Prize literary award (Russell 1998, 174 n. 65).

During a year of fieldwork on the yellow cabs in Waikiki, however, I found that my informants' accounts of their liaisons with foreign men did not narrate any such blank thralldom to the black penis; the women I knew insisted that they pursued brief encounters with gaijin men, black or white, because they were "frustrated" with Japanese men and experimenting with possible alternatives. Among the women with whom I spoke, gaijin men were desired not primarily for their amatory prowess (or penis size), but for their *yasashisa,* glossed as kindness, gentleness, or chivalrousness. Karen Ma has called Japanese women's belief in gaijin yasashisa a "Western chivalry fantasy" applied "indiscriminately to every gaijin man [whom women] meet" (1996, 92). However, for the yellow cabs the point of the gaijin male's alleged yasashisa—as well as his supposed sexiness, English ability, sophistication, and good looks—was that these qualities were claimed to be entirely absent in Japanese men. "Gaijins are more masculine than skinny, unhealthy-looking Japanese men," said one tourist in Waikiki. Another woman said, "Even in sex, I mean, if a gaijin is really telling you 'I want you, I need you, I want you,' you get in the mood, right? Not like with some stone-faced Japanese guy who tries to push you into a hotel all of a sudden" (in Murota 1987, 7). Journalist Kudo Akiko, in the women's magazine *Fujin Kōron*, quotes a young woman: "When I go to visit a British or Italian guy, they always . . . serve food and drinks themselves. But when I go to a Japanese guy's place . . . he tries to make me clean his room and cook his dinner!" (1990, 408). Kudo went on to summarize women's complaints: "The reasons Japanese women reject Japanese men are not just physical. . . . Women evaluate them badly in all areas—'they are childish and disgusting,' 'they have a bad attitude toward women,' 'they are fake and dishonest,' 'they are narrow-minded,' 'they are bad-mannered,' 'they can't take care of themselves,' 'they can't do housework.' . . . Japanese men are the opposite of the Japanese GNP—they are the lowest in the world!" (411).

I will return later to the political motivations and effects of such gleeful and hyperbolic repudiation of Japanese men. For now, I note that the yellow cabs of the 1980s and 1990s used their liaisons with foreign men as temporary avenues of escape from, and critique of, Japanese gender relations and Japanese men. By speaking and writing on the charms, sexual and otherwise, of the foreign male, Japanese women communicated to themselves and to Japanese men their rage against the gender status quo. The yellow cab phenomenon can be seen, then, as one locus of potent and influential negotiations between Japanese women and men over present-day and future gender relations in Japan. As novelist Kajiwara Hazuki argued, "The yellow cabs are not only a women's problem. I think it is time for overworked Japanese men to start changing. . . . I don't care how rich Japan has become; any country that has to export women's frustrations is just not right" (1991, 58). The import of the yellow cabs' discourse transcended Ieda Shōko's own personal journalistic credibility, which was shattered in 1992 when George Sarratt, an African American man who had apparently acted as Ieda's assistant in her research for the book *Yellow Cabs* (1991a) (and who had previously published his own similar book; Sarratt 1992), released an announcement to the Japanese media exposing Ieda's methods and findings as fraudulent and admitting his own culpability in promoting them (see Toyoda 1994, 49–50). Shortly afterward, one of the many scandal-mongering television exposés on interracial sex on the American bases in Japan was revealed to have been staged, and after a brief flurry of anti-Ieda activity in the media, the yellow cab phenomenon faded from the scene.

Nina Cornyetz has observed of Japanese women's pursuit of African American lovers, "By taking on an African American sexual partner, the Japanese woman, who is socially, economically, politically, and otherwise subordinate to her male counterpart, liberates herself and threatens Japanese male heterosexual subjective agency." Cornyetz notes, however, that the taking of the black lover "sidesteps the issue of Japanese male dominance" (1994, 127). Indeed, for the yellow cabs, too, the pursuit of the foreign male (black or white) was in no sense a permanent rejection of Japanese patriarchy; it was, instead, an appropriation of the late-capitalist methods of the patriarchal state to "mirror back" Japanese men's so-called failings to them. This appropriation was then disavowed in a discourse of passivity. "It was men who made us act this way," claimed many of the women interviewed by Ieda and with whom I spoke in Waikiki, or "Foreign men are an addiction." Russell observes that "the metaphor of addiction allows these Japanese women to deny female agency while still flaunting their delinquent identity. At the same time, it indicts Japanese men, since it implies that had they performed their function as lovers and companions properly, these women would not have strayed" (1998, 137).

Ambivalence over female sexual agency permeates women's own accounts of their interracial sexual pursuits, making it difficult to read the yellow cab phenomenon as a protofeminist rebellion. For in the end, it was women's ambivalence over sexual agency that prevailed, reaching its fullest expression in about 1990, with the emergence in New York City of a group known as the Ierō Kyabu o Kangaeru Kai (Group to think about yellow cabs). From that year, this group, comprising mainly of Japanese female professional writers and journalists residing in New York, instituted an aggressive media campaign against Ieda Shōko, which had as its apparent goal the complete eradication of public discussion of the yellow cab phenomenon. Kangaeru Kai members began by claiming that as a result of the yellow cab coverage, many Japanese and foreigners had come to associate loose sexual behavior with all single Japanese women living abroad, regardless of their professional standing. As serious career women, members were outraged to be associated with the sordid yellow cab behavior sensationalized in the media and objected to the growing harassment of internationally active Japanese women that had emerged in Japan as a result of the yellow cab fracas. Toyoda notes that what ensued was an "image battle" that "legitimate" study-abroad students lost and male writers won by successfully perpetuating in the salacious men's weeklies an image of women abroad as sexually depraved (1994, 115). According to some, women with overseas experience interviewing for jobs in Japan were being confronted with smirking insinuations about their sexual behavior abroad.

The Kangaeru Kai held conferences and seminars and published articles in major Japanese magazines insisting, accurately, that the term *yellow cab* was not widely understood, let alone employed, among American men to refer to Japanese women, and criticizing its usage in Japan as both racist and sexist. Through this group's organized efforts, which became known as "Ieda-bashing," Ieda Shōko found her already questionable reputation in ruins (at least temporarily). The group continued to meet regularly in New York through at least 1993, to publish articles in American magazines and newspapers denying the validity of the term yellow cab (see Tanaka M. 1993; "Are Yellow Cabs Real?," 1993), to petition Japanese publishers against using the term in publications or listing it in dictionaries, and to hold meetings in Japan devoted to dispelling what they called the yellow cab "myth."

My own encounter with Kangaeru Kai members at a meeting of the Japan–Afro-American Friendship Association in Tokyo in November 1993 was not a success: one member objected to the fact that I focused on white men instead of black, and that I took yellow cabs seriously as women with their own agendas of gender and sex. It is easy to understand the consternation of serious Japanese professional women at being associated with the yellow cab phenomenon. Toyoda and others have argued that the anti–yellow cab media frenzy can be interpreted as a Japanese male backlash against increasingly independent and mobile women, and a form of revenge against women's intensifying criticism of Japanese men's own sexual practices, from the enslavement of military comfort women during World War II to contemporary sex tours to Asia (Toyoda 1994, 105). However, in their efforts to remove themselves from this association, Kangaeru Kai women and their supporters seemed to argue two contradictory points: that yellow cabs did not exist except as a fiction invented in the racist and sexist Japanese male imagination, and that they themselves "were not like" yellow cabs, suggesting that the latter not only existed but engaged in behavior embarrassing to serious Japanese women. The Ieda-bashing campaign was also striking in its mean-spiritedness, although this seems to have originated not with the Kangaeru Kai but with the Japanese media, which demonstrated a hypocritical eagerness to cast off Ieda after fully exploiting her work for several years. Although Ieda's work was eventually discredited, at the same time it seems that she was made into a scapegoat to bear women's rage and to satisfy the media's desire for a new controversy.

In any case, the determination of the Ierō Kyabu wo Kangaeru Kai and other professional Japanese women to "disappear" the yellow cabs by "eliminat[ing] the term from the Japanese vocabulary . . . and the American media" ("Are Yellow Cabs Real?," 1993, 52) reveals the degree to which

Japanese women's sexual agency vis-à-vis foreign men has proved to be a source of ambivalence and conflict for internationally active women themselves. Kangaeru Kai rhetoric reinforced an image of Japanese woman as victim, a perpetually injured party vis-à-vis all men, Japanese and foreign. Although the Kangaeru Kai too eventually faded from the scene, its legacy of denial and disavowal of the possibility of Japanese women's racialized desire for foreign men continued. Thus, when at the tenth annual International Conference on AIDS in Yokohama in 1994, a Thai researcher, Dr. Sairudee Vorakitphokatorn, reported her research findings that 70 percent of Thai beach boys in Phuket had claimed to have had unprotected sex with Japanese female tourists (see Vorakitphokatorn, 1993), a number of Japanese women in the audience reacted emotionally by denying the validity of her findings and demanding an apology from her (Ma 1996, 68).

The Yellow Cabs and the White Man Although I have so far finessed the distinction between black men and white men in the yellow cab discourse, the distinction, obviously, is important. As Russell describes in his analysis of the black man as sex object in Japan, the black man's body has received the lion's share of media attention, driven by the literary output of Ieda Shōko and Yamada Eimi, as "object of female empowerment and transcendence . . . a site of creation, resistance, [and] self-discovery" (Russell 1998, 124, 135). Russell notes that the works of Ieda and Yamada

> privilege discourse about blacks while effectively precluding any dialogue, since the black is perceived as already known. In silencing the Black Other, the speaker reasserts the very racial boundaries she boasts of transgressing. . . . Unlike the White Other, the Black Other is a singular presence, he is *medatsu* [conspicuous], dominating all that surrounds him, capturing the gaze like a black hole sucks up ambient light and ensuring that those who enter his singularity never escape the promise of fame and notoriety. Yamada, Ieda, and the mass media have exploited their proximity to this overpowering black "presence" [*sonzaikan*] to perpetuate literary careers or boost television ratings. (130–32)

But what of that White Other whom Russell quickly passes over? In my research in Waikiki, it was white men, not black, who commanded the most intense interest from Japanese female tourists and who comprised the overwhelming majority of playboys. Accounts in women's magazines lauded the acquisition of the white, not black, lover and constituted him as the most coveted status symbol and route toward social upward mobility. *Cosmopolitan Japan* gushed, in an article accompanied by pictures of diminutive Japanese women on the arms of tall, well-coiffed, and heroic-looking white men, "We'd all like to be seen walking down the street arm in arm with a gaijin boyfriend, wouldn't we, girls?" ("Gaikokujin kara mita anata no otonado," 1988, 49). A twenty-five-year-old English student in Hawai'i asserted, "We can walk a little taller. We think, '*You* go out with men from the same country, but *I* go out with men from a different country.'" The term *gaijin* itself, literally meaning merely "foreigner" or "outsider," in actual usage is employed primarily to refer to white foreigners. Thus, the discourse of the gaijin lover is most often a discourse of whiteness. Indeed, what distinguished the rhetoric of yellow cab women was its shrewd and insistent comparison—a kind of "comparison shopping" among races and nationalities. In men, as in other things, rarity brought status; this status was coveted, and its effect calculated (see Figure 14). Black men had their own market "niche," but white men enjoyed a far wider appeal. Why was the white man's role continually minimized?

Ieda writes in one of her books:

> I have written that Japanese women find blacks irresistible, but, in fact, whites are also quite popular. Then why are they overlooked? If there are two couples, one black–Japanese and the other white–Japanese walking down a street in Roppongi, which will draw attention? . . . Obviously, it will be the black–Japanese couple. Using Americans as an example, in the case of the average black it may be that his brown skin gives him presence . . . but it's also because he is large and fashionably and colorfully attired. In comparison, the somewhat smaller white, casually attired in sneakers and jeans, is hidden in the shadow cast by the black, and leaves a shallow impression. (1991b, 226; quoted in Russell 1998, 133)

"Still," Ieda concludes, "the really gorgeous white Americans are more popular and successful than blacks" (226). The "smaller" white man lurks in the black man's shadow, repressed, diminished, and yet effortlessly triumphant. He is "gorgeous" and "successful," yet unworthy of comment. Is

14. Foreign and Japanese men compared. Cartoon by Chūsonji Yutsuko, a cartoonist then resident in New York City. Text reads in part: "I check out New York men by inviting them to dinner and serving them tempura. The white yuppie drinks his miso soup first; he's a gentleman! The black rapper eats with his hands; he's so passionate! The Latin American takes it home to his family; he's so domestic. The 'Oriental'? (as Japanese man noisily slurps up tempura broth). Well, let's just try to avoid stereotyping." Source: *AnAn* (14 January 1994): 22. Reprinted with permission.

he not unworthy of comment because of his all-encompassing "success"? Do not his supposedly more modest phallic endowments release him from the restrictions and compulsions of the exclusively racialized, sexualized body, and cast him into a much broader field of potential signification?

The notorious television documentary *Yellow Cabs* featured not a single white–Japanese couple. The director is quoted as explaining why: "They weren't interesting [*omoshirokunakatta*]. Don't get me wrong. It's not that relationships with whites aren't interesting. It just turned out the couple weren't interesting as characters [*kyarakutā toshite omoshirokunai*]" (in Russell 1998, 138). In fields of meaning, those things that are deemed "not interesting" are precisely the objects of the most deeply repressed anxieties and desires. If the white man cannot be singularized as a "character," then what is it that he represents in his generality?

Unlike the solely erotic fetish of blackness, whiteness functions in Japan as the transparent and free-floating signifier of upward mobility and assimilation in "world culture"; it is the primary sign of the modern, the universal subject, the "citizen of the world." "Whiteness," Russell remarks, has "acquired a kind of transparency that . . . enables Japanese literally—and literarily—to see past it in a way blackness does not" (1998, 117). Whiteness in advertising, Russell observes, "hawks objects Japanese associate with sophistication, purity, and aesthetic grace" (52). White men appear in women's media as sensitive, refined, and without sexism. They are *redī fāsuto jentoruman* (ladies-first gentlemen), "sophisticated romantics who treat women with a respect and gallantry not found in Japanese men" (153). They figure, as sensitive (*yasashii*) husbands, as the heroes in the mythos of *kokusai kekkon* (international marriage), and, as egalitarian employers, in the narratives of cosmopolitan careers I have introduced (see Figure 15).[2] Indeed, as I have shown, in the roles of husbands and employers they occupy the position of gatekeepers to the "universal" realm of the West. Marriage and employment, after all, are not only sites of the fantasy West; for Japanese women, they represent the only two methods available of acquiring permanent residence in Western countries. Whiteness here—that is, white masculinity—becomes too important to be spoken of lightly; it is rendered unspeakable.

In 1992 at a presentation on the yellow cabs I gave at the University of Hawai'i, several Japanese women students in the audience who were mar-

15. Japanese woman showing off her white husband to envious friends. Text reads: Wife: "This is my husband. He's even British!" Friends: "Oooh, you're so lucky!" Source: Miyazaki Chieko, "Hansamuna gaikokujin dansei wa hontōni 'risō no dārin' ka?" (Is a handsome foreign man really your "ideal sweetheart"?), in Ishida Yōko, ed., *Marugoto onna no tenki: Itsukara demo yarinaosō* (The complete women's turning point: It's never too late to get your life in order). (Tokyo: Asupekuto, 1997) 136.

ried to white men objected to my work. "How can you claim," each demanded in so many words, "that race has anything to do with my relationship?" "I love X because he is X," they went on, "not because he is white!" At the time, this reaction bewildered me; my presentation had not touched on the topic of white male–Japanese female marriage, or indeed on any Japanese women other than the marginal subcultural group of yellow cabs. I had explicitly emphasized the transitory nature of yellow cabs' affairs and their lack of interest in lengthy commitment. I had not spoken of "love" at all. I have pondered that reaction to this day. Indeed, I have encountered it so many times since (I came to think of it as the "*tama tama gaijin* argument," after the phrase *boifurendo/shujin ga tama tama gaijin datta* [my boyfriend/husband just happened to be a foreigner]), that I am led to wonder what this invocation of love, in these circumstances, by Japanese women married to white men, signifies, as if it forecloses politics, negates

146 ≈ Women on the Verge

race. "I love X because he is X, not because he is white" forms a flawless opposite counterpart to the yellow cab discourse about black men: "I don't love Mack because he's Mack," Ieda quotes a young woman as saying, "I love him because he's a *brother*" (1991b, 41). The white man is accorded the individuality that the black man is denied in a zero-sum racial economy: if the black man is all race, the white man is no race at all. In this rhetoric, the white man achieves transcendence of race. My interlocutors' insistence on the "racelessness" of their white husbands or partners, as well as their own attraction to them, suggests that this transcendence of race encompasses the woman associated with the white man as well.

Of course, love (as well as desire, affection, and intimacy) is never (or rarely) reducible simply to race. At the same time, however, I argue that this insistent refusal to countenance race as an element of attraction is a form of the denial that inevitably accompanies desire. This denial functions on both individual and societal levels, where it is predicated on what Dorinne Kondo has called the "liberal humanist assumption" that individuals "are shorn of history and beyond or outside power relations" (1997, 230). Ruth Frankenberg, in her important work on interracial marriages, has shown the ways that such "race evasiveness" "preserves the power structure inherent in essentialist racism" (1993, 147). I would add that discourses of love and romance have similarly functioned in the liberal West, often in association with such color-blind racial discourses, to disarm potential scrutiny of gender, racial, and sexual politics. "Love knows no color," runs the contemporary liberal mantra, allowing "the effects of a racist society [to be] relegated to the subconscious where [they] resurface in more subliminal ways" (Farman 1992, 7). That these discourses still exert their effects is apparent in the extraordinary resistance—exemplified by the Ierō Kyabu Kangaeru Kai but just as common, I found, among Western audiences—to interpretations of the politics of Japanese female–white male attraction not only as a trope of Japanese women's victimhood as Orientalized Madame Butterflies, but as site of women's potential cosmopolitanism and active (rather than passive) desire for the white man in his specificity and his generality.

It seems worthwhile and necessary, however, to attend closely when an author such as Kawataki Kaori, in one of her books on international marriage, writes:

You often hear women with foreign boyfriends say that their partner "just happens to be a foreigner" [*aite ga tama tama gaikokujin datta*], but that certainly wasn't the case for me. . . . My husband is American, and for me, the fact that he was an American who could speak English . . . , that he was a totally gorgeous, handsome foreigner like a movie star . . . , that the instant I looked into his blue eyes the blood rushed to my head, and I thought, if I could only have a wonderful person like this as a lover I would close my eyes to his faults, that I would sacrifice anything—I mean, it may sound like I'm exaggerating, but this is no exaggeration; I was completely beside myself. (1993, 232)

This is akogare personified. Japanese women (and men) operate in a world in which "Westernness" and "whiteness," conflated, are not simply objects of fantasy and desire but hegemonic constitutive elements of want, if not need. Indeed, as women I spoke with repeatedly told me, the akogare for whiteness—white maleness—is powerfully encoded in some of Japanese women's most formative experiences. As my informant Nagaki Mitsuko recalled of the American television shows she had watched growing up (including *I Love Lucy, Father Knows Best,* and *Bewitched*), "We Japanese got the idea that to have an American family was to live in a big white house with a great big yard in front, with a spacious entry, and pictures of the family all over, and there's a big cake or pie that Mom just baked, and lots of ice cream, and homemade jelly. . . . It's an image of abundance [*yuta-kasa*], and big, really big, love [*aijō*]. You feel like you want to be inside that, that you want to be one of those people, and that akogare is why you want to marry a foreigner." Nagaki related that this message was only confirmed in the fairy tales she read as a child: "The stories Sleeping Beauty and Cinderella were just so seductive [*akogareppoi*]. And of course all these picture books, and Disney stories, all had princes who had white faces." She went on: "That's why we have so much akogare for the West! Because Japanese fairy tales are not about love or romance . . . they're *moralistic* [*dōtoku kyōiku*]! Not the kind of stories that feed little girls' dreams. . . . Of course, there were princes and shōguns in Japan from long ago. But no one has akogare for that! Shōguns? [Makes a face] Japanese shōguns were no gentlemen. . . . But those princes of Western stories never had affairs, they were kind to women, they were gentlemen, they didn't abuse women but protected them, so naturally Japanese girls all just flew to their side." If whiteness is hidden in its "colorless multicoloredness" (Dyer 1988, 46), then yellow cabs—and women like Kawataki and Nagaki—defy this peculiar transparency, but reinscribe its power, when they name the white man as object of desire: when they say they want a man like a movie star, or the prince in a fairy tale.

It is Japanese female writers themselves who continue to voice some of the most insistent constructions of the white man as sex object and romantic target. Soft-core pornography written by women for women, including the popular and widespread genre of semipornographic "ladies comics," frequently employs the white man in the role of stud. For many years, covers of the popular monthly ladies' comic book *Comic Amour* featured a full-color photo of a white man and a Japanese woman locked in embrace; the comic continues to open with a three- to five-page full-color glossy feature depicting a white male–Japanese female fantasy sexual encounter, usually involving some kind of role play. The March 1996 issue featured a Japanese woman as a "love slave" in an SM scenario with a white male "capitalist," and the February 1996 issue showed a kimono-clad Japanese woman instructing a German "Gunther" in how to make love without removing her kimono (see Figure 16). Meanwhile, the December 1994 issue of the ladies comic *Loving* includes the story of "Maya," a Japanese woman who falls in love with a series of Mafia operatives in New York.

The white male fetish is not limited to comics; in a much publicized 1992 project, a newly established high-end pornography viewing salon for couples solicited pornographic videos from two well-known directors, one male and one female, with the aim of creating a pornography that would appeal to a female clientele. The male director produced a standard soft-core piece that left viewers cold, but the female director won acclaim for a misty, soft-focus fantasy featuring a Japanese woman in a ménage à trois with a blond, Caucasian couple in an exotic Western setting. In yet another example, it wasn't until 1993, well after the yellow cab moment, that the popular male strip club called J-Men's opened in Tokyo, featuring a cast of seven muscular white male dancers and one black, who stripped before an audience of Japanese women. At the climax of each performance, scream-

蜜

壺に入ってきたユキの指の力だけで私は引っかけられて抱き寄せられて…ぬるぬるに濡れてしまう。

「ああん、ダメッ」脱がしたらもう、
着れないんだから」
「えッ!?　何だって?」
「キモノ、自分では着れないの。だから、
脱がさないで……」
「自分では着れない?　では、いま着て
いるのは、どうやって?」
「ビューティ・パーラーのような所でお
金を払って着せてもらうの。いまのヤー
パン・ガールは、皆そうよ」
なるほどね。伝統の文化が忘れられて

いくのはドイツでも同じだよ。しかし、
それなら尚、どうやってセックスを楽し
むんだ?　さっきも、僕たちと一緒に、
キモノを着た女のコが何人も、このホテ
ルに入っていったけど……。キモノを脱
がずにどうやって……」
そう言いながらギュンターは、むしゃ
ぶりつくように私の首筋に生温かくねっ
とりとした舌を這わせてきた。

「さあ、教えておくれ、キモノを脱がさ
ずに、いったいどうやって……」
「意地悪……」
「へ……。べつに、これが初めてというわ
けではない。しかし、いままで相手して
きた日本人の男のコは皆、『どうやっ
て?』と訊くまえに、私の着物の裾……

そうっと捲くり上げていた……」
「どうしたらいい?　ねぇ──」
ギュンターが、さらに手を私の胸元
に差し入れてきた。彼の芸術家らしい繊
細な指を持った美しい指先が、私の、すで
にコリコリに硬くなった乳首の周りをく
ねくねと展開する。瞬間、歓喜の波が押
し寄せて噴出しそう。「ああ……ンン……あ
部でしっかりと受え止めた。
「この結を解くりとげるのかい?」
「どうやって?」
「ここのこと?」
今度は、裾を割ってギュンターの指先
が、獲物を狙う蛇のように私の股間に這
い迫ってきた。恥ずかしさで両方の内股
を、硬く閉じ合わせたが、彼の中指の腹は
膣口をシュンッと一直布の上から私の局
なのよ……」
「さあ、自分で捲って……ン──」
下半身がビクビク馬打ち。

16. She teaches "Gunther" how to make love without removing her kimono. Soft-core porn in a "ladies comic." Source: *Comic Amour* (February 1996): n.p.

ing women tucked fake U.S. dollar bills (bought before entering the theater at a rate of five bills for 1,000 yen) into the fluorescent G-string of the foreigner of their choice, in exchange for a kiss.

Even after the yellow cab media scandal faded, the yellow cab image was appropriated by other women for whom the white male continued to serve as a reflexive icon in a commodity-driven project of complaint. In 1993, for example, Iizuka Makiko, a journalist residing in California, wrote a book entitled *The Guys Who Can't Even Hitch a Ride on a Cab* (Kyabu ni mo norenai otokotachi). In seventeen chapters with titles such as "Men Without Dreams Must Be Dumped," "Men Who Can't Express Their Emotions Must Be Dumped," "Control Freaks Must Be Dumped," "Men Who Are Too Lazy to Improve Their Bodies Must Be Dumped," "Infantile Men Must Be Dumped," and "Thankless Men Must Be Dumped," Iizuka systematically justifies Japanese female sexual and romantic preference for Western men by indicting Japanese men's "deficiencies." She concludes the book:

> The question is, why are Japanese men so charmless? It is common knowledge that although since long ago Japanese women have been popular all over the world, Japanese men haven't been popular at all. And so, I decided to write this book, based on the experiences of myself and my friends, to focus on the question of "why?" Recently the women who run to foreign men have been criticized as "yellow cabs." But isn't the fundamental reason for that phenomenon the lack of appeal [*miryoku no nasa*] of Japanese men? If Japanese men were more appealing [*miryokuteki*] Japanese women wouldn't have to turn to foreign men. Of course that is not all there is to it, but there is no question that Japanese women generally want to escape from the kind of Japanese society that Japanese men stand for. . . .
>
> I want Japanese men to try harder. Not only at work, but at love too. That's why, by writing this book, which can perhaps be criticized as a somewhat excessive form of "Japanese man bashing," I have tried to make them see the side of love that women are thirsting for. I want men to comprehend the fairness [*feanesu*] in male-female relationships that women are seeking. . . .
>
> There must be many gentlemen who will respond by scowling and

calling us "disgusting foreign-lovers," but even so, I wrote this book to express the quiet wish of Japanese women that Japanese men would become this kind of internationalist [kokusaijin]. (1993, 210–11)

Here the discourses of internationalism and erotic desire have merged. For Iizuka, women's search for true internationalism can only lead them into the arms of Western men, who embody, even in their most romantic and intimate moments, the democratic, modern ideal of "fairness." The difference between yellow cabs and internationalist women here appears to lie more in method than in motivation. Yellow cabs did not emerge independently of the internationalist impulse expressed in women's sky-rocketing rates of travel and study abroad, but indeed were part and parcel of it; their rejection by the Japanese establishment has less to do with their own behavior than with both mainstream society's and internationalist women's own ambivalence about women who combine sexual aggressive-ness with transnational mobility. As good late-capitalist subjects, the yel-low cabs merely transformed into sexual commodities those men whom modernist internationalism understands primarily as enlightened agents of democratic change in the world.

Meanwhile, the romantic or sexual rejection of Japanese men was also an integral part of the internationalist trajectory. One woman mentioned a friend, a jet-setting diplomat, who "won't even speak to Japanese men. She hates them, *hates* them! She says if she were to say even one word to a Japanese man it would be rude, so it is better not to say anything at all." Another commented impatiently, "I never date Japanese men now. I don't have a chance to, really. No, let's be honest—I don't *make* a chance." On two occasions women spontaneously drew strikingly similar graphs for me (on restaurant napkins) illustrating their contention that the majority of women had "evolved" too far to be content with average Japanese men and were "forced" to turn their thoughts toward romance and marriage with white men. Most Japanese men, by contrast, were, according to the graphs, only "good enough" for Southeast Asian and other "Asian" women (see Figure 17). In this way Japanese men and women, white men, and Southeast Asians (or Asians more generally) are fixed in a grid of value reflective of their position in a global erotic economy. As recently as 1997 an essay appeared in a woman's self-help text on finding a "handsome

JAPANESE WOMEN

Sophisticated, attractive, and talented Japanese women who will only be satisfied with a Western man

JAPANESE MEN

Top Japanese men who are "good enough" for Japanese women

Average Japanese women who can "be satisfied with" a Japanese man

Average Japanese men rejected by Japanese women, who are forced to turn to Southeast Asian women

17. Informant's graph illustrating the erotic hierarchy among Japanese and foreign men and women.

foreign man" as a method of turning around a stalled life (Miyazaki 1997). This essay takes a newly ironic tone: "A sweet, masculine, and kind husband, adorable children, a life full of love, the envy of your friends—a rich foreign husband will bring you all of these—NOT!" (134). It rejects the tropes of romance for a more efficient market approach, advocating the use of commercial dating clubs and Internet dating services to sift through "chaff" and quickly locate an "elite" and educated white man who earns a good salary and, ideally, speaks Japanese. However, what has not changed is a persistent discourse of monetary valuation based on race and nationality, with the white man representing success, black men not mentioned, and Asian (i.e., Southeast Asian, South Asian, Chinese, and Korean) men rejected. "I'm certainly not a racist," says one young woman quoted in the article, "but I paid all this money to go to a matchmaking party that advertised 'nothing but elite European and American businessmen' and the only ones there were these Asians! . . . I say I want to live 'abroad,' but that really means Canada or England. What I'm really looking for is a good-looking blond Canadian or British guy" (143); (see Figures 18 and 19).[3] Although the methods evolve, access to the status of the white lover or husband continues to be a commodity worth paying for.[4]

Before moving on, let me be explicit. I am not claiming that what we know as affection, love, or intimacy cannot or do not prevail in Japanese female–white male involvements, or that such couples are illegitimate or suspect. I am also not claiming that there are no cases of Japanese women intimately involved with nonwhite, non-Western men. What I am claiming is this: just as countless scholars have shown that racialized and sexualized meanings adhere to the Asian female body that exceed any individual's "intentions" or will, and that are irretrievably connected to histories of Orientalism and the eroticization of the Oriental woman, so—it scarcely seems necessary to say (and yet how telling that it is)—racialized and sexualized meanings adhere to the bodies of white men, meanings that have nothing to do with either the good will or the political impulses of individual men, but that are deeply imbricated in histories of modernity, colonialism, and white hegemony in the West and globally. Lest it seem that I am unfairly singling out Japanese women for scrutiny here, I hasten to add that the same examination of the politics of white male attraction could be, and indeed should be, made in the case of white (and other)

18. Text reads: "At home I'm just a skinny, broke guy, but somehow in Japan I'm a ladies' man!") Source: Miyazaki Chieko, "Hansamuna gaikokujin dansei wa hontōni 'risō no dārin' ka?" (Is a handsome foreign man really your "ideal sweetheart"?), in Ishida Yōko, ed., *Marugoto onna no tenki: Itsukara demo yarinaosō* (The complete women's turning point: It's never too late to get your life in order). (Tokyo: Asupekuto), 144.

19. At a mixer party featuring foreign men, various "Asian" men greet Japanese women in their own languages. Woman: "Ugh, this is a washout!" Source: Miyazaki Chieko, "Hansamuna gaikokujin dansei wa hontōni 'risō no dārin' ka?" (Is a handsome foreign man really your "ideal sweetheart"?), in Ishida Yōko, ed., *Marugoto onna no tenki: Itsukara demo yarinaosō* (The complete women's turning point: It's never too late to get your life in order). (Tokyo: Asupekuto), 143.

women as well. As Frankenberg and others have shown, white women have long accorded white men the role of their self-chosen "defenders" from the threatening sexuality of the men of other races (1993, 76–77). Here too the unspoken and unspeakable assumption of the universal "preferability" of white men over all others (acknowledged only in private talk, and then only rarely) enacts, through this public silence and private "sanctioned ignorance," histories of racism in which white women are accomplices as well as victims. "White Man as savior," Frankenberg observes, "would founder without White-Woman-who-must-be-saved" (1997a, 12).

In each case, these histories have constituted the white man as an individual without race who exemplifies all the "successes" of the modern West, which in turn adhere potentially to the female subject who aligns herself with him. The yellow cabs and even more so the response to them in Japan and abroad suggest a conflation of whiteness and the West as object of desire and agent of "liberation" for transnationally mobile, cosmopolitan Japanese women, not merely in the crude sexual sense enacted by the yellow cabs, but in the realm of imagination and fantasy as these are linked to the seductions and opportunities of transnational capital, to the now global hegemony of liberal humanist discourses of modernity, and to the "continuing racism defining America [and other Western countries] as white" (Kondo 1997, 192). These seductions and opportunities create the conditions for a domestic gendered critique and resistance that transcends Japan's national borders and interjects some internationally inclined women into an emergent transnational class constituted by its own distinct erotic economy.

Status, Money, Race, and the White Man That white men have been viewed in Japan as coveted erotic commodities linked to a kind of transnational social upward mobility in ways that transcend the yellow cab moment can be seen in a survey of three women's texts, dating from the 1970s, 1980s, and 1990s, which show the evolution of these discourses of money, sex, and race over time. In this section I briefly discuss Kirishima Yōko's *The Lonely American* (Sabishii Amerikajin, 1975), Takahashi Fumiko's *How to Date a Foreign Man* (Gaikokudansei to tsukiau hō, 1988), and Kida Midori's *Women! What Do You Want from America?* (Joseitachi yo! Amerika e itte dōsuru no?, 1998). In these three texts the image of the white man shifts steadily in keeping with the changing economic status of Japan and Japanese women vis-à-vis the West, yet remains embedded in a persistent discourse of value and evaluation of the white man as lover within larger hierarchies of racial and class status.

Kirishima Yōko's *The Lonely American* (1975 [1971]) was an influential book by an author who came to be known as much for her unconventional lifestyle (she bore three children as a single mother at a time when this was virtually unheard of in Japan) as for her accomplished and prolific writing (1982, 1987, 1990). Although it is a personal account of her two-year sojourn during her early 30s in late 1960s Los Angeles, *The Lonely American* predates the emergence of the female internationalist genre treated in previous chapters; in the late 1960s few young Japanese women had the resources to spend extended periods abroad, let alone to return and write autobiographical accounts of them. *The Lonely American* is also a much more ambitious and complex piece of writing than most works of the internationalist genre. In it Kirishima makes a quasi-sociological analysis of American racial, sexual, and class mores based on her experiences in the L.A. dating scene, which she negotiated using the personal ads in the *Los Angeles Free Press,* an underground newspaper that was read, she tells us, by hippies, antiwar activists, "wife-swappers," "swingers," and sm afficionados.

As she relates only near the very end of the book, Kirishima's reason for coming to the United States was to accept a "super-rich man's offer of marriage" (1975, 196). Three days after coming to live with her children at his mansion, however, she leaves this man (she does not explain why) to be taken in by an American male friend. An unspecified time later she enters the dating fray. First responding to others' ads, and later placing an ad herself, Kirishima markets herself in the *Free Press* as an "Oriental woman" in search of a wealthy white sponsor. Kirishima does not romanticize this search. Her total absorption in and allegiance to the standards of monied white society, her open contempt for blacks, hippies, the poor, and other marginal groups, and her exclusive association with a series of white men who appeared to constitute her entire social network, all reveal an extraordinarily pragmatic calculation of the American race and class structure and a single-minded determination to use whatever racial, sexual, and class "distinctions" she had at her disposal to insert herself advantageously into it.

Interestingly, Kirishima displaces her "Oriental" female identity onto the figure of a Chinese alter-ego, "Miss Lily Yang." This persona of a twenty-five-year-old Chinese woman so sheltered that she was "not even allowed to walk out alone during the day" seems intended to inflame the interest of white men enamored of an Asian female rescue fantasy, while eliding Kirishima's own agency and projecting her state of dependence and vulnerability onto the figure of a passive, victimized Chinese woman. "I hope to find a kind friend," she tells us she wrote as Lily Yang, "who will let me taste the freedom of America" (10). Although the six men to whom she sent this letter all responded eagerly to her solicitation, each proved disappointingly inadequate, and still as Lily Yang Kirishima continued her quest. She writes that through the personal ads she quickly made a circle of "close friends," consisting of "high-level" individuals such as executives, doctors, journalists, scholars, lawyers, architects, and other "intellectuals," all of whom were white and most of whom were wealthy (20).

What distinguishes Kirishima's text is that while she uses the personal ads to pursue sexual encounters and "make friends" (the distinction is one she seems to leave intentionally vague), she at the same time reacts to the ads as sociological phenomena, evidence of American social dysfunction. American personal ads, she writes, are cries of loneliness: "What frightened me were the cries of people starving for love. I was horrified to find myself touching the open wound of people's loneliness, and hastily drew away my hand. There were just too many lonely people here. In America, escalating sexual freedom had only made more and more apparent the human isolation that is beyond the reach of sex" (22). She tells of one lover, a highly successful psychoanalyst, so starved for companionship that he pathetically paid her to come to his office weekly and let him lay his head in her lap and pour out his woes. However, she does not let her ambivalence about the raw pain lurking beneath the surface of the personal ad network prevent her from continuing in what she comes to call her "addiction," using various "boyfriends" to investigate a series of lovers whom she quickly discards for failing to live up to her image. "America is a land of many strong and masculine men," she writes, "although it is a tragic environment for men who are not strong" (33).

For most of the book Kirishima's total absorption in white men is not so much stated as implied: with only one exception, no other kind of man (or woman) figures in her book, or apparently in her life in the United States. Her investment in the white establishment becomes explicit only in chapter 6 when, briefly, a black nationalist named Freddy appears with whom she has an extended debate. This debate is significant not only for its substance, but for its tone. In contrast to the elaborate, indeed exaggerated level of polite and feminine language she employs in her conversations with white men (as rendered into Japanese in the book), with Freddy her language is simplistic and vaguely mocking, as if speaking to a slightly slow child. "I wonder if America is really such a bad country?" she admonishes Freddy. "I wonder why there are so many people lining up who very, very much want to become Americans? You might not want to be here, but for someone like me to stay here I have to go again and again to ask the Immigration Office to let me stay!" (175). Kirishima expresses nothing but contempt for the black nationalist position and sympathy for white hostility to it: "Freddy's heart was already armed. On top of that he and his friends took up rifles and armed themselves in public. No wonder white citizens were terrified of them" (175). Ultimately, black men are rejected as potential lovers: "I wouldn't have the courage to marry a black or bear a black child. I suppose if I were to really fall for someone, ultimately it wouldn't matter if they were black or red, but rationally I just pray that this does not occur. I have never made love with a black" (170). She sums up, "They're just too racially different [*ijinshū*]; it would be hopeless to live with one, and we'd be too out-of-synch even to work together" (171).

She has a similar response to some hippies she encounters in Berkeley on a visit accompanied by a "conservative white gentleman." After a long, increasingly hostile dialogue with a young hippie couple marked less by a mocking frivolity than by an escalating rage and outrage on her part, the hippies accuse her of "sounding like a PR agent for the American government." Kirishima retorts, "I'd rather do PR for the republic than for you hippies! I don't think the American nation is as rotten as you all seem to believe. It may have some problems, but it's too precious to simply destroy! *For my own benefit I want to preserve America!*" (183; emphasis added).

Ultimately, Kirishima is explicit about the benefits she hopes to accrue through her sojourn in the United States. She describes them in the final chapter, in which she relates the results of her own ad in the *Free Press*: "I had two motivations for deciding to place my own ad," she writes; "the first was that I wanted to be the one in charge. I didn't want to pick ready-made clothes off the rack; I wanted to buy them 'made-to-order' " (191). Second, living alone had become inconvenient: "Everyday life in America is extremely inconvenient for a woman who doesn't have a man to help her. First of all, men earn more than women, but even apart from the financial aspects, running a household without someone to handle the roles of driver, electrician, carpenter, cleaner, babysitter, and bartender is quite difficult. To buy these services short-term is so expensive as to be practically impossible, and who has time to call and arrange them?" (192). In ascending from the ranks of the chosen to the chooser, Kirishima attempts to shift her position in the market economy, using the mechanisms of the market to purchase services previously beyond her reach. In short, Kirishima is attempting to sell her race (and sex) to buy class.

Kirishima's ad reads as follows (in its original English, reproduced in the text): "I am absolutely not possessive, but would like to try cooperative life with stable male companion with mutual respect for freedom and privacy. He must be under mid-40's, high IQ, adventurous but responsible, financially secure with ability and will to enjoy life. I am 32, petite, slim Oriental female. Artistic, cultured, well-traveled. Not domestic type, but intelligent and sensitive enough to run a comfortable home in good taste. Have beautiful little kids, and need good books, fine food, ocean, and interesting people. Photo and phone pls to NX c/o R. Hill, Box 868 Manhattan Beach 90266" (192). Kirishima relates that she employed all of her skill as a former ad writer to sell herself to maximum effect on the dating market. The "catch phrases" of "respect for freedom" and "privacy," she writes, "were even more effective than I had hoped," and clearly revealed, in her view, that "American men are constricted by [American] women's possessiveness and prevented from enjoying true freedom or privacy" (203). Similarly, "Oriental" had an "astonishing degree of effect": "There are still many men for whom the mere mention of the word *Orient* has some kind of romantic sound to it. Those men who are disillusioned with American women are especially prone to idealize and long for women of the Orient" (204). She attempts to add class distinction by describing herself as "cultured" and "well-traveled."

Kirishima tells us that she had her "boyfriends" John pay the cost of placing the ad (as a Christmas present), Chuck deliver it to the *Free Press*, and Bob provide the mailbox; these men also served as her "intelligence agents," making background checks on the men who responded. Her efforts were successful: she received a total of fifty-six responses. However, the ad did not yield Kirishima a sponsor. The series of rich respondees she dated proved, she tells us, to be either impotent, domineering, or too old. With only one man, Ron, did Kirishima feel a potential bond; unfortunately, Ron was broke. Kirishima writes that she was on the verge of casting aside her financial scruples and allowing Ron to share her apartment, when she was dissuaded by John, Chuck, and Bob. She quotes Chuck: "This is how Oriental women get taken advantage of! You've been in the States two years and you still don't know the rule that financial status is the most important part of a man's character?" (226). With that, abruptly, Kirishima gives up. She writes, "Standing amidst the loneliness of so many Americans made me feel ill, as if I had drunk too much bad wine, and I gradually lost my appetite. I became homesick. Enough, I thought. I've had enough of America" (226). The book ends with her departure for Japan.

The Lonely American illuminates a moment when an exceptionally bold, single Japanese woman was able to claim the personal mobility and financial resources to spend an extended period abroad in an effort to escape disadvantageous circumstances in Japan; however, it was a moment when women's expectations still hinged overwhelmingly on a male protector. To Kirishima, the United States was a land of wealthy white men who had the power to magically bestow on her, an independent but struggling young mother, the money and class status she craved, money and status almost certainly beyond her reach as an unwed mother in Japan. With the unapologetic pragmatism of a participant in arranged marriage negotiations (*omiai*; indeed, she employs that term for her meetings with respondents), Kirishima evaluates her own market value and employs all of her skills as a writer to sell herself to her public. The status she craves is an explicitly racialized status: only white men, repeatedly referred to as "gentlemen" (*shinshi*), qualify as potential objects of her search, in an ascending hierarchy rising from her circle of "intelligence agents" to the rich and successful executives, doctors, lawyers, and others whom she targets. While Kirishima's ambivalence about the men she encounters, the personal ad mechanism itself, and the overwhelming "loneliness" of life in the United

States permeates her book and complicates her experience, ultimately she cannot see white men as anything but sources of money and status. When she is unable to acquire the services she seeks, she gives up and goes home.

Takahashi Fumiko's *How to Date a Foreign Man* (1989), written by a former Pan Am stewardess married to an American man and residing in the United States, reveals a very different moment in Japanese women's experience with the West. Published at the height of the bubble economy, originally as a series of essays in the travel magazine *BIANCA*, *How to Date a Foreign Man* consists of short chapters on the men of twenty-five different countries, including Western countries such as England, France, Italy, the United States, and Canada as well as non-Western countries such as China, Nepal, India, the Philippines, Egypt, and Morocco. Although the publication of the book coincided with the emergence of the yellow cab controversy and undoubtedly was conceived to capitalize on it, *How to Date a Foreign Man* was not written by or for the yellow cabs themselves. At the time of writing the book Takahashi was already in her mid-forties, married for many years and the mother of one child. Her stated purpose in writing the book, as expressed in the introduction, was to provide the increasingly sophisticated and well-traveled young Japanese women then emergent in the late 1980s with the necessary information to safely and successfully date foreign men—ideally, with the goal of making a high-status marriage—without falling prey to "loose" or "undignified" behavior: "The purpose of young women's foreign tourism is not just to see the sights and shop, but also includes the desire to get to know foreign people, particularly charming men [*sutekina dansei*]. There are only two sexes in the world; I think we should try seeing not just the men of our own country, but the charming men of other countries as well" (5). Yet, although the book appears to take a broad-minded, ecumenical approach to men of all colors and nationalities, in fact Takahashi is exclusively interested in white "Anglo-Saxon" (her preferred term) men, and the agenda of the book is to instruct young Japanese women in how to acquire one of these while being on guard against the advances of inferior types who deviate from the white Anglo-Saxon ideal.

This theme is introduced in the first chapter, "The English Gentleman: Once Rejected He Won't Ask Again." Takahashi writes, "The first thing one thinks of regarding English men is the image of the gentleman [*shin-*

shi]. The custom of ladies first—giving way to women on elevators and trains, rising from one's seat when a woman stands up from or sits at the table—these are lovely manners, but we don't encounter them often outside of England. . . . But in England it is indeed difficult to find a man who is not a gentleman" (18–19). Takahashi's reverence for the English man is permeated with racialized meaning: he is unlike Gallic or southern European men who stare rudely at women, "Latins" who can't take no for an answer, and certainly unlike Indians and Pakistanis in England, who she shudders, crudely importune women on the street. Indeed, for Takahashi, the English gentleman is inaccessible, particularly to Japanese women. Therein lies his mystery and charm, for his is both a class and a racial inaccessibility. According to her, the true English gentlemen will almost never date or marry a nonwhite woman. Thus, one of Takahashi's chief regrets, she writes, is that she was "never blessed with the chance to date an English gentleman" (14). As a cautionary tale, she relates at length her failure to take advantage of a chance meeting with a delightful English lawyer in a London restaurant:

> A tall, slender man elegantly dressed in a well-cut suit approached our table. He kissed [fellow stewardess] Janice's cheek, and held out his hand to me, saying "How do you do." . . . Throughout the meal, without betraying the least sign of boredom, he listened to our conversation, with elegant gestures quietly pouring out tea into our teacups, and savoring its flavor and fragrance. Occasionally he contributed a refined joke or amusing witticism. I felt that here I had encountered a true English gentleman. How different, I thought, from those noisy American pilots who slurp up their meals! From then on whenever I flew into London, I took out his card, which read "barrister," but I never dialed his number. Why? I thought at the time that a refined English gentleman like he could only be interested in a white woman. Surely I'm too short, I thought. I had quite a feeling of inferiority. Several years later when I ran into Janice, she told me he had waited eagerly for my call. Hearing that, I felt the most extraordinary sense of disappointment and regret. (17)

Thus, Takahashi has this advice for Japanese women: "If you should ever, for whatever reason, be asked on a date by an English man, realize that it is a most unusual opportunity. Quite the opposite of those Latin men who will importune you repeatedly, if you refuse he will never ask you again. . . . And if love should grow between you, and you wish to nurture it, you must take your time and patiently allow things to develop. To hurry things along is an affront to the manner of the gentleman" (18).

Takahashi treats Canadian and Australian men as only slightly inferior inheritors of genuine British manners, and warns Japanese women not to offend potential conquests with affronts to their fastidiousness (for example, by the touching of one's hair during mealtimes; 148). American men, however, are treated much more ambivalently, described in places as "noisy," "unrefined," "cold," and "cheap." Much of the chapter on American men is taken up by the story of Takahashi's betrayal by an American who asked her to marry him, failing to mention that he was already married. Nevertheless, she gamely offers advice on how to meet an "elite" American man, and finishes with what she calls a "Cinderella story" of a Japanese stewardess who finally lands a rich American "Prince Charming" on her third marriage. Takahashi, however, in general mourns American men's loss of "virility" since the appearance of the "women's lib" movement. She concludes with a certain skepticism, "Of course, I wonder if their appeal when I first arrived was due to the strength of the dollar then" (169).

In contrast to the generally reverent treatment of Anglo-Saxon men, French, Italian, and Spanish men are depicted as seductive but dangerous, and Takahashi devotes most of her space to warning young women against falling too easily. "Among the playboys of Paris and Rome, Japanese women have the reputation for being extremely easy," she admonishes; "this seems to arise from Japanese women's vagueness and inability to clearly say yes or no" (28–29). While acknowledging the allure of their "soulful eyes" and "skillful praise," Takahashi urges her readers to be adequately prepared should they accept a date with a Frenchman and "not be seduced by the delicious food and champagne and the sparkling, enchanting lights of Paris" (29). However, it is when Takahashi moves into a discussion of nonwhite or non-Western men that her attitude abruptly changes. About Greek men she urges women "not to let them spoil your trip" (61), and about Indians she warns against marriage, relating a cautionary tale of a Japanese woman who found herself the victim of an oppressive Indian extended family. Her chapter on Cairo is entitled "Don't Be Pleased If You're Popular in Cairo" and consists of a series of unpleasant incidents with "pop-eyed, large-nosed, typically Arab-faced men" (205).

The chapters on non-Western men in *How to Date a Foreign Man* almost invariably devolve into either accounts of charming white English or American men encountered in non-Western countries, or else half-hearted praise of the local men for the degree to which they approximate the appearance and manners of Anglo-Saxons. Thus, in the chapter on Thailand, Takahashi tells the story of a fellow Japanese stewardess "Cinderella" in Bangkok who met and married an American "prince," "as handsome as a movie star and a highly cultivated individual, anyone's ideal man" (120). The chapters on the Philippines and Argentina praise the local men as "Westernized": Argentina she describes as "a white person's country where Europe breathes" (188), and Filipino men as "having the deeply carved face of Europeans" and "understanding the European manner of escorting a woman" (107).

There is a euphoric quality about *How to Date a Foreign Man* that characterizes much of the internationalist women's writing of the late 1980s, as young, highly mobile, and economically independent single women first found themselves with the unexpected freedom to explore every sensation the world had to offer. As Japanese women fanned out as tourists around the globe, they increasingly came to recognize their own value on the global romance market and that, here at least, their hegemony over Japanese men was complete. Takahashi relates with delight a Singaporean friend's quoting of the hoary adage that a man's happiness lies in living in an American house, eating Chinese food, and having a Japanese wife. She exclaims, "It might seem that Japanese women have become Westernized recently, but . . . we still very much have an image of being ideal wives— sweet and feminine" (93). Meanwhile, as she states in her conclusion, "Japanese men are the least popular among all the men of the civilized world. . . . Added to their meager physiques," she writes, "is their clumsiness in treating women and their lack of gentlemanly manners" (236). Takahashi loses no opportunity to berate Japanese men: "In skill at flirting there is no comparison between Parisians and tongue-tied, ham-handed Japanese men" (30); "Italian men may love their mothers, but this is nothing like the mother dependency of Japanese men with their Oedipal complexes" (42); "Northern Europeans drink a lot, but they are as night to day compared to Japanese men who clamor and hoot as soon as they get a drop of liquor in them" (67). Telling the story of a Japanese man with whom an American friend became involved in Mexico, Takahashi writes, "He was such an ugly man that seeing them together was like 'Beauty and the Beast'! It was most extraordinary" (175).

Takahashi takes each potential fault of a foreign male and justifies it as preferable to similar behavior on the part of a Japanese man, while making any potentially attractive quality of a Japanese man evidence of his inferiority compared to foreigners. Thus:

> There might be many short men among Latins as well, but unlike Japanese men they are attentive and forthcoming. Compared to them, Japanese men, who have no custom or practice of ladies first, are simply incapable of actively approaching a woman, praising her, or wooing her with soft words. . . . Japanese men might be generous in picking up the check on dates, especially compared to those American men who scowl at the bill, calculating each and every line. . . . But among Americans this is merely a case of Western rationalism, which makes them unwilling to conclude a transaction until they have thoroughly satisfied themselves about its correctness. It is nothing unusual, and nothing to be ashamed of. They express themselves clearly. They are not vague like Japanese men. (237)

Takahashi criticizes Japanese women's akogare for "blond-haired, blue-eyed foreign youths" (208), but this is a bit disingenuous, for *How to Date a Foreign Man* makes the blond-haired, blue-eyed Anglo-Saxon male the ultimate object of desire, the entry point into a world of refinement, prestige, and good manners. "You're such a nice American man" (143), she tells us she said to a young passenger who "charmingly" helped her lift her bags to the luggage rack on a crowded flight (he was Canadian, and not, apparently, pleased at this compliment); but in the context of *How to Date a Foreign Man,* one cannot imagine Takahashi praising anyone as "such a nice Korean (or Indian, or Egyptian) man." Despite the fact that race is never explicitly mentioned in the book's 238 pages—or rather, precisely because race is never mentioned—the white man is isolated as the object of desire, he who can be acquired only through the Japanese woman's mastery of Anglo-Saxon standards of behavior, through her careful acquisition of the tropes of global class distinction.

Kida Midori's 1998 *Women! What Do You Want from America?* marks a new trend in women's writing about the West. Composed of a first part entitled "New York Job and Career Facts" and a second entitled "New York Love and Marriage Facts," it openly combines the concerns of career, sex, and marriage in a supremely pragmatic informational guide for women who wish to relocate abroad. The author, a journalist who at the time of writing had lived in New York City for eight years, tells us that she had a single purpose in writing the book: to urge on fellow young, single, internationally minded Japanese women the need for a realistic, pragmatic "strategy" (*senryaku*) to achieve their goals overseas, goals that she simply assumes include both a professional career and a white husband or lover. "When I go home to Japan I find many girls who tell me they want to go to America, live in America, marry an American," she writes in the introduction, "but they have no long-term vision of what it is they wish to accomplish in their own lives" (1). "But just like in business, for a woman to achieve happiness she needs a solid strategy, as well as effort and luck" (4). The purpose of *Women!*, she writes, is to provide the stories of potential role models for young women to learn from: Japanese women who have "made it" (and some who have not) in New York City.

The first half of the book follows the conventions of the typical internationalist text, describing professional opportunities for women in New York, differing only in its bluntness about the reduction in such opportunities since the Japanese recession and Japan's "decline in importance to American business" (69). It is the second half of the book that distinguishes *Women!*, not only from other internationalist texts, but also from the grim tone of Kirishima's *The Lonely American* and the giddiness of Takahashi's *How to Date a Foreign Man*. Kida is above all impatient with her readers. She has no time for dreamy-eyed idealization of foreign men and heartily blames Japanese women for their reputation abroad as "easy conquests." According to Kida, too many Japanese women throw themselves away on men with no resources and no prospects, misled by their own Hollywood-driven akogare for "tall blond-haired, blue-eyed Adonises—the kind Japanese females can't resist" (82). Nevertheless, "You've come all the way to America, and it would be a terrific waste if you didn't hook up with the kind of fine man [ii otoko] you almost never see in Japan" (80).

Kida is unrepentantly materialistic. "Beware of men with no earning power," she begins her discussion; "don't choose the wrong man; make sure you have a solid strategy for finding the right kind" (84).[5] The right kind is emphatically not a military man; Kida devotes a chapter to the stories of women who met and married mainly black Army men on U.S. bases in Japan, only to find themselves stranded in the United States with alcoholic husbands, or abandoned, poverty-stricken, and on welfare. Kida is entirely unsympathetic: "You can make various excuses that they picked the wrong person or had bad luck, but the fact is, it's the fault of their own ignorance [ninshiki no amasa]" (97). "Unlike Japan where 90 percent of people are middle class," she admonishes her readers, "America is a class society" (98–99). She sums up, "I'm not saying marry a rich white man, and I'm not saying money will make you happy. But you in Japan simply cannot imagine how miserable life is in America without money or connections" (105).

In the effort to find a rich, young, elite white man, Kida quotes Chinese military strategist Sun-tzu: "Know the enemy, know yourself, and you will win a hundred battles." She begins by instructing her readers in the class geography of New York City: "Brooklyn, the Bronx, and Queens . . . are where the lower half live . . . (racially speaking, blacks and Hispanics)" (112). She warns women to avoid these areas and to focus their energies on Westchester and Greenwich, "where you find the crème de la crème" (112).

Ultimately, however, Kida urges women to set their sights beyond the merely rich. She advocates finding a genuine "WASP," a "member of the American ruling class, descendents of the Puritans who came over on the *Mayflower*" (121). This is not just money but "old money" (ōrudo manē), to be found among the "blue bloods" of Park Avenue on Manhattan's Upper East Side. To meet these young scions, she urges attendance at the Friday evening charity parties held at Sotheby's, Christie's, and the Guggenheim. Kida freely acknowledges that class and race prejudice characterize blue-blooded American society and argues that such prejudice is "perfectly natural" and a kind of "universal exclusionist feeling" (125). The only way around this, she insists, is to gear up for battle and "give everything you've got." She insists that Japanese women learn how to "sell their charms" (*onna o haru*) to overcome racial opposition to their acceptability as potential wives.

In her afterword, "Japanese Women, You've Really Got What It Takes!" ("Nihonjosei, ōi ni waza ari!"), Kida describes the special "secrets" that Japanese women bring to this battle, derived from centuries of oppression and the corresponding imperative to develop "the weapon of our womanhood" (*onna to iu buki*) under adverse conditions. Japanese women's legendary charm, according to Kida, derives from their "traditional skills [*waza*] in . . . knowing how to thoroughly control events from behind the scenes, and manipulate circumstances to accomplish our own gain without the enemy even being aware" (155–56). She continues, "Today, it is Japanese women who have reaped the benefits of the postwar prosperity, and who are now the richest consumers in the world, traveling to New York and Paris buying up designer products. But on the eve of the twenty-first century, Japanese society is undergoing an immense shift. The 'corporate unity model' has collapsed and we're now in an age when both men and women must earnestly struggle to discover their own ikikata and life foundation [*yoridokoro*]. . . . It is an era of intensive competition in which individuals must learn to live by their own strength" (156–57). She concludes, "In the coming competitive era, our hard-won 'woman's weapon' will serve us well" (157).

With Kida we have come full circle. The quest for the white man has led back to the internationalist imperative, mediated by Japanese women's "essential" marginality on both corporate and familial levels. Women must seek inclusion in the unstable realm of deterritorialized capital not by such simplistic means as buying up designer products in New York and Paris, but by using the marks of their marginality to sell themselves to white men in order to buy an upper-class white lifestyle. The white man is still a means to an end, but in this case he is not simply a financial sponsor for a woman in need, or a glittering, elusive ideal, encountered on brief travels, racially inaccessible. Rather, he is an entirely obtainable, if elusive, quarry, promising Japanese women, now independent agents of their own fate and unhampered by social or familial restraints in Japan, the chance to establish "the good life" outside of Japan in an internationalist age. Total self-reliance is Kida's motto, based on the individual's prudent manipula-

20. The Japanese woman in kimono through the gaze of the white man. Poster for a kimono school.

tion of "Japanese womanhood" as value-added commodity in a competitive international marketplace of work and marriage.

In this way, it is not only the white man who is commodified but also the Japanese female self as seen through his eyes. When a major yearly fashion show in Kyoto showcased Japanese and Italian fashion through the theme of a love affair between a kimono-clad Japanese woman and a suited Italian man, a female fashion journalist who covered it wrote that the plot made her "rediscover the true appeal of the Japanese woman wearing her traditional costume" (Miyauchi 1993, 273). The Japanese woman in kimono as seen through the eyes of the white man is fetishized in a variety of female-targeted media, including ads for kimono and bridal classes (see Figure 20). In one 1994 television commercial for a kimono company, a blond man in nineteenth-century dress stands on a deserted beach, gazing unsmilingly at a Japanese women in kimono enclosed in a cage. Heavy with symbolism, this commercial constitutes the kimono-clad Japanese woman as the white man's object; it is his gaze that renders her "truly" Japanese.

This commodification of the Japanese woman as seen through the eyes of the white man has recently been made even more explicit in the bilingual *Hiragana Times* cross-cultural communication magazine, which now sponsors a monthly competition among Japanese female readers for the prize of appearing on the magazine's cover paired with a white male model (see Figure 21). However, constructing the Japanese woman as the white man's desired object hinges on a competition with white women: the vanquishing of the white woman as rival for the white man's affections. Thus, a persistent theme in writing about the white lover is an insistence on Japanese women's special ability to please white men and to liberate the "inherent" masculinity in them that, according to the writers, has been tragically suppressed by aggressive, mannish white women. Takahashi Toshie writes of her American fiancé Herbie, "He was delighted with a Japanese woman's delicate, natural care and considerateness, so different from American women. Of course as far as I was concerned I was just acting normally" (1989, 196–97).

Competition between Japanese and white women for the heart of the white man is one of the subtexts of the 1988 biography *American Lover* by Miyamoto Michiko, introduced in chapter 1. The climax of this story of a decades-long illicit love affair between Yuriko and Bart, a married American ex-G.I., comes when Miyamoto travels to the United States in the mid-1980s to interview Bart, now in his seventies, and to meet Bart and Yuriko's illegitimate son, Eddie. Miyamoto relates these events in the book's epilogue, entitled "Japan's Women" ("Nippon no onna").

Miyamoto first sets up a contrast between Yuriko (now called Yuri), whom Bart described as "a little flower, delicate and weak," and the American women whom Bart had known before: "lively, smart, active, pushy women . . . who spoke their minds just like men" (174). That Bart chose Yuri—"the kind of woman," in his words, "who made a man feel stronger and more manly"—Miyamoto interprets as proving that "Yuriko's 'little flower act' had awakened Bart's manhood, and the inborn protective instincts that had been smothered, even forgotten, from dealing with American women" (177).

In case the reader misses her point, Miyamoto makes it again in the context of her first meeting with Yuri and Bart's son during their drive from the L.A. airport accompanied by Eddie's American fiancée Debra. Here she sets up a contrast between Eddie ("gentle and handsome" and

ステキな国際生活マガジン
Magazine for a Beautiful Global Life☺
ひらがなタイムズ

HIRAGANA TIMES

9
September
2000 No. 167
¥390

COVER MODELS WANTED!
表紙モデル募集！

特集 / Feature
日本で学ぶ―日本文化を継承する外国人
Learning in Japan — Foreigners Inheriting Japanese Culture

外国人成功物語
旭鷲山　昇

Foreigner Success Story
Kyokushuzan Noboru

スペシャル・レポート
「アメリカに来てはいけない娘」

Special Report
"A Girl who shouldn't come to the States

ビザ
離婚外国人配偶者

VISA
A Case of Divorced Foreign Spouse

Japanese-English Bilingual Magazine　日英バイリンガル表記

21. Each month the *Hiragana Times* sponsors a competition among Japanese female readers for the prize of appearing on the cover with a white male model. Source: *Hiragana Times,* January 2001. Reprinted with permission.

"slim and subdued") and Debra, who, rather alarmingly, has a "square face and jutting jaw" and "white attractive teeth that seemed to fill her mouth." She relates an exchange among the three: "In the car Eddie whispered something to Debra that I could not hear. Debra's loud penetrating voice rang out, 'No, we can't take her there for dinner! That place is common, and the food isn't any good. We have to take her to a decent seafood restaurant!' I spoke up from the back seat, 'it's my treat, so please pick your favorite place, even if it is a bit more expensive. . . .' Eddie began to reply but was instantly drowned out by Debra: "Oh you mustn't; we planned to treat you!" . . . Debra, with her body half twisted around facing me, talked on and on" (185–87). Later in the evening Miyamoto is again riding in Eddie's car as he and Debra return her to her hotel:

> I sat back in Eddie's Toyota, soaking up the smell of the ocean and the feel of the dry California air, and listening to Eddie rhapsodize about life in California. Suddenly—"Eddie, you're going the wrong way! The scenery isn't pretty this way! Stop and go back! Go the opposite way! Right now!" "I can't turn here," Eddie objected, "I mean . . ." "What do you mean 'I mean'? If you want to see the ocean at night I said you can't do it from this road!" Eddie instantly obeyed Debra's sharp command. Debra seemed to think of something. She twisted around in her seat and looked at me happily, "I'm nothing like a Japanese woman, am I? I'm not very obedient!" (192–94)

Miyamoto's mind goes back to a conversation Yuri had once spoken of, in which Yuri had asked Bart to marry her if his wife, Frieda, should die first. Yuri had related that she told Bart then that she wanted to have the chance to care for him when he grew old and feeble, to cook for him, and even change his bedpans. Yuri repeated to Miyamoto, "I want to do everything for him. I want to see him through to the end. Then I can die." She went on, "It's funny, when I asked him that, he was so overcome he started to cry. He said to me, 'Oh, what a Japanese woman you are! You're so Japanese!'" Miyamoto recalls Yuri asking aloud, "Am I such a Japanese woman, I wonder?" (195–96). Back in the car Miyamoto whispers to herself, "Yes, Yuri. You are a Japanese woman [*japanīzu uōman*]. A Japanese woman [*Nippon no onna*]." Debra swings around, asking, "What? What did you say? Who is Japanese?" "Nothing, nothing, I was just talking to myself," Miyamoto replies, and ends the book: "Settling into the back seat, caressed by the dark ocean breeze blowing in from Laguna Beach, I shut my eyes" (196).

The transnational signifier "Japanese woman" (*japanīzu uōman*) functions here in a fantasy of displacement of the white woman. Miyamoto's heavy-handed juxtaposition of the helpless, selfless Yuri and the loud, castrating Debra allows her female readership to project themselves in turn as saviors to misunderstood and harassed white men, the victims of white women's "phallic theft."

Mutual Attractions Traise Yamamoto has summarized the Japanese woman as represented in Western erotic fantasy as a "fetishized . . . super-feminized exotic object in whom the soul of the geisha resides. . . . ontologically mysterious, sexually available, and hungry for contact with the West—via the white Western male" (1999, 22). She notes that although American images of Japanese women have evolved over the past hundred years, what remains unchanged in American representations is the Japanese woman's "ideological alignment with the West in contrast to and often against the negative aspects of Japanese culture and the threat of the Japanese nation-state" (24).[6] In Yamamoto's analysis, the Japanese woman is always "she-who-must-be-saved" (24) and is granted agency in Western accounts "only insofar as it has served the interests of those other than herself . . . she has been used to both feminize and dominate Japan in ways that obscure the imperializing impulses of the West" (60).

I have shown some of the ways that Japanese women have indeed been imagined by Americans as aligned with the West against the Japanese state, especially after World War II. Yet, what Yamamoto's analysis and others like it fail to take into account is the possibility that some Japanese women may appropriate this fetishized image of themselves to their own ends. As should now be apparent, this is what internationalized women have sought to do in the realm of career and ikikata, and what the yellow cabs and their predecessors and followers have sought to do in the realm of sex. As I have shown, some Japanese women have constructed *themselves* as "she-who-must-be-saved," requiring rescue by Westerners from "the threat of the Japanese nation-state." They have made what they consider their exclusive claim on the sympathies of Westerners the very foundation of a repudiation of Japanese "culture." And they have made what they construct as their exclusive access to the white man, through romantic or sexual involvement, a route to assimilation in the liberating realm of the West. This is why Matsui Machiko, in her study of Japanese study-abroad students in the United States, rather smugly remarks that Japanese women have an advantage over their "Oriental male" counterparts in being able to assimilate through marriage to white Americans, an opportunity she insists is out of reach for Japanese men (1994, 137–38). The exclusivity of women's opportunity to "marry in" to the West is invoked in the slogan about the U.S. green card introduced earlier: "To get the Green Card women marry, men cook" (gurīn kādo o toru niwa, onna wa kekkon, otoko wa kokku).[7]

Ishizaki Reiko, the twenty-four-year-old woman who had studied for two years at U.C. Santa Barbara, explained to me, "Japanese guys feel more inferiority than girls do that they are racially despised by the world. With Japanese girls, you are popular just for being a Japanese girl. For us, it's almost an advantage. But Japanese men have no standing [tachiba ga nai]. Race becomes a problem for Japanese men, but for women, race is 'excused' [yurusareru]." I suggest that in Japanese women's case, race is not so much excused as fetishized. Japanese men, by contrast, like the Asian American men described by Ebron and Tsing in a 1995 article, are seen as representatives of too much tradition in a regime of modernity that defines the traditional as "outside, ineffective, and already having lost the game" (397); (see Figure 22).

The Asian American parallels are illustrative here. In 1971 an anonymous Japanese American woman published an essay, "White Male Qualities," in which she summarized what she called the "white male stereotype": "(1) tall, (2) handsome, (3) manly, (4) self-confident, (5) well-poised, (6) protective, (7) domineering, (8) affectionate, (9) imaginative" ("White Male Qualities," 44). "These are all Prince Charming characteristics," she observed, and noted, "It seems that Oriental girls who marry White men are looking for this stereotype and will not settle for the short, ugly, unconfident, clumsy, arrogant Oriental man that we are all plagued with" (44). She concluded, "More and more Asian American girls are seeing that

Is It a Nerd? Is It a Brain? No, It's Salaryman!

By John Burgess

Japan may make fun of its workaholic managers, but it hasn't found a replacement for them

BY DAN HUBIG FOR THE WASHINGTON POST

22. "Is it a nerd? Is it a brain? No, it's salaryman!" Source: *Washington Post National Weekly Edition* (7 September 1987): 24. Reprinted with permission.

there is a better life—dating the White male. He treats her as the woman she really is" (44). This view is little changed in the late 1990s, as we see in Claire S. Chow's 1998 book about an Asian American female coming of age in America, *Leaving Deep Water*: "What I most ardently sought [was] a man who took my breath away. A white knight who desired me above all others. A man in whose liquid blue eyes I could see reflected the promise of limitless possibility" (1998, 94). She goes on:

176 ≈ Women on the Verge

For myself, I never dated or even considered dating a single Asian man, never had any desire to do so. . . . In my desire to discard my ethnicity, I spent many years trying to distance myself from what I saw as these studious, unathletic, conservative, and fundamentally uncool acquaintances. I found Asian men physically unattractive in the same manner that I considered my own Asian features to be undesirable. . . . And although I could not have articulated this thought at the time, I believed that if I married a white man, it would raise my self-esteem. A guy with blond hair, who had his pick of women with blond hair and Anglo last names, choosing me? (112).

Prince Charming, white knights. This American racial hierarchy sets the stage for both Japanese men's and women's experiences in the United States. A Japanese man with extensive experience working in the United States told me, "I thought since foreign men come to Japan and can have all the girlfriends they want, that I would be able to go to the States and be equally popular. But no, it doesn't work like that. To Western women Japanese men are invisible. They look right through you."

Back in Japan the effects of this now transnational libidinal economy find their peculiar expression in the sexual mechanisms of the Tokyo dating scene. In the Roppongi district, where foreigners and Japanese meet and mingle, Japanese men are few and far between, except as bartenders. One of my informants told me, "I know one guy who refuses to even set foot in Roppongi because the women completely ignore him." Another woman said that, in her observation, some of the few Japanese men who entered this zone at all were reduced to pretending to be foreign, attempting to converse with Japanese women in English in an effort to pull off an Asian American persona.

Meanwhile, there is a well-established circuit of "international singles parties" held regularly in venues around Tokyo and elsewhere that either explicitly exclude attendance by Japanese men and Western women both, or else discourage it by all means possible. A Japanese male journalist who attended one of these parties in a professional capacity related his shock that there was not a single foreign woman to be seen: "There was none! Simply none! Absolutely none" (Nakaya 1994, 7). He goes on, "Since there are no foreign women, Japanese men inevitably feel small. This is because all the Japanese women want to talk to foreign men. There were even some foreign men who bluntly claimed that 'Japanese men are in the way' " (8).

That there is an explicit sexual economy at work here is apparent in the monetary exchanges that accompany these encounters. According to Karen Ma, only the Japanese women participants are charged admission to these parties, sometimes at rates of nearly $100 per party (1996, 121). One less "exclusive" cruise party I managed to attend in 1993 had only a small percentage of Japanese male and white female guests compared to white men and Japanese women (as far as I could tell there were no other racial/ethnic groups on board).[8] As the evening wore on and couples steadily paired off, Japanese men were increasingly left behind, occasionally paired with a Japanese woman, but rarely, as far as I could tell, with a white woman.

Thus, an economics of white male scarcity prevails. At the many "English conversation lounges" scattered around Tokyo, which also serve as pick-up spots, Japanese women are required to pay dearly for the privilege of speaking to foreign men. At one of the smaller ones that was operating in 1993, the Corn Popper in Shibuya (which featured on the cover of its brochure a photo of two white men playing pool with two miniskirted young Japanese women), foreign visitors were charged 500 yen for a whole day at the lounge (and admitted free two days of the week), while Japanese visitors were charged 700 yen for the first hour alone. Such conditions are, predictably, magnified at the international marriage services in Tokyo that broker marriages between Japanese women and foreign men. Western men (over 90 percent white, according to one source) are charged between $300 and $400 to join such services in search of a Japanese wife. Japanese women, meanwhile, are charged almost $3,000 (Ma 1996, 125) for membership.

According to Yoshimura Fumiharu, the president of Dandies Minami Aoyama, the largest and most well-established international dating and marriage service in Japan, even charging women these prices he cannot keep up with demand. "It's absolutely crazy," he said. "I'm deluged with calls, even at the outrageous prices I charge. Thousands of women call me, at least five hundred to six hundred women a year for the past seven years." However, Yoshimura told me later that his business is limited by the inadequate "supply" of acceptable white men in Tokyo:

Ninety-five percent of the women who contact me are looking for a white man. There will be one or two who are looking for a black man or Indian, Indonesian, or whatever. But we deliver a good "product," and they know it. We guarantee that our white men meet three conditions: they are educated, they have a steady job, and they're serious [*majime*]. We make them sign a contract that says they have taken an AIDS test, that they are sincere, and that they are looking for marriage, not one-night stands. A lot of guys read the contract and get scared off. The ones who stay are quite high quality. But there are very, very few white men who fit our conditions. This is the limiting factor to my business. It cannot grow beyond the scale of acceptable white men in Japan. Basically, we've already reached the limit; we've reached saturation point of white men. Of course, our black men are actually "super blacks" [in English]. I mean, they're super elite. Really inside they are completely white.

Yoshimura went on to elaborate the nature of the market:

With the women I ask right off on the phone, "What's your height and weight?" The guys hate fat ones. Other than that, educational level, English ability, and motivation. Based on that I accept or reject them. If a heavy one calls who is otherwise good, I will tell her to call me back when she's lost 2 kilograms. The men always say they want intelligence, but that's a lie. They want looks. And plus, they want a Japanese woman to get away from big, mannish, aggressive Western women. They know a Japanese woman is going to care for them and be feminine. Plus, she'll keep her figure. The guys tell me when they take their wives home their friends' wives have all gotten fat, and then they feel really good.

Occasionally I will get a Japanese man calling in who says, "Japanese women won't pay any attention to us so we want a blonde Western woman." And occasionally a white woman will call in and I think, "Oh good!" but they only want "elite white males" like everyone else. They're not interested in Japanese men. Yoshimura continued, "Of course, according to the white guys who work in my office, Japanese man–white woman couples have absolutely no chance of working out. The reason is that Japanese men are too short, too narrow-minded, and too sexist."

He concluded, "I have to agree that white men are more interesting than Japanese men. They're more open-minded, active, definitely interesting. But they do have faults. They're cheap, they go bald, and they age fast [laugh]."

Yoshimura's local preeminence as international marriage impresario of Tokyo perhaps accords him the capacity for amusement. However, in some cases Japanese men's exclusion from this interracial sexual economy can lead them to preemptively reject the Western woman and what she represents (see Figure 23). Fifteen-year-old high school student Fujita Chikako told me, "The majority of my female friends have a romantic interest in Westerners, but not the guys! The guys *definitely* would rather avoid them." Hasegawa Katsuyuki, the publisher of *Hiragana Times* and someone who has devoted his life to promoting "international exchange," writes that American women "are not in the least attractive to Japanese men. They're just large and have some kind of strange pride because they're American. They insult people from other countries. And on top of that, they're unrefined" (1991, 182). Hasegawa concludes this description with the lyrics of the 1970s song "American Woman" by the group Guess Who: "American woman, stay away from me; American woman, mama let me be; don't come hangin' around my door; I don't wanna see your face no more; I got more important things to do; than spendin' my time growin' old with you" (183).[9]

Traise Yamamoto observed that in Western fantasies of Japan, Japanese men are eradicated from the feminized Japanese landscape as "the necessary mechanism of a paradigm in which Japan, femininely infantile and sexually exotic, may be mastered" (1999, 61). We have seen this effect in the context of the U.S. Occupation discussed in chapter 1, and it continues unabated to the present day. Thus, Pico Iyer's well-known account of his sojourn in Kyoto, *The Lady and the Monk*, is relentless in its depictions of failure of Japanese men with white women. Describing a scene in a Kyoto disco, he writes, "Two goofy salarymen in their fifties got onto the dance floor with two American escorts, absurdly tall and elegant girls who must have been pulling down three hundred dollars apiece just for teetering over their dates" (1991, 111). Elsewhere, he describes an international party at which a "diligent [Japanese] salaryman kept sidling up to one foreign girl after another, whispering something in each one's ear and then

23. Japanese men rejecting the frightening white woman. Source: Gregory Clark, *Understanding the Japanese* (Tokyo: Kinseido, 1983), 7.

standing erect and nodding solemnly as he got the bad news, receiving each rejection like a gift" (21).

American sexual ridicule of the Japanese male reached a climax of a kind when an American female cartoonist going only by the pseudonym "Kasumi" wrote a 1992 book called *The Way of the Urban Samurai*. Bearing the subtitle *The Japanese Male Exposed*, this book, a series of comic drawings accompanied by short satirical text, purported to humorously "explain" the absurdities and failures of the Japanese man for a foreign audience. Under headings such as "a glossary of urban samurai terms" ("extramarital sex: the only way to get any"; "foreplay: a golf term"), "quizzes" ("are you repulsed when your wife accidentally brushes against you . . . ?"), and a "glossary of terms for the wife of the urban samurai" ("body fakes: pretending you like it"), the author indulges in a mockery of the Japanese man that would be called racist in any other context (see figures 24 and 25).[10]

Again, however, there are some Japanese women authors who have appropriated for their own purposes these Western Orientalist representations of the abject Japanese man as universal failure. This happens not only in yellow cab discourse, but in mainstream writing as well. One

181 ≈ Fetish of the White Man

24. "Pass the Soy Sauce, I'm Coming!" Illustration from *The Way of the Urban Samurai*. Source: Kasumi, *The Way of the Urban Samurai: The Japanese Male Exposed* (Rutland, VT: Tuttle, 1992), 81. Reprinted with permission.

common convention in internationalist writing, for example, is "the Japanese man seen through the eyes of the foreign woman," which constructs the Japanese man as pathetically incapable of consummating a normal adult relationship with a non-Japanese woman. In Iizuka's *The Guys Who Can't Even Hitch a Ride on a Cab* (1993), the second part of the book, entitled "Strange Japanese Men as Seen by Foreign Women," ridicules a series of Japanese men for failing, in the eyes of their foreign girlfriends, in everything from holding an intelligent conversation to consummating the sexual act. Similarly, Tanimura Shiho, in a 1996 book on men's "inability" to find wives, devotes a chapter to what she calls "unsuccessful love affairs with foreign women," describing three Japanese men's painfully humiliating involvements with, respectively, a Filipina prostitute, a Chinese "sadist," and a half-French psychotic who sets her lover's apartment on fire.

Even when they are not depicted in scenes of abjection and failure with foreign women, Japanese men in women's internationalist writing are often infantilized. A case in point is *Chocolate Orgasm* (Chokoretto ōgazumu, 1993), a novel about the lives of two Japanese women friends in the United States by Nonaka Hiiragi, a popular fiction writer who lived in California for a number of years. The character of Kazuhiko, the only Japanese male to figure in the novel, first appears poolside, with his swimming cap "pulled down almost to his shoulders," looking "just like a boiled egg . . . with his smooth hairless face" (54). Nonaka goes on: "In his small, shiny, smooth-skinned face . . . Kazuhiko's evenly-spaced features—his large, round, black eyes, delicate, small-nostriled nose, and fleshy, crimson lips with their overbite—made him look adorable, like a little girl. You would never think of this as the face of a 25-year-old adult male. Scrutinizing his face Mayuki felt, as always, that she wanted to call him 'my little boy [*boku-chan*]' and tickle him beneath his chin" (56–57). Kazuhiko's role in the

25. Urban samurai kissing techniques. Illustration from *The Way of the Urban Samurai*. Source: Kasumi, *The Way of the Urban Samurai: The Japanese Male Exposed* (Rutland, VT: Tuttle, 1992), 79. Reprinted with permission.

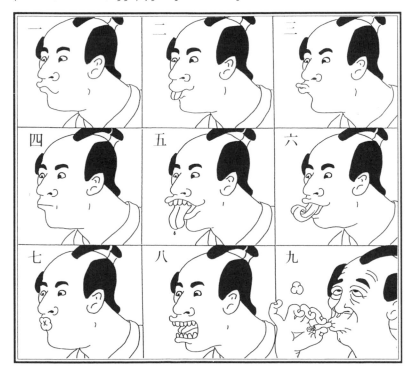

story is to listen sympathetically to Mayuki complain about her American boyfriend and to eventually fall in love with a Japanese woman in America who rejects him. That Kazuhiko is accorded any heterosexual agency at all is unusual in this genre. In Toshiko Marks's *England, Country of Adults; Japan, Country of Children,* Japanese men don't even qualify as fully heterosexual: "The men can't separate from their mothers, and the mothers don't treat their sons as real men. For this reason, the men of Japan are all, to put it bluntly, either homosexual or gay [*sic*]" (1992, 151). Marks assures her readers that while English men may have worn makeup and elaborate costumes in the Tudor and Elizabethan periods, they always behaved in a "manly" fashion toward women (151).

That the ultimate legitimation for women's sexual mockery of Japanese men derives from a Western Orientalist impulse is revealed by a kind of circular feedback loop between Western men's and Japanese women's discourses that emerges in women's literature. Returning to Iizuka's *The Guys Who Can't Even Hitch a Ride on a Cab,* we find the first chapter simply titled "Japanese Men Have No Dicks" ("Chimpo ga nai"), which "fact" the author derives from a barstool conversation with an American man named Terry: " 'Japanese men have no dicks,' said Terry, the American regular, jokingly. 'Japanese men aren't men. With that arrogant attitude, they can't please a woman.' 'It's true, it's true,' sadly chimed in a nearby [Japanese] woman in her forties who'd been in many international love affairs, 'I've traveled the world, and dated a lot of foreign men, but Japanese men have no appeal at all' " (1993, 7). Later in the chapter, another Japanese woman tells Terry she has broken up with her married Japanese lover. He responds in a gratified manner, " 'See I told you that Japanese men have no dicks!' 'That's right,' she replied. She agreed with him" (11). Here, perfect accord has been achieved between the emasculating impulses of Western Orientalism and the oppositional agendas of internationally bound Japanese women. The Japanese man is effectively rendered sexless—literally impotent—incapable of either satisfying or controlling the transnationally mobile cosmopolitan woman (see Figure 26).

In the international meeting places I visited, Japanese men's phallic lack was staged for them in a variety of ways. Not only were they the excluded element, but they were directly or indirectly ridiculed. Gus, a middle-aged American writer hanging out at a Roppongi bar with a Japa-

26. Cover of *The Guys Who Can't Even Hitch a Ride on a Cab*. Japanese male (on far right) watches from the periphery as sexy Japanese women are ogled by a white and a black male in Waikiki. Source: Iizuka Makiko, *Kyabu ni mo norenai otokotachi* (Tokyo: Hara Shobō, 1993).

nese male "friend," said to me, "My poor friend here really, really wants to meet white women. He's been trying for two years, but poor guy, no luck." Leering at me, he asked, "Why don't you go talk to him?" What emerges is an openly phallic competition between Western and Japanese men in which the stakes seem to be no less than penile adequacy. Ken, a manager at IBM in his mid-forties and one of the white men at the singles cruise party I attended, said to me during our conversation, "I can understand Japanese women with white guys, but I can't understand white women with Japanese men! I can't see what they get out of it, unless they like being treated badly. The guys cheat, stay out late. . . . And they have small dicks, too, right?" An American man in Roppongi snickered to me that the Japanese men he'd seen in the shower at his gym were "hung like hamsters."

The feedback effect reached an apotheosis of a kind in the pages of the *Hiragana Times* in 1994, when it ran a cover story entitled "Why Are Japanese Men So Unpopular?" ("Naze motenai, nihonjin dansei?," 1994).

In the article a succession of Japanese women, foreign men, and foreign women weighed in on the vexing topic of Japanese men's inadequacy, setting off a debate that continued into many subsequent issues. This debate did not question Japanese men's total sexual failure, which was taken for granted, but centered only on its cause. In opinion pieces with titles such as "Why Japanese Men Are So Boring," "Japanese Guys Have to Try Harder," and "Isn't It Inevitable That Japanese Men Are Intimidated by Foreign Women?," the whole world, it seems, lined up behind Japanese women in their rejection of Japanese men. In the pages of the magazine, at least, Japanese women had achieved perfect inclusion.

In this way, the Orientalist West has already established the racial hierarchy of potency and impotence that sets up its own mimetic appropriation in Japanese women's domestic strategies of resistance. Orientalist imagery creates the conditions for an act of revenge against the patriarchal Japanese nation-state that is potentially devastating in its intimacy. A West which is "now everywhere" complicates any simple *domestic* formulation of female marginality/male centrality such as that from which women's narratives claim to gain their rhetorical (and moral) force.

Bruce Robbins (1994) has argued that the cosmopolitan, upwardly mobile woman who desires the white man without necessarily seeking marriage is enacting a new resistance, one that eludes middle-class moralities. He sees in the female subject who sleeps with the white man without marrying him a subject moving "laterally," in "a postmodern allegory of a decentered society in which movement may be neither rise nor fall" (141). However, what Robbins here disregards is the continuing power of white men to fix women's position in a transnational "grid" of sexual access to white men themselves and the realm of power they inhabit. Women have the opportunity of sexually mediated upward mobility only insofar as they have been "anointed" by white men as among the desired and desirable of the world. Yet, as we have seen, recognition of the politics of such racialized desire is repressed in a powerful mechanism of denial that operates now globally. As Abou Farman writes in his essay "An Archaeology of Interracial Relations" (1992), an economics of "privatization" has allowed the sexual fetishizations of raced subjects to be removed from public scrutiny and analysis under a rubric of liberalism. There is a gap, he notes, between the real mechanisms of racism and their almost total denial in the space of interracial relationships. This is the denial that allowed Kangaeru Kai and other women discussed in this chapter to categorically deny race as an element in romantic or marital attraction to white men. It likewise permitted the author of the essay "White Male Qualities" to conclude, after systematic exaltation of the white man as lover, "My fiancé and I don't dwell upon my being Japanese and he being white—we think much more about being a man and a woman" (1971, 45). Farman observes that when the foundations for the choice of a lover are questioned, "everyone becomes uncomfortable, feeling attacked on a personal level" (1992, 8). I will return to this in the conclusion.

Global Marketing of the White Man In this section, I turn to the realm of Japanese popular media to examine the racialized desires that operate in the selling of white men as commodity markers of upward mobility. Focusing on Japanese television commercials, I wish to explore the role of domestic and transnational capital in marketing the imaginative iconography that enables and in turn delimits the scope of women's cosmopolitan desires.

It is well-known that white foreigners are conspicuous on Japanese television. According to one estimate, 30 percent of Japanese commercials feature foreigners, and 85 percent of these foreigners are white (Forum for Citizen's Television 1991). It has been argued that the prevalence of white people in Japanese advertising is an indication of Japan's power to "domesticate" white others in projects of reverse Orientalism (or "Occidentalism"; see Creighton 1995). It is true that the commercials attempt to fix white men in a relation of subordination, subject to the viewer's and potential buyer's gaze. At the same time, however, white men, or white maleness, transcends that attempted relation. Not only is it impossible to separate the "domestic" and the foreign when whiteness as a signifier circulates globally, emanating from and marketed by Western institutions such as the Hollywood film industry and multinational corporations, but domestication as an analytical concept does not account for the degree to which white people function in a globalized public sphere as an unmarked category, that from which all difference emanates outward. As Karen Ross has written, "Whiteness is taken as the profoundly unproblematic norm against which all 'others' are measured" (1996, 4).

Recent whiteness studies in the United States have done much to complicate what was previously an "invisible" racial category; however, they have not attended in large part to circulations of whiteness globally. I argue, however, that white men in particular are the possessors of a kind of global phallic authority that accords them the "leverage . . . to manufacture a sense of inclusion . . . in the dominant" (Frankenberg 1997a, 13–14). That this inclusion may be to varying degrees "illusory" (14) does not alter the effects of this leverage when it operates transnationally, at the level of fantasy and desire. Whiteness has become the object of racialized aspirations all over the world under conditions of deterritorialization (although it is certainly resisted as well). If the postcolonial subject is one who is "not quite / not white" (Bhabha 1994, 92), then how is that subjectivity perpetuated by the effects of transnational capital on a global scale?

By studying the multinational nature of whiteness we may approach what bell hooks has called, in a domestic U.S. context, the "terror" of whiteness, as it insinuates itself into the minds of those who must respond to it as a global icon, symbol, and site of power (1997, 172–78). Although whiteness is not at present an object of terror in Japan, it is certainly an object of intense anxiety. John Russell has written that in Japanese media, "the Japanese self emerges as white, near white, or aspiring to whiteness" (1995, 12–13).[11] As a result of their signification of the normal, white men in Japanese media are accorded the authority to evaluate Japanese ability to "pass" into the white sphere. It is this capacity to "pass" that becomes the site of anxiety and struggle in Japanese television commercials. White men become the fetish objects onto which Japanese desires for inclusion into "global society" are projected.

To date, it has been the white woman's body that has been problematized in critiques of Japanese media. Observers both Japanese and foreign, feminist and otherwise, have decried white women's objectification in Japanese media (Forum for Citizen's Television 1991). However, little attention has been paid to the precise ways that white women as signifiers are employed. In the vast majority of Japanese television commercials and other media contexts, however, the white woman functions merely as a vehicle to the larger authority of white men. I give examples below.

Tempstaff Temporary Employment Agency: Three elegant, young, white women in pale miniskirt suits stride purposefully through a busy office building filled with white people. They are flanked by two older white businessmen, one talking on a cellular phone. Later, one woman is shown individually, standing and speaking earnestly before an older white male boss who is seated behind a large desk. Japanese narration: "She's overflowing with a bright power; she's developing her flexible career; her skills shine; each one is an instant hit."

Toyota Chaser Avante Ltd. Automobile: An attractive young blonde woman drives a Chaser through Western city streets. She pulls up in front of the wide steps of an immense stone building. She emerges from the car, sexy legs first. She is the car valet. She turns to an older, gray-haired white man in an expensive suit descending the steps, whom we see only fleetingly, from the back. She looks into his eyes / the camera, holds up the keys, smiles flirtatiously, and says, meaningfully and in English, "Nice choice." (See Figure 27.)

In the Tempstaff commercial, the highest career aspirations of women are shown to be bounded by the authority of white men, who frame them, observe and evaluate them, who indeed constitute them as subjects. In the Toyota commercial, the superficial objectification of a lovely young blonde car valet obscures yet also fetishizes her servicing of the suited male subject who invisibly gazes on her. "Nice choice," she tells him / us: But what is it that is chosen? There is a metonymic relationship in her legs, the keys, and the car itself, as well as the international "success" the car represents. In other words, as an object, the white woman confers prestige; but as a subject, the white man holds power. This power, in the Toyota commercial signified by the keys of car ownership, is elsewhere signified by tropes of dress. While white women appear conspicuously underdressed, at the very least with attractive legs exposed, white men are clothed in the trappings of power: expensive suit, doctor's coat. They descend from large stone buildings and sit behind large desks.

White men are also depicted to an extraordinary degree as speaking and writing subjects. In contrast to white women, who recite nonsensical ad copy, white men instruct, harangue, philosophize. They speak in their native tongues, which, in the confines of a thirty-second spot, may be scrupulously translated with dubbing or even subtitles. They speak "adult" language that communicates knowledge and the authority to make and impose meaning.

27. The white woman in service to the white man. Still from commercial for Toyota Chaser, 1995.

Sunstar G-U-M Medicated Toothpaste: A white man wearing a white dentist's jacket stands facing the camera with a pointer in hand, lecturing before a large diagram of a tooth. He states forcefully (with Japanese dubbing that allows the original English to be heard), *"The point is,* periodontis and gingivitis are fearful things that can *destroy* your gum tissue *before you know it."* Closing shot of a young white girl smiling beatifically and brushing her teeth. In a later version, he gazes down benevolently on her as she sleeps.

Thus, whereas white women are interchangeable simulacra, white men are more often represented as individuals with recognizable identities. A number of commercials go so far as to employ "real" personages: not necessarily celebrities, but living symbols of refinement, achievement, and the good life, such as the conductor of the Berlin Philharmonic or, in the case below, a French skin diver.

Yazaki Solar Panels: Shot of the profile of Jacques Maillor, a French skin diver, with his name, profession, and a diving diagram superimposed. Maillor dives in the ocean and swims with dolphins. Next, he is sitting at night by a campfire, where he intones pensively in French (with Japanese subtitles), "Why do I dive? The answer *must* lie in a deep place—in the 'Great Blue.'" Japanese narration: "Yazaki's answer is to create energy in harmony with nature."

In an Uchida Yōkō office equipment company commercial, an influential German architect even has his curriculum vitae reproduced on the screen.

Uchida Yōkō Office Equipment Company: German architect Herman Helzberger sits at a workdesk scattered with books and drafting tools. His name and a short c.v., listing the architectural prizes he has won, are shown on screen. He looks intently into the camera. He says seriously, in German, "I always plan my designs with a person at the center." Montage of his architectural drawings transposed on actual buildings, with features captioned in his own handwriting. Dissolve into miscellaneous architectural drawings all captioned with his handwriting. Japanese narration: "Human-scale space, human-scale information. Total design of information and space. Uchida Yōkō."

The nature of white male authority, the *akogare* directed toward that authority, and the commodity-mediated resolution promised to the mixed feelings that authority elicits differ dramatically depending on the target audience, which is distinguished broadly according to gender and age. Commercials that target young working women, for example, "sell the fantasy that involvement with white males will lead to personal fulfillment," Russell writes. "The Japanese woman becomes more desirable, more independent, more herself in the white man's presence" (1995, 14). The study cited earlier by the Forum for Citizen's Television showed that Japanese women–white men pairings were the most common type of Japanese-foreign pairing used in television advertising (1991, 21).[12]

Lotte Crepe Ice: Two teenage girls sit on a park bench eating a Lotte Crepe Ice (an ice cream cone in a crepe). The first girl exclaims, "Lotte Crepe Ice is so *Parisian,* isn't it?" Instantly, a red carpet unfurls before them, and a young, handsome, tall, blond, tuxedo-clad French male appears, holding a single long-stemmed red rose. With a flourish he tosses the rose into the first girl's lap, crying dramatically, "Bonjour, Mesdemoiselles!" They gasp ecstatically and cry out in unison, "Bonjour!" and take a bite out of their Crepe Ice.

Nescafé Instant Cappuccino: Attractive, conservatively dressed Japanese woman in her late twenties takes a box of Nescafé Instant Cappuccino from a supermarket shelf and, to the accompaniment of a soaring Italian operatic tenor, is transported back in memory to a visit to Italy.

28. Selling romance with the white man. Still from commercial for Nescafé Cappuccino, 1993.

There, she visits an artist's studio, where she is instructed by a handsome young blond Italian in the art of china painting. A teapot steams, and he stirs her a foamy cup of instant cappuccino. She smiles, takes the cup, drinks; suddenly they gaze into one another's eyes, and to an operatic climax, kiss (see Figure 28). Voice-over: "Man, woman—the foam rises [*otoko, onna, awadatsu*]." Commercial ends with the woman back in Japan, sipping a cappuccino and smiling secretly to herself. Voice-over: "Creamy, foaming Nescafé Cappuccino."

In some cases, the symbolism is explicitly phallic.

SeaBreeze Shampoo: Shot of a wide blue ocean. A long white submarine surfaces, parting the waters. A Japanese woman and a white man in white bathing suits emerge from the ocean and climb atop the submarine. They each wash their own hair, gazing at one another significantly. The white man stands with a showerhead and holding it up, sprays the Japanese woman, now seated below him. In the closing shot the two stand together, his arm around her waist, gazing out across the ocean. Song lyrics in Japanese: "I can't see love; I can't swim in your ocean anymore. More than kindness, I want a kiss."

Elsewhere, white men act as the gatekeepers who adjudicate Japanese female ability to successfully compete with white women and "pass" as erotic objects on an international stage.

VO5 Basemaker Shampoo and Conditioner: A sexy young Japanese woman runs through a shopping mall in some Western country, attracts the attention of a handsome, tall, blond white man, flings herself down an escalator handrail, and lands in the arms of the man, who now stands waiting for her at the foot. She says, "There's no way it won't all come together for you! [*matomaranai hazu wa nai*]," *matomaru* (come together) being a play on words that refers both to personal style and to a sexual or romantic relationship.

Vidal Sassoon Hair Products: A fast-paced Parisian fashion shoot. Four models—three white, one Japanese—are made up by white male makeup artists and hairstylists. The shoot is presided over by Vidal himself. All four models are photographed, but it is the Japanese woman who is chosen for the cover of *Elle* magazine. Commercial closes with shot of cover.

Thanks to Vidal, the Japanese model vanquishes her rivals, white women all, and achieves sanctification as global glamour standard.

Media that target an older male audience feature a different sort of competition, one not sexual but phallic, and one that is achieved through projects of technological and/or linguistic mastery.[13]

Asahi SuperDry Beer: Yamagiwa Junji, a nonfiction writer (named), stands in a white shirt and tie among a group of dungarees-clad white male aviation engineers on an open runway in Arizona (identified). The scene is labeled "Next generation passenger plane development." When the experimental plane, a giant sleek silver jet with a pointed nose, successfully takes flight, the white men and Yamagiwa cheer, flashing the thumbs-up sign and shaking hands. The closing shot shows Yamagiwa alone, drinking a can of Asahi SuperDry.

The anxiety of adequacy is resolved with the commodity-promise that, indeed, the Japanese male can best the white man at his own game, even in his own language.

Alfa One Mg Cigarettes (Japan Tobacco): Four good-looking people—two white males, a white female, and a Japanese male—play cards in an elegant French apartment. The Japanese man and one of the white men are arguing heatedly in French (with Japanese subtitles), the white man insisting that the Alfa cigarettes taste better than other "one mg tar" cigarettes. The Japanese man insists that, on the contrary, all one mg.s taste the same. He refuses to give in, even after tasting Alfa and realizing that it is indeed better (revealed by a voice-over of his private thoughts in Japanese). The Frenchman grows enraged over the Japanese man's obstinacy and begins shouting and waving his arms, disrupting the game and irritating the French woman, who sneers at him. The commercial closes with a shot of the Japanese man, alone, savoring an Alfa One Mg in private.

The stakes here are ambiguous: if the white man, in his loss of control, relinquishes the white woman's regard, the Japanese man's self-control leads not to her sexual possession, but to solitude. Indeed, potential sexual union with a white woman is, on the rare occasions when it is depicted, represented as a terrifying and potentially castrating encounter.

Ippei-chan Instant Ramen: A childlike, sexually ambiguous Japanese male (Ippei-chan), who works in a ramen stand in a strange, *Blade-runner*-esque underworld of neon-lit, crowded street markets and rainy, dark sidewalks, is suddenly accosted by a platinum blonde foreign woman with enormous breasts. She cries out, in a screeching sirenlike voice, "Ippei-chan!" and clutches him to her substantial chest. Ippei-chan struggles wildly, looking back terrifiedly at the camera as she leads him away into the night.

Elhaven Weiner Sausages: An obese white female opera singer in garish makeup and clothes screeches "ЕЕELLLUUUUUHAAA AA VEN" to piano accompaniment. The scene cuts to the small, thin Japanese male piano player, smiling weakly, and then back to a close-up of the opera singer, who crunches down on a weiner with a fiendish grin.

As we can see, the denouement of encounters between Japanese men and Westerners far more commonly lies in the Japanese man's solitude and self-sufficiency, drinking and smoking alone (or with an understanding Japanese woman), in blessed relief from the deafening clamor of white people's demands.

Kyabejin Heartburn Medicine: A young Japanese male is eating a Western business dinner with a blond foreign man. He talks energetically in

English, after which he gets heartburn from stress. He takes Kyabejin and in the final shot is shown having recovered enough to be able to enjoy late-night romancing with his Japanese girlfriend at a traditional Japanese restaurant.

Frontier One Mg. Cigarettes: An English conversation class in a Tokyo office building. The teacher is a severe-looking, tailored, middle-aged blonde British woman; the students are all stylish young Japanese women, with the exception of one hapless-looking middle-aged male at the very back. As the teacher drills the class in an English phrase (containing the word "frontier"), she strides to the man and, looming over him from behind and peering intently into his face, taps his shoulder and demands aggressively, "Mr. Kobayashi! One more time!," waving her hand under his nose. Tensing, he stumbles through a garbled, incomprehensible string of words. She grimaces and shakes her head. He, stone-faced, breaks into a sweat (see Figure 29). Commercial suddenly shifts to a shot of the man alone against a blank background, reaching out for a cigarette floating toward him through the air. Voice-over: "Light is good; one milligram." He draws on the cigarette contentedly. Scene shifts back to the English school building; the man, late for class, races up the stairwell, passing the teacher coming down. "Linda!" he cries, holding out a box of cigarettes, "*Fron-tier!*" "No, no," she admonishes, "*Fron-*tier!" He grins weakly and sprints up the steps.

There are, of course, other ways that the relations of white people and Japanese are represented; like all such struggles of identification and disavowal, the one enacted in the world of Japanese media also produces fantasies of projection, displacement, and reversal. In some television commercials, this is played out in the figure of a diminutive young man or woman who subdues physically large, threatening white men, rendering the men infantile and ridiculous objects of their will.

Aquarius Ion Drink: A young, slightly built Japanese male plays volleyball on a field. He is knocked to the ground and pants with thirst, activating a "thirst rescue squad": a crew of four hulking, sunburned white male lifeguards in old-fashioned blue bathing costumes and bathing caps. They hop on surfboards and "paddle" from the beach to

29. Fear of the overbearing white woman. Still from commercial for Frontier cigarettes, 1995.

the volleyball field, delivering Aquarius. They line up behind the Japanese male; he drinks and is transformed into their leader (see Figure 30). They shout "Thirst rescue!" and execute a foolish pose; he points off-camera and they run in that direction; he follows.

Hagoromo Canned Tuna: A Japanese female camp leader directs a troop of thirty hefty white male "campers," dressed like children with little red caps and neckerchiefs. They childishly follow her lead in making a simple tuna pasta salad. She sings "Me so satisfied—hee, hee, hee [*bokuchan manzoku usshishi*]." They repeat, simpering and making infantile gestures.

Certainly, the present reading does not exhaust possibilities of interpretation of these commercials within a Japanese cultural setting. Japanese consumers are among the most sophisticated in the world, and irony abounds both in their reception of commercials and other media and in the media productions themselves. What I question here, however, is the scope of a "Japanese cultural setting." Where are the boundaries of Japanese "culture" in an era of multinational capitalism and transnationally circulating images? The male-targeted media I have summarized advertise the products of domestic Japanese companies (Asahi Beer, Japan Tobacco) and operate in a primarily domestic loop. Many of the female-targeted commercials that employ the idiom of Japanese female desire for the white man, however, are the creations of Western multinational companies such as vo5, SeaBreeze, and Vidal Sassoon. This raises the question of whose fantasy they represent. Whose anxiety over white male authority do they

30. Infantilizing the white man.
Still from commercial for Aquarius
Ion, 1995.

inscribe? Brian Moeran's (1996) ethnography of a Japanese advertising agency suggests that the micropractices of individual members of foreign management do indeed shape foreign companies' advertising strategies in Japan. We must consider the possibility that fantasies of Western male corporate executives travel in tandem with transnational flows of commodities and capital. This, of course, leaves open the question: If these fantasies do travel, do their meanings stay the same?

A commercial shown in 1995 for Philip Morris Tobacco's Parliament cigarettes was targeted at Japanese males, but tells a tale of romance between a white man (Charlie Sheen) and a supremely "exotic" Japanese woman in New York. We see the New York City skyline on a rainy blue evening and the Chrysler Building from above. Sheen, in tuxedo, is driven in a limousine through the misty dark streets. He takes a small Japanese ornament from his pocket, gazes pensively at it, and is transported in memory to a time in Japan when he met and fell in love with an exotic, mysterious young Japanese beauty in kimono, who gave him the ornament as a keepsake. His reverie is interrupted when his car pulls up to the broad steps of a magnificent building into which people in evening wear are ascending. He steps out and pauses on the wide stone steps to smoke. Then he looks over his shoulder and sees, approaching him on the sidewalk, the very Japanese woman from his past, this time dressed in a form-fitting scarlet gown, the height of Western elegance. She has followed him to America. He descends the steps toward her. A shot of the skyline. Japanese narration: "The aroma of freedom and relaxation. Stylish Blue Parliament."

197 ≈ Fetish of the White Man

The commercial posits the Japanese woman as the exotic object of multinational desire, a border-crossing Madame Butterfly in an era of late capitalism. The commercial tells us that only by assuming the potency and allure of the white man can Japanese men hope to keep the newly mobile Japanese woman from the lure of the "stylish" West. The absent Japanese man projects his fantasy/anxiety of mastery onto the duplicitous Japanese woman. Yet he, beguiled but excluded, is now exposed in his failure, longing, and shame; his only chance to regain authority over his own women lies in the purchase of the Western cigarette. The commercial for Parliament cigarettes narrates the struggle over the heart (and body) of the spectacularly cosmopolitan Japanese woman. Her desire for the West strikes at the center of Japanese men's erotic subjectivity, but the commercial holds out the promise of control. What is never questioned is the fact of the global power and sheer sexual allure of the white man himself (it is Charlie Sheen, after all). In the absence of careful ethnography, it is difficult to know the industrial micropractices by which this commercial came to take shape, yet this Orientalist fantasy is one that reinscribes the narrative of white men's global phallic authority and that communicates the leverage of white men to broker others' access to the world dominant.

Akogare and the West Before moving on I want to turn again to the question of reception. Women viewers do not simply or simplistically accept sexualized images of white male phallic mastery; rather, they observe these commercials, and the other imagery described in this chapter, with skepticism, ironic distance, and humor. Women with whom I spoke in Japan and the United States were alternately saddened, ashamed, amused, and disgusted at the circulation in Japan of these sorts of representations of the white man. They were dismayed too at what they took the popularity of such fantastic akogare-driven narratives to mean for the standing and credibility of Japanese women in Japan and abroad. A young woman residing in Portland, Oregon, who came to one of my talks, shook her head incredulously at the videotaped commercials I played. "I've been out of Japan for so long," she said, "I forgot how stupid these things are."

Many of my informants rejected the common image of the white man as "prince on a white horse" (*hakuba ni notta ōjisama*). They did not necessarily disagree with the hierarchy of white men over Japanese as desired partners. But for women whose deep and passionate commitment to ideals of equality, human rights, and democracy had led them to a lifelong investment in internationalist work, the reduction of the West to the eroticized body of the white man as sexual commodity was evidence only of the lagging consciousness of young Japanese women who uncritically accept the delusions of akogare.

Many of the women I knew turned their critical gaze instead on the real effects of Western Orientalist fantasies on women's lives, accusing Western men who pursue Japanese women of being "losers" who could not make it in their own country, and who prefer Japanese women only for their reputed docility. Kitahara Satoko remarked drily, "The story that I hear is that the men who come to Japan in the first place are already strange. I mean, they have some kind of thing for the Orient, for Asian girls, and that's why they look for work here." Nozawa Yuka, a thirty-two-year-old bilingual secretary in an American securities firm, commented disgustedly, "I don't like the foreigners who work in Japan. I think over 50 percent of them could not survive in their own country. They come over here and get all the nice girlfriends just because they have long legs and blue eyes. I am so sick of it." Hosoda Maki, a woman in her mid-twenties employed at one of the largest American brokerage houses in Tokyo, spoke disdainfully of the foreign men in her office, who, she said, used the workplace to hunt for women: "There are two foreign guys in the company who are only there to find Japanese wives. As soon as a new woman enters the company they walk up to her and say, 'Let's go out,' or even 'I want you to have my baby!' "

Some women also objected to white men's ridicule of the Japanese male. "I really can't stand it the way foreign men come to Japan and don't have even one Japanese male friend," Nozawa Yuka said, "not one. Not even just a guy to play tennis with. Nearly all the foreigners in my company are like that. They treat Japanese men as if they were invisible, or else they just ridicule them. The favorite pastime of the guys in my company is to bash Japanese men."

Women critiqued as well the depredations of the Tokyo interracial sexual economy, discussed earlier, that has led to the "overvaluation" of white men as scarce resources. One woman, a public relations officer for a foreign-affiliate advertising firm, remarked unhappily to me, after relating the story of a recent breakup, "Foreign men get spoiled after they've been in Japan for a while because of all the attention they get from Japanese women. And then, after a year or so, they leave. It's virtually impossible to find a serious, responsible foreign man in Japan." Nagaki Mitsuko echoed this view, telling me sadly that Japanese women are seen to constitute a highly "convenient" (*tsugō ga ii*) supply of sexual partners for foreign men, but are not treated as legitimate marital candidates. "It's sad," she began. "I've met and corresponded with a variety of white men in Japan. But I think they are really just ridiculing me [*baka ni shiteru*]. They don't respect me. They just want someone to sleep with, and they just assume that, because I'm Japanese, I'm going to go to bed with them." Nagaki gave an example:

> There was one interesting man who was forty-five, divorced, with an eight-year-old daughter. He said he was searching for a Japanese wife. I asked him, "Why Japanese?" He told me, "I don't have much money, I'm divorced, and I have a kid, so a white woman would never marry me." He thinks a Japanese woman will take anything he dishes out without complaint. A Japanese woman does tend to work hard for the man she loves. But it seems like that side of us is being exploited by white men. Anyway, I told him that he had a bad attitude. He seemed to be offended at that! I mean, the reason he likes Japanese women is that we're not supposed to say things like that. But to me, that just means he's not respecting Japanese women's personhood.

In this way, the search for "personhood" can eventually lead women to a critique of Western as well as Japanese men, and to a distancing from the claims of Occidental akogare on their lives. The textual sources that narrate an uncritical akogare for the white man elide, or ignore, the ambivalences of real women about their encounters with the actual West and actual Westerners. Having sketched the terms and the mechanisms of akogare, then, it is necessary now to attend more closely to internationalist women's own evolving understandings of self and other, their emergent skepticism at oversimplified binaries of good West/ern man and bad Japan/ese man, and their acquisition of experience and knowledge that moved them away from akogare-driven fantasy to a critical perspective on their own ambivalent "locatedness" on multiple borderlands. Shioyama Norie, a twenty-eight-year-old professional translator with a master's degree in women's studies from Sarah Lawrence College, commented in a letter to me (in English) after the completion of my fieldwork:

> I too am uncomfortable with the idea of akogare, and I wish that there were no—or at least less—akogare for white culture among my sisters. But the reason that I feel this way is not because I don't believe that akogare exists (far from it!) but because so many Japanese women are influenced by nonsense which is not in our DNA, but which has just been thrust on us by the mass media, etc. Japanese women just don't even try to see that their admiration for the West may be problematic on different levels. The trouble is that there are so few opportunities for us to learn how problematic it may be to automatically adopt the ideas, customs, and values of the so-called civilized West.

Texts alone, frozen in the time of their writing, do not reveal the fluidity of women's understandings and identity. Many of the internationalist women I knew in Tokyo grew to distrust easy assumptions about the redemptive power of the West and the white man, and came eventually to put their faith, above all, in themselves. This skepticism did not make women autonomous from the continuing hegemonies of race, gender, sex, and class that constitute transnational space. It did, however, reveal the ways that discrepant cosmopolitanisms yield over time the "plurality of vision" and "contrapuntal awareness" that Said has written is the primary characteristic of the exile (1984, 172).

4 ≋ (Re)Flexibility in Inflexible Places

U.S. not always the promised land, young women from Japan discover.—HEADLINE, *Daily Yomiuri* online, May 15, 1999

The Search for Home Behind the ideal of living in two worlds is a
parallel danger of being able to live fully in neither. Women may find
themselves trapped in the space betwixt and between Japan and the foreign, outsiders both in Japan and abroad, belonging nowhere. The new
selves unearthed with such exhilaration abroad or among foreigners in
Japan are said to wither and fade in the face of Japanese family and corporate pressure. The question of whether or not to reside in Japan becomes
urgent: Women debated with great intensity the decision to leave, to not
return, and, once having returned, to leave again. Internationalist women
struggled with an ongoing sense of, in Gotō Kayoko's words, "being split
apart in the space between two cultures" (1994, 183). In this chapter I trace
the narratives of "homelessness" that inevitably accompany the internationalist trajectory and inquire into their resolution in some women's
enunciation of a hybrid identity later in their lives. I also query the effects
of such inscriptions of "flexibility" for internationalism as an oppositional
movement potentially aligned with feminism, in Japan and elsewhere.

A melancholy letter, printed in *Cosmopolitan Japan* in 1993, captures
the sensation of homelessness experienced by many overseas-returned
women in Japan. Written by a young woman who had studied abroad in a
small English town for one year, the letter begins, "Each time a letter
arrives [from England] I get just a little down." It goes on, "Five long years
since coming back to Japan, I often find myself not caring what happens to
me. Sometimes I think that you just can't have dreams in Japan. . . . But at

times like that I shut my eyes and recall that small town by the sea, and I force myself to remember the decision I made back then. My life in that village is just a memory now, but knowing that the people I met there are somewhere on this earth doing their best makes me want to do my best too." She concludes, "Someday soon I want to be reunited with the 'me' that walked on the shore of that village" (Yoshida 1993, 118). The authentic self is one that comes alive abroad and can only be recalled in memory in Japan. The reunion with this authentic self is anticipated, for this woman and for many others, in a second study-abroad sojourn. For Fuke Shigeko this is not merely a second trip overseas but a return to the embrace of the desired other/self, the West as lover. "My body was in Tokyo, but my heart was still lost in the streets of New York," she writes. "Finally, I decided I had to go back. . . . I took my seat on the plane as agitated as if I was going to meet my lover. . . . When the plane landed at Kennedy Airport, I felt a peaceful sense of having returned home" (1991, 60–65).

Yet, once finished with their studies, women have few options for remaining overseas without permanent residency status. As this is available only through company sponsorship or marriage, it remains out of reach for many. The result is a condition of perpetual discomfort that forces internationally inclined women to continually shuttle between Japan and the West, seeking a home without ever finding one. Morimoto Tomomi, thirty years old when I met her while she was visiting family in Tokyo, had been roaming back and forth between Japan and a variety of Western countries since her initial "awakening" to the West on a family trip to Europe at age fourteen. By eighteen she was in Hawai'i studying English, and although a year and a half later she had to return to Japan, at twenty-eight she left again, this time for Australia. After one year there, still unwilling to go back, she moved to the United States to begin life as a student in an English-language program in Tennessee. When that was finished she entered a B.A./M.A. program in accounting at the University of Texas. At the time I met her she was shortly to graduate and anxious that if she didn't somehow obtain a Green Card she would have no choice but to return to Japan. Her case was not unusual and, as I discuss below, reveals the vital importance of the Green Card (or other forms of permanent residency status) in internationalist women's calculations. Yet even the acquisition of the Green Card does not resolve the struggle for home. Novelist Kyoko Mori, for example, writes in her memoirs of her twenty-some years of permanent residency in the United States, "I am a balloon cut off and floating away into the blue sky. I have nothing to hold me anchored to the country of my birth, and yet I feel out of place among people who look nothing like me" (1997, 250).

Researcher Alice Lachman (1998) has observed that many Japanese women newly returned to Japan from abroad attempt to deal with the difficult adjustment by establishing wide-ranging support networks through the use of letters, newsletters, and e-mail newsgroups. They also associate with the foreign community in Japan through participation in international volunteer organizations such as Amnesty International and Greenpeace, or in social organizations such as Toastmasters International, a meeting of which I attended once in the company of an informant. The attraction of Toastmasters, my companion told me, was that it offered a chance not only to speak English and mingle with foreigners, but above all to continue honing her skills of individual "self-expression," in danger of withering otherwise.

Nevertheless, in many cases the predicament of homelessness left many women perpetually wistful for another time, another life, another country, and the other self that, they insist, emerges only abroad. On the whole, informants expressed themselves in subtle ways: a vague sigh, an unfinished sentence. After speaking for over an hour about the difficulties of pursuing her volunteer activities in Thailand, Mori Mayumi paused, sighed, and said, "It's not that we want to live somewhere else; it's just that we somehow want to run away from here!" Tanabe Minami, a former UC-Santa Cruz History of Consciousness student reduced at the time of our first interview to working as an OL at a small trading company in Osaka, said at the end of our interview, "How I envy you. I know it's hard and you are struggling with your dissertation, but look at you! You're doing exactly what you want. Not like me . . ." Statements such as "How lucky you are" and "I envy you" cropped up not infrequently in my interviews with women in Tokyo. For some, the very fact of my appearance before them as a female graduate student conducting fieldwork in a foreign country, with funding and a husband (but apparently unhampered by familial or societal restraints), seemed to represent the freedom they had enjoyed while abroad and lost on return.

The Limits of Internationalism Age harassment may be what women are fleeing when they make the decision to leave Japan; it is also the primary problem that confronts them with renewed force on their return. Okada Aki, a thirty-one-year-old public relations manager for a gaishikei advertising firm, told me of her return to Japan after two years of study abroad, "When I came back, I was so full of energy and eager to develop a career in Japan, to do something new. So I went to see my old boss at Dentsū advertising agency, and I expected him to ask me all kinds of questions about my experience abroad and my hopes and plans for the future. But all he said to me was, 'How old are you?' I was twenty-four. And then he said, 'Oh, you're going to have to get married pretty soon.'" Kitahara Satoko recounted with sad amusement her attempts to explain this age pressure to American college friends: "I said to my friends, 'I might not be able to get hired in Japan.' My American friends asked why not. I said, 'Because of my age.' And the Americans said, 'Oh, because you're too young?' Can you imagine?! [laugh]."

Their age may also prevent women from finding the very type of job they originally sought education abroad to obtain. This is because, as I have written, Japanese companies, at least until recently, so rarely hired anyone, especially women, for responsible posts in midcareer. One young woman sadly explained of her low-wage, low-status OL position, "You see, when I came back from two years in the States, I was already twenty-three, not twenty-one like everyone else. Wherever I went I was told 'sayonara.'" The renewed pressures of age may ultimately compel a second, and permanent, alienation from Japan, as in the case of Mori Mayumi's sister-in-law, who had previously lived in Hong Kong and Africa for several years: "She was already thirty when she left for Africa. . . . Now she's back, and working at an NGO in Tokyo, but her salary is so low that she has to live with her parents. . . . And she's faced with this choice: marry or pursue a career? Her parents pressure her constantly, relentlessly, to get married. . . . She's already thirty-three now, and to hit thirty-five and still be single in Japan means that companies probably won't even hire you! It's so hard for her in

Japan that she's thinking of going abroad again, and looking for work in an NGO in England or the U.S. I feel bad saying it, but really, if she stays in Japan much longer, she's going to have a nervous breakdown."

Women who succeed in finding work often discover that foreign expertise is not sufficient to overcome the deeply entrenched gender hierarchy of the Japanese workplace. Sakakibara Yoshitaka found in his research on former study-abroad students in Japan that whereas nearly 90 percent of the men expressed contentment with their lives, almost 33 percent of the women found their current professional situations unsatisfactory or "frustrating," and over 50 percent of the women claimed to have experienced serious readjustment difficulties in all realms of life (1984, 153, 160). Tanabe Minami, mentioned previously, was perhaps the most poignant example. A passionate, dynamic, deeply intelligent young woman of twenty-three when I met her, she had just returned from two years of study abroad at UC-Santa Cruz's History of Consciousness program. She spoke intensely of postcolonial feminist and race theory, the writings of bell hooks, and her own position as an Asian woman in the United States. Yet, on her graduation from college, Tanabe could find work only as an OL in a small trading firm in Osaka, with no opportunity to employ her English skills, let alone to pursue her intellectual aspirations. Two years later Tanabe managed to find a position in a cash-strapped feminist NGO devoted to Asian women's issues, but in doing so sacrificed a living wage and benefits. Now forced to live at home, Tanabe told me when I last saw her that she dreamed of going to graduate school in the United States (to study the politics of "imperialist Japanese feminism" in Asia), but could foresee no opportunity to do so in her current financial circumstances.

As the number of women pursuing language study and study abroad has skyrocketed, the relative value of this background has also declined. As one thirty-five-year-old woman told Matsui Machiko, "There are too many returnees with American degrees. . . . I don't expect much." She concluded ominously, "I've done what I wanted. I'll pay for it" (in Matsui 1995, 374). Matsubara (1989) quotes several senior executives in major Japanese corporations who criticize professional women for being overly dependent on language skills and overseas experience and for being unwilling to do the whole range of work necessary in a corporate job. Women, however, respond that too many Japanese companies still give preference to males even in jobs involving English and other foreign languages. One frustrated woman interviewed by Matsubara stated, "Companies will pay men to go to a language school and study English, but they won't hire a woman who is already fluent" (86).

Meanwhile, those who worked at gaishikei did not necessarily find the realm of perfect gender equality they anticipated. Some claimed that the reason lay in the gaishikei's increasing "Japanization"; as many gaishikei now employ only a small proportion of foreign staff, it is argued that the "gaishikei effect" is diluted. Kitahara Satoko told me, "It's still a male-dominated society in my gaishikei, but that's because everyone I work with is Japanese." Women also insisted that even those gaishikei that guarantee women's status inside the company cannot change circumstances in the male-dominated Japanese corporate world outside. Kitahara continued, "Even if my company is all right, you step one foot outside the company and it is Japan. My immediate superior is Japanese, but he recognizes my ability and lets me work on important things. But even now, once we step outside the company, when I'm with him, I'm treated as 'the briefcase holder,' not a colleague." Nagata Hiroko observed, "Even in gaishikei, men still have an advantage over women because Japanese clients want to deal with men."

And yet, informants revealed other discriminatory practices of the gaishikei that suggested inequalities embedded in the political economy of the gaishikei itself. Bilingual secretaries at major gaishikei stock broker-ages in Tokyo, for example, were subject to the whims of the young, inex-perienced white male traders under whom they worked. These traders, who generally could speak and read no Japanese at all, were completely dependent on the bilingual secretaries to contact and negotiate with clients and rival firms, to filter market information, to interpret at meetings, to handle correspondence, and to facilitate their personal adjustments to life in Japan, handling paperwork regarding taxes, insurance, large purchases, and children's schooling. One woman observed caustically that the firm could survive for a week without the foreign traders, but could not survive a day without the bilingual secretaries. Another described the numerous errors, amounting to hundreds of thousands of dollars, made by her American boss over the period of her employment, and the hasty, behind-the-scenes efforts required of her and other Japanese female secretaries to cover for his mistakes. Despite these heavy responsibilities, each of these women earned a secretarial wage, while the foreign male staff were not only given lavish salaries but provided with yearly trips home and large, luxurious apartments (and in one case, an enormous, brand-new house) in the most prestigious neighborhoods of Tokyo.

Secretaries were not the only ones so treated. Matsubara Junko relates the case of a thirty-five-year-old financial analyst with an MBA from MIT employed in the Tokyo branch of an American manufacturer. This woman, originally hired in the United States for a high-level management position at the main headquarters in New York, had been transferred, like any American employee, to the Tokyo branch. Whereas the American employees received a package such as the one described above, however, she received nothing (1989, 67–70). When the woman confronted her boss he dismissed her complaints, saying, "If you want a 'package' so much, become an American" (70). Matsubara concludes, "It is indeed foolish to believe that just because you have an MBA from a top-ten school, you can compete equally with white males. They say America is equal, but if a white male and a Japanese female with the same academic record come for an interview, it's natural that the company will choose the white male" (68).

Yet, acknowledgment of such discrimination was expressed only uneasily in internationalist women's accounts. Miyajima Kazumi, a bilingual legal assistant employed in a foreign-affiliate law firm, commented, "At this firm, all the lawyers are white men, and all the assistants are Japanese women. It's the official policy. The partners don't want any Japanese males here. They say Japanese women are easier to control." She later foreclosed a discussion of race by saying, "It pisses me off, but what can you do? Aren't all law firms sexist?"

Green Card Cinderellas As may be expected, single women face particular contradictions in their efforts to bridge internationalist experience and a Japanese environment. The simple fact of years spent abroad will have pushed women nearly to the edge of or beyond the *tekireiki* (marriageable years), making them less viable on the marriage market and reducing the pool of males to choose from. Single women confronted unceasing pressure to marry. One told me, "Sometimes I feel like giving in. But other times I don't want to compromise, so I just keep working. My friends who quit their jobs all became 'rice-cooking hags' [*meshitakibabā*], and then they can't get a decent job ever again." Meanwhile, women's own cosmopolitanism works as an obstacle to marriage; people around them fear their "excessive" intimacy with the foreign may have somehow tainted their purity as Japanese. Nozawa Yuka explained the problems that can emerge: "Girls who are able to speak English with foreigners have to be able to say yes or no clearly. We have to be aggressive. Sometimes I forget who I'm talking to. For example, if a foreigner asks you out on a date and asks you what you want to eat, you have to stop and think, and say, 'Well, I had curry today and pasta last night, so tonight I want xyz.' But if you were to say something like that to a Japanese guy, it would be a disaster! You're supposed to say, 'It's up to you.' Sometimes I forget. He says, 'How about Mexican?' and I say 'NO!' [laughs]." She continued, laughing sadly: "Japanese guys are afraid of me now. If I meet someone and tell them I work for a gaishikei, he instantly disappears. They just run away! I say, 'Wait, don't run away,' but they're gone. . . . They just assume that I'm aggressive and that I will date only foreign men."

Even women who seek to marry a Japanese man may find that Japanese men have rejected them in advance. Kitahara Satoko explained, "It is sad. It's not like I'm a workaholic career woman or anything, but I have a job with responsibilities and I work at a gaishikei and I get a pretty decent salary, and it seems Japanese men don't care for that. I meet men and tell them I work for gaishikei, and they say, 'Oh, you must be earning a lot,' or 'You must go overseas all the time.' And I say, 'Well not all the time, but I do go abroad sometimes,' and that's it, end of conversation. That really bothers me!" Okada Aki related an incident with a young TV producer who had lived in Paris for a number of years that occurred at a party one evening. This man accosted Okada and demanded that she arrange a date for him with some "cute, quiet Japanese girl." "But I don't know anyone like that!" Okada exclaimed later. "All my friends are like me, aggressive and tough." She went on disgustedly, "You'd think he would be different because he'd been abroad, but no! He said he's sick of aggressive women and wants a 'docile Japanese girl'—no gaijins. He wouldn't talk business with me, he just started making comments about my boyfriends and love life and other bullshit [in English]. He started saying to me, 'You're over thirty! If you don't settle down soon, nobody is ever going to want you.' It was just awful!" Okada recalled. "I mean, it's already on my mind every single day as it is—marriage, work, my age . . . ."

Pressure of this kind can cause what my informants called a "Japan allergy," leading some to reject their Japanese nationality and become, as one woman described a friend, "non-Japanese Japanese," for whom Japan is no more than an exotic vacation spot. Mori Mayumi told me that she had "thirty friends" in the United States trying to get Green Cards: "They don't want to come back! It's not that the U.S. is so good, but that Japan is just too awful." Such women often say that they will return "when Japan changes." In the meantime, to avoid a return they may endure continual uncertainty abroad. One journalist wrote that the women he met in the United States were willing, for the sake of the Green Card, to endure "illegal alien status, illegal hiring practices, and a life in the shadows" (Koike 1990, 24). In this context, the U.S. Green Card becomes permeated with the weight of unfulfilled longing. That it is sometimes referred to as the "gold card" or "platinum card" shows the degree to which its possession conflates financial security with social upward mobility (Sakuma 1992). The Green Card is proof that its bearer has truly "arrived."

This is the point at which political economic conditions begin to bear in on the would-be deterritorialized imagination. Capital, it has been pointed out, moves much more easily across borders than people do: people, unlike capital, need Green Cards. For internationally mobile Japanese women, marriage, as one of only two paths to permanent residency status abroad, comes to bear a burden of expectation that transcends any discourse of akogare such as was introduced in previous chapters. The eroticization of the white man as liberatory agent does not account for the legal and financial constraints on women's search for a foreign spouse to realize the dream of escape. Yamamoto Michiko, with her usual flair for language, summarizes this as the "need-to-marry syndrome" (1993b, 159). She describes its effects on her own life during the lengthy period in which she lived as an illegal immigrant in California: "Previously I had always considered marriage a mere formality," she writes; "I only wanted someone whom I loved and who loved me. . . . But that was a sentiment I could only enjoy in Japan. In the U.S., where I had no legal standing, I could not afford such an attitude, because the Green Card was always dangling in front of my eyes" (160). As Yamamoto anxiously awaited a proposal from her boy-friend Robert, she was forced to acknowledge that, "if Robert didn't make the decision to marry me, the question of where I would work, where I would live, could never be resolved. Regardless of whether I did or did not love him, he held the key to my life [*kare wa watashi no jinsei no kagi o nigiru sonzai datta*]" (161).

This state of dependence on the will of lovers raises the possibility of abuse. Takako Day, a well-known journalist formerly married to an Ameri-can man, wrote a controversial 1991 piece in the prestigious news maga-zine *Asahi Journal*, arguing that Japanese women who seek white hus-bands in the United States will be treated as no more than Asian servants, forced to work to support white men: "Japanese women are so eager to have careers just like white women, that they end up being used by white men. They think they are so independent, but in reality they are no more than obedient Asian females working to support their men" (1991, 8–9). This piece instantly drew fire from the Tokyo-based internationally mar-ried Japanese women's organization Kokusai Kekkon o Kangaeru Kai (Association for International Marriage), among other groups, which defended the legitimacy of Japanese women–white men marriages. Of course, the legitimacy of individual marriages does not require defense. However, among women living overseas, far from family and social net-works and anxious to acquire permanent residency in an effort to avoid illegal alien status, the potential for abuse exists. This became apparent in stories told to me by women about friends who found themselves victims of domestic violence after marrying American men out of desperation for a Green Card. One commented, "The women aren't stable; they need someone to depend on, especially since they're in a foreign country. The woman wants a commitment and the guy won't make one, and they have a bad time. The guy might be abusive, and an American woman would kick him out right away, but a Japanese woman has this 'grin and bear it' mentality. And then also Japanese women put up with things from foreign men that they wouldn't tolerate in a Japanese man. Like being unem-ployed, or cheating. I have some friends who would say that even an abusive foreigner is better than a good Japanese." Morimoto Tomomi told me, "With a Japanese man I'd require that 100 percent of my demands be met, but with a white guy, I'd settle for 50 percent if it meant I could stay in the U.S. Because he comes with the place attached [*machi ga tsuiteru kara*]."

A foreign man's refusal to marry his Japanese girlfriend can thus have serious consequences. Kawataki gives one account of a woman in the United States who month after month allowed herself to be exploited at work in the vain hope that her employer might someday sponsor her working visa, or that eventually her boyfriend Rick might propose. In time, one of Rick's friends offered her a "paper" marriage just for the sake of the Green Card. But still Rick did nothing. An artist, he had told her in the beginning, "I'm a loner. I hate making commitments. I can't be creative when I'm tied down" (in Kawataki 1993, 222). In general, Japanese women, raised in a society in which the pressure to marry weighs nearly as heavily on men as it does on women, were frankly incredulous that American men so often expressed an unwillingness to "commit." Yamamoto Michiko writes that among the Japanese women she knew in California, American men's unwillingness to marry was a source of constant dismayed comment. The women who did manage to marry she refers to as "Green Card Cinderellas": "My feelings toward these 'Cinderellas' were a confused mix of envy toward the women and personal humiliation" (1993b, 162–63).

The majority of women I interviewed, however, several of whom still fervently desired a U.S. Green Card, shunned the foreign husband as a means of acquiring one. An international journalist argued, "I don't agree with the idea of marrying anyone just to stay in the States. You should go to do what you want, and then if you meet someone good while you're there, you can marry him. To look for a man just to stay there is too dependent. That's a really Japanese woman's way of thinking." Indeed, as time passed women residing in Japan reevaluated their need for permanent residency abroad at all. Kitahara Satoko and Nozawa Yuka both married Japanese men, Nozawa remaining in Japan and starting a family, and Kitahara eventually transferring to a California branch of her company along with her husband. Tanabe Minami later reflected, "From UC-Santa Cruz I came to realize that whites are the 'haves' of the world. . . . Now I don't want a Green Card. I realized that if you are not white, the more you worship white culture and try to 'move upward' like that, the more you degrade yourself."

The Flexibility to Be Japanese Women's views of the foreign/West are thus not static but constantly shifting. According to different women, and at different times in their lives, disillusionments with Western governmental policy and the apparent failure or hypocrisy of liberal political rhetoric (particularly during the Gulf War, ongoing at the time of my fieldwork), experiences of racism and sexism at the hands of Western male superiors in foreign firms, a questioning of the merits of "individualism" and other Western values, particularly within personal relationships, and reevaluation of the virtues of "Japaneseness" (often expressed in explicitly self-Orientalizing terms) led to skepticism and a distancing from the enthusiasms and akogare of earlier years. One woman who had previously extolled the attractions of marriage to a white man looked back in a later interview and reflected, "You know, white men are overrated. I used to think all I wanted to do in life was marry a white man and move to Canada. I wanted to actually *become* Canadian. But now I don't think so. Now I think I want to stay in Japan and make it here. If I can make it here, I can make it anywhere." In one discomfiting moment with Odawara Yumiko, the fellowships coordinator at the United Nations University in her mid-forties, I found myself on the receiving end of a stern lecture about U.S. atrocities against Iraqi civilians during the Gulf War. Accustomed as I was by that time to often uncritical praise of the West, I congratulated my interlocutor on her "astuteness": "Not many Japanese would take such a critical stance," I intoned. "And I suppose you think Americans would?" she shot back, leaving me red-faced and stammering.

Women also came to criticize the Western values they had previously embraced. One woman said of the "individualism" she saw in practice at her gaishikei bank, "It's so extreme, it's absurd [*hijōshiki*]! . . . I simply can't believe the way they act at my office, without any regard whatsoever for the feelings or the standpoint of people around them." Another told me, "I can only feel 'love of company' [*aishashin*] for a Japanese company. If my gaishikei went bankrupt, I wouldn't care less, but if I worked for Daiwa Securities and it went bankrupt, I'd be heartbroken. Because Daiwa is a family, but my company is just a bunch of individuals." A few women even came to reject the assumption of gender equality in the West. Hamamoto Tamiko, a high-ranking manager in the international section of a Japanese company, exclaimed, "If there is no gender discrimination in America, why is it that all the English letters I get from American companies are addressed to *Mr.* Hamamoto?! Why is it that at our conferences in the United States, *every single attendee* is male?! Why is it that when I go to tour American plants I don't see a single woman executive?!" Hamamoto went on, "I see a few at management level, or in sales, but when I talked to one she said she has to get up at 5 A.M. to cook breakfast for her husband, work all day, come home, cook dinner, and take care of the kids. This is equality?"

Criticisms of the West may at times lead to a version of the state-sponsored nationalist *kokusaika* (internationalization) that rejects any transformation of the ethnic or national self in favor of an assertion of that self, seen as fixed and unchanging, on the global stage. Cartoonist Chūsonji Yutsuko, for example, ridiculing "wannabe California girls" who "dye their hair blonde, find a surfer boyfriend, and learn to speak crude English slang," writes, "Do you think it's international to become just like foreigners, and do exactly the same things that your foreigner friends do? As a matter of fact, it's just the opposite. . . . The real issue is, can you be confident as a Japanese overseas? Because if you can be confident as a Japanese, that's going to be something amazing that no foreigner can imitate!" (1991, 126–30). At other times, the critique leads back to an inward-looking nationalism, as Matsubara Junko relates of her own case at the close of her book *I Can Speak English* (1989): "When I was younger . . . I had a stage where all I did was criticize Japanese men in my mind, and I planned on living abroad. I imagined having a cute little 'half' baby, and I was just thrilled." She goes on, "Looking back now, I can't believe what an ignorant, stupid woman I was. . . . Recently I don't even want to speak English anymore. I find myself thinking, 'Why do I have to speak English? I'm a Japanese. I don't have to grin and grovel to Westerners'" (202–6).

Such critiques amount to a repudiation of akogare. Matsubara writes, "If I thought that speaking English, having white friends, and knowing all about foreign countries made me more 'advanced,' in fact, it was nothing but a simple case of 'West worship' [*seiyō sūhai*]" (1989, 270). Akogare, always projected elsewhere, is here projected as symptom of immaturity onto the prior self. In feminist Tajima Yōko's case, submission to akogare was exemplified by her youthful eagerness, while studying in England, to accept an offer of marriage from the dashing youngest son of an aristocratic Belgian family, an offer she characterized as "Cinderella's shoe held out before me". Ultimately, however, she came to recognize her own needs for independence as a scholar and writer. Invoking Virginia Woolf, she writes, "I realized I didn't need any more horses or tennis courts or parties or castles. What I really wanted was a room of my own and a pen" (1994, 59).[1] In this way, Western men as the fetish objects of akogare (in Tajima's case, literally a prince) are also repudiated. One woman who had devoted a number of years to the vain search for a white husband told me: "Recently I've begun to think that, well, to put it bluntly, Japanese are better! Foreigners are immature. They say wonderful things but don't back them up. When I think about where I'll live, where my children will be born—long-range, serious things—I begin to think a Japanese man might be a better bet." It was common for women to reevaluate the very qualities of the white man that they had previously admired. Asano Minami, a thirty-four-year-old vice president at an American securities firm, told me, "Foreigners—particularly Americans—are good at compliments. They say nice things all the time, but it doesn't necessarily mean that they are really supportive or understanding. . . . So I don't particularly want to marry a foreigner right now. I don't have a strong desire to get married at all. To tell the truth, I don't have any desire to get married. And I would prefer to live in Japan."

I found that the process of acquiescing to the demands of Japaneseness was not abrupt, but slow, gradual, and cautious. It seemed to entail less an embrace of nationalism than an acceptance of ambiguity. Women who had resided in Japan for many years embodied a cosmopolitanism that was not entirely located in the foreign: in one sense, they were equally at home both in Japan and the West (to which they still traveled frequently for both business and pleasure); in another, they were equally jaundiced about the possibilities for fulfillment or a new ikikata in any geographical region of the world. They continued to defend their right to a career based on their extensive international expertise and experience. They remained intimately involved with economic, political, artistic, and social trends abroad, and maintained this involvement through frequent overseas travel (one even traveled to Denmark for a long weekend just to visit an exhibition of one of her favorite artists). Their networks of foreign friends and colleagues were often larger than their Japanese circles. However, they resisted any essentializing identification of the self with either Japan or the West.

This was exemplified by the story of Nagata Hiroko, mentioned previously, who was when I first met her a successful public relations manager in her mid-forties in an American securities trading firm. Years earlier, she had earned an MBA at an American university and had gone on to a successful career on Wall Street. Her company offered to sponsor her Green Card application, and her future seemed assured. One day, however, while visiting the Metropolitan Museum of Art, she experienced, in her words, a revelation. She had been eagerly exploring the Impressionism exhibit and studiously avoiding the Asian art collection because, as she describes it, she was "crazy for white peoples' culture." Then, by mistake, she turned a corner and found herself face to face with an enormous, ancient Korean mural of the Buddha. As she recounts, "It was as if, seeing the round, peaceful face and narrow eyes of that Buddha, I for the first time realized a different side to my identity. . . . That's when I came to realize myself as Japanese, as Oriental."

Shortly thereafter, Nagata turned down the Green Card and returned to Japan, where she took up a prestigious post in an American securities firm. Devoting her weekends, however, to volunteer work for an overseas aid NGO in Tokyo, she soon came to question the international division of labor that had brought wealth to Japan and Western countries while impoverishing other parts of the world. After a few years (and shortly after our first interview), she quit her high-paying job to take up a public relations position at the NGO for which she had been volunteering, at starvation wages. Her job now takes her to Laos and other Southeast Asian countries several times a year. She told me in a letter that her new life goal was "to work to become a human being who knows the joy of life and fosters true equality."

Women like Nagata resisted any attempts on my part to pin them down to a single set of allegiances. In interviews they would speak of themselves as "Japanese" and as comfortably connected to Japanese "tradition" when conversational circumstances called for distancing from women they considered akogare-driven and naïve. Yet in the next sentence, they would speak as "internationalized globalists" (chikyūjin) to distance themselves from what they considered the insular, exclusive, narrow-minded world of

Japanese male corporatism. They moved lightly across different identifications, choosing their self-representations strategically, almost in self-defense, forestalling circumscription. The West was not external to their identity and Japan was not internal; identifications with both were contingent and above all pragmatic exercises in hybridity.

In this sense, such women, even though resident in Japan, enunciated what Stuart Hall has called a diasporic identity: an identity that "lives with and through, not despite difference . . . [and] hybridity" (1994, 402). Accepting hybridity, women described themselves as molding an identity and an ikikata in which both Japanese and foreign allegiances could coexist. As Kitahara Satoko described it, "I used to want to fight all the time, to assert myself against Japanese society. But now I know that you just exhaust yourself doing that. So now I think it is better to work in a 'womanly' way, suppressing what has to be suppressed, and just asserting myself in a few places, in a moderate way." Noda Kaori's poem, "Walk Again," with which she ends her book, expresses this acceptance of hybridity: "The water flowed noisily by / And the wind blew / I hope it's a bright wind / A bright new start." The poem ends, "Yes, now, once more, slowly / 'Walk again!' / Farewell New York / The skyscrapers of Manhattan" (1992, 241–42).

This invocation of hybridity, however, should not be seen as a final humanist resolution to the problems of internationalist women's multiple enmeshments in dispersed, scattered, and contradictory hegemonies. Anthropologist John Russell has asked: Are women's emergent awareness of themselves as "Oriental" still embedded in the white culture they now reject? (personal communication, 10 October 1996). Whose authenticity is privileged in claims of racial and cultural identity, and how are these images marketed? Visweswaran cautions that "while all identities may ultimately be multiple and shifting, surely there are also hierarchies of hybridity" (1994, 132). In the next section, I turn to the tensions between internationalist discourse and feminist activism, both domestic and Western, to begin to approach the question of the scope of the radical potential of internationalism, and other such "imaginative" agencies, in effecting social change in deterritorialized spaces.

Feminism, Dependence, and the Refusal of the Collective Women's focus on the achievement of a flexible personal hybridity means that internationalism does not serve as the catalyst for a feminist movement intent on remaking discriminatory corporate practices or cultural norms of the age-driven life course in Japan. Internationalism is represented as a means—the only possible means—for each individual to avoid what can only be an inevitable submission to those norms. Nagata Hiroko put it, "You have a choice of doing nothing in Japan or going abroad." It is true that for many women the turn to the foreign is cast as an aggressive act of revenge against a Japan they feel has ignored and humiliated them. Noda describes one young woman studying accounting in the United States who "shivered with glee" in anticipation of correcting the English telegrams of the men in her company who used to "oppress" her (1992, 64). However, correcting telegrams was the extent of this woman's oppositional intention.

Although their internationalist rhetoric echoed many of the claims of first-wave Western feminism, particularly the effort to gain access to the Enlightenment category of individual personhood (Fox-Genovese 1982), women consistently rejected what they understood to be the goals and methods of both Western and Japanese feminists, even those that had led to many of the professional opportunities they traveled abroad to exploit. Asked to describe her impression of American feminism, one college student responded in English, "It's bullshit." American-style feminism, which they assumed to be based on legalistic tactics of confrontation with and competition against men, was criticized by Japanese women for having caused American women to lose their "femininity," which was associated with marriage and childbirth. Otani Fumiko, a freelance writer with extensive overseas travel experience, told me, "American women's success outside the home has led to sacrificing the family. Women have sacrificed cooking and cleaning for careers. But women are suited to family life, more than men. So, Japanese women will never try to have a women's movement." Others suggested that Western women's feminism had destroyed the strength and goodwill of Western males, who rather must be valued and praised as women's liberators. In her book *England, Country of Adults; Japan, Country of Children* (1992), Marks dismisses American feminism as "terribly aggressive" and expresses relief that it has not yet infected English men, who still understand what it means to be nice to women by helping them on with their coats and holding doors open (153–54). Nagaki Mitsuko said, "I was born and raised in Japan, and I guess I still have the belief that a good woman is the kind who stands behind her man and doesn't challenge him. So when I look at Western men I see them as being *tired*. Western men want a chance to be selfish, but they can't because they always have to serve Western women."

Women with whom I spoke insisted that activist tactics, even if they were worth pursuing, have no hope of success in Japan. According to Tanabe Minami, "There was a women's movement in Japan when I was a child. But they didn't even have the support of most other women, let alone men, so I think they decided, 'even if we try to change things, we can't.'" Fushida Kazuko, the twenty-three-year-old student of Burmese, told me, "If we women fought for the things we want, things would change. But we feel like it's just too much trouble. There was once a women's movement in Japan, and those women had to suffer so much. So now women my age think we'd rather just take it easy."

Although none of the women I interviewed seemed inclined to "take it easy," many admitted to ambivalence over the idea of devoting themselves singlemindedly to a career, internationalist or otherwise. Women spoke of "having an expectation that a man will support me" or "believing that a good woman doesn't challenge men." Okada Aki said quietly at the end of an interview, "I would definitely prefer to live in the States, and of course the best way is to be independent. But you see, as a Japanese woman, somewhere inside I want to be dependent." Women I spoke with somewhat ruefully recognized that their desire for dependency contradicted their earlier statements about seeking freedom, emancipation, and a new self abroad. In Nagaki Mitsuko's words, "Japanese women want to be *enveloped* in something big and safe. They want to be protected by a big and strong man. They don't want an equal relationship, or a partnership, but rather to be held and protected by a big man." Nagaki went on, "In the past, Japanese men were bigger than women, but now men have diminished. So women are dissatisfied." When I remarked that this seemed to contradict her earlier claim to be seeking "equality," Nagaki laughed: "Right! That's the problem. We're greedy. We want everything!"

The contradictoriness of internationalist women's desires reveals the degree to which gender relations in Japan have been destabilized without reaching a resolution in a direction that women find acceptable. Dissatisfied with their position, internationalist women cast blame onto Japanese men, whom they accuse of being at once too strong and too weak, and hold them responsible for the larger structures of the Japanese economy, which, if they benefit men more, also weigh on them more heavily. These ambitious and talented women wish for change, but place the onus of change on men's shoulders, while also ridiculing men for their subjection to the same economy that excludes them.

Matsubara Junko, in her influential 1988 analysis of working women and feminism in Japan, *The Croissant Syndrome* (*Kurowassan shōkōgun*), argued that contemporary Japanese women are socialized from childhood to "dependency" (*izonshin*). Matsubara suggests that because of this, despite their increasing entry into the workforce, they remain uninterested in fomenting large-scale social change on behalf of women's rights; the women she interviewed for her book, she writes, seemed to be "simply waiting for some outside force to determine their fate" (217–18). Discourses of internationalism also posit what is literally an "outside force" as a solution to women's oppressions in Japan. Kawachi Kazuko concluded her editorial (introduced in chapter 2), "I look forward to the day when the U.S. administration denounces Japanese firms for having achieved prosperity at the expense of women" (1994, 6).

It is critical to note here that this kind of antifeminist internationalism is only one subject position in a wide field of women's activity in Japan.[2] There is an active and varied feminist community in Japan, and there are many Japanese feminist activists who in turn disdain internationalist discourses, and who indeed reject the West as a model, seeking solidarity with Asian women against the depredations of both Western and Japanese capital expansion (see Matsui Y. 1989; Buckley 1997a; AMPO 1996). These feminists are in profound disagreement with internationalist women's rhetoric and methods, and some of them have written scathing critiques. Journalist Hisada Megumi, for example, wrote a fictionalized parody of "new self" rhetoric entitled "Horseback Riding, English, Beautiful Young Men, and Everything British: She Loves Them All," in the working women's magazine *Nikkei Woman*:

> Keiko likes England. That is, Keiko doesn't just like England; she loves every single thing associated with England. She loves Mother Goose and

London Bridge. She loves the misty Thames River and the sound of Big Ben. . . . She loves England so much that she believes that only in her imaginary English world is she truly alive. . . . Wearing her flower-print cotton dress with the hand-woven lace collar, Keiko tells her friends, "I'm crazy about England. I'm in love with England." . . . And if her English teacher isn't quite as handsome as Hugh Grant, the way he behaves so chivalrously toward her quite sends Keiko's heart a-flutter. . . .

As long as Keiko stays in her English dream world, Keiko never has to grow up. She can be a child forever. But someday soon Keiko is going to wake up and find out that she is an unmarried office lady nearing 30. And then, just like all those other Japanese women, Keiko is suddenly going to realize that she is all alone in her tiny, lonely little craft pitching in the rough Dover Straits. (1993, 130)

The grand image of the lone exile fleeing an oppressive Japan for glorious liberation in the West has been replaced by the pathetic figure of an aging, unmarried, and possibly deluded OL paddling a dinghy beneath the forbidding white cliffs of Dover. It is the very inwardness of internationalism that Hisada here critiques—its intensive focus on the self and rejection of communal identity, whether derived from national or feminist solidarity.

This tension between individualist internationalism and feminist communalism is exemplified by the 1993 film *Looking for Fumiko* by filmmaker Kurihara Nanako. In the film, Kurihara, who has a PH.D. in performance studies from New York University and resides permanently in New York, travels back to Japan to interview five women formerly active in the Japanese women's liberation movement of the 1970s. The film (inexplicably retitled *Ripples of Change* in its English edition) sets up Kurihara as a kind of transnational free agent, liberated from what are represented as the mind-numbing, soul-killing demands of communalist Japanese national identity and cultural identification. The film glamorizes Kurihara from its opening scenes, showing her strolling alone, self-sufficient and free, through the streets of New York, breezing by huddled masses of camera-wielding Japanese tourists. From this exalted vantage point Kurihara as filmmaker proceeds to write the obituary of the Japanese women's movement.

One of the underlying agendas of the film seems to be to justify and legitimate Kurihara's own flight from Japan. By denigrating, with varying levels of subtlety, the allegedly broken-down lives and shattered hopes of former "women's lib" activists who remained in Japan, Kurihara can convince herself and others that Japan continues to be a backward, sexist, and oppressive nation for women, a nation lagging far behind the opportunities and emancipation offered by her adopted country. Continually contrasting the freedoms of life in America with the implied failures of these five women who remain in Japan, Kurihara, as Linda White observes, "[uses] an invisible West . . . to evaluate and gaze down upon the positions of Japanese women and the *ribu* [lib] movement" (1997, 12).

Some of the feminist women Kurihara interviews, however, respond with barely concealed outrage at the implicit condescension of her questions, and stoutly defend their life choices as based on deeply held values of community and family. Funamoto Emiko, for example, founder of the groundbreaking (now defunct) feminist magazine *Onna Eros,* now in her fifties and single, lives at home as the sole care provider for her invalid and senile mother. Kurihara remarks, "Some people might look at someone like you and say you're all alone and pathetic . . . can you really say you've accomplished any of your ideals?" Funamoto, incredulously, responds in turn, "Surely it's better than just clinging [to some man] with no independence!" She goes on, "I've got many friends and colleagues, so the basis for that judgment is fundamentally wrong. Pathetic is not a word I'd use to describe myself!" (Kurihara 1994, 165).[3]

If feminism demands that society change, internationalism puts the locus of change in the self. As in the days of Tsuda Umeko, internationalism places women's hopes in foreign pressure to change the ways of Japanese men and does not advocate a commitment to women's own activism. The numerous volumes of women's internationalist writing produced each year, despite their striking generic similarity, emerge in virtual isolation from one another. Each is presented to the reader in an unmediated first person as a purely private and entirely original experience. Cumulatively, they suggest an active refusal of the collective. The West is valued precisely because it permits the individual self to be discovered and cultivated. To make the exodus to the West a collective event would be to strip it of its meaning. This revolution begins and ends in solitude, or at least not in the company of other Japanese.

Thus, the cosmopolitan imagination that potentially provides the grounds, and the means, for new collective social action on a global stage has resulted, in this case at least, in a "social movement" that denies sociality, a vision of emancipation that is relentlessly private. I wrote in the introduction that women's discourses of Western akogare are expressive of desire that functions within an overarching logic of capital. It is in the contradictions and impasses of internationalism as a potential feminist social movement that we begin to see the limitations of imagination and desire as subversive forces in a now transnational regime of commodity capital. Desire here is anticipated and recuperated by commodity logic, a logic that operates in increasingly subtle registers. Internationalist women in late-capitalist Japan, particularly those with demanding professional careers, reject any simplistic commodity resolution to their discontent in the form of, say, shopping trips to New York or Paris, but nevertheless work within a larger and inescapable logic of the fetish. That is, desiring "liberation" and believing they lack it, they have fetishized the West—in the last instance expressed metonymically in the white man—to fill the lack. But the referent of a fetish is always illusory and this fetishization forecloses real political engagement.

This is certainly not to suggest that women's fantasies of the West have been either static or ineffective. Tsuda Umeko found in Victorian America an ideal of the educated wife and a source of financial support for her school. Mishima Sumie saw in prewar and wartime America a model of democracy and the "enlightened husband." Some women active in the Occupation saw America as righteous military victor, promising individualized courtesy and regard for women's "personhood" embedded in specific legal and constitutional reforms, and embodied in the actions of individual G.I.s. Contemporary internationalist women manipulate all of these images (and others) into a new "West" that is not limited to (although it is still dependent on) the United States, a West that promises newly mobile and highly educated women discursive and material means for the rejection of the patriarchal nation. What sets the current moment apart, however, is that the fantasy West has come to proliferate as a decontextualized mediated image, an empty signifier that is infinitely manipulable but ultimately politically empty as a feminist emancipatory mechanism. Internationalist desires derived from this fantasy image give birth to no *social* movement. That they remain so persistent in the face of repeated failures of the "real" West indicates what has been called the "Disney World syndrome," in which the simulacrum is more compelling than the model. The danger here, Anne Allison observes, is that the simulacrum can come to "take on a life of its own, becoming a crucial determinant of who and what we are" (2000, 18).

As we have seen, the "West" has taken on a life of its own in the century or so of development of the female internationalist narrative in Japan, becoming an end in itself, an all-encompassing trope of goodness, cultural advancement, and unattainability that obliterates the particularities of Japanese (and other) pasts and futures. In its latest incarnation, under deterriorialized regimes of mobile capital, the desire for "liberation" expressed in such a fetishized West is perpetually deferred. Such desires are seamlessly absorbed into the global economy that, in Godzich's words, "takes hold of individual imaginations and exploits them for private rather than collective ends" (1993, xvii).

Godzich argues that in such an economy, "there can be only subjects and no society, that is subjects . . . deprived of any access to potentially subversive subject positions" (xix). This, however, is going too far. For the image—or perhaps the act of imagining—is also powerful; it changes women's lives and, in turn, the lives of those around them. For certainly, internationalism must be counted as a form of oppositional practice at least on an individual level. Mariko Tamanoi has argued that examples of Japanese women's resistance to Japanese patriarchy must be looked for not in Western-style political/legal "stimulant[s] to profound social change" but in individual women's "everyday social practices" (1990, 26–27). Indeed, the women I knew in Japan acted with courage and determination to create new opportunities for themselves by demanding acknowledgment of a different and alternative world "outside." Daily they resisted the hostility and pressure of an uncomprehending community, family and friends who attempted to push them into marriage and a corporate environment that seemed set on excluding them, both despite and because of their painstakingly acquired international experiences and passionately held internationalist beliefs. Despite their disappointments they continued in their convictions, forging alternative occupations and lifestyles for themselves that challenged the gendered assumption of Japanese patriarchal nationalism.

Without a doubt, internationalist women's colonization of the international realm has provided individual women with an important alternative to early marriage and childbearing and is intimately connected to other signs of domestic gender "distress" in Japan, including the dramatically falling birthrate and delayed age of marriage. Internationalist women's persistent critique of Japanese ikikata and gender roles and enunciation of a hybrid identity are an integral part of a larger challenge to long-standing assumptions in Japan governing women's (and men's) life courses, as well as the institutions that impose them.

"Personal choice" is one of the hallmarks of modernity, which has valorized it over the roles and expectations associated with national "tradition." Perhaps it matters less precisely what kind of ikikata women are choosing—Western-derived or otherwise—than that they are choosing at all, or rather, that they are naming ikikata itself as an object of scrutiny. Women's naming of Japanese ikikata *as* ikikata and their critique of the gender ideologies fundamental to it show the degree to which taken-for-granted operations of Japanese family and corporate systems have been shaken; it reveals the emergence of a discourse of value and morals that, in its radical skepticism, stands to impose the ruptures of a disenchanted modernity in the intimate gendered spaces of the Japanese home and company.

The unilinear drama of modernity, however, does not exhaust the possibilities for either liberation or oppression in deterritorialized spaces. Although it is undoubtedly true, as Tamanoi reminded us, that everyday social practices must be counted as sites of resistance, "everyday practices" do not exist in a pristine cultural space that constitutes their total field of meaning. In transnational contexts, "everyday social practices" have transnational implications. That is, social practices that are dependent on a fluid, almost infinitely mutable circulation of images and mutually imbricated desires of the Other, also yield unintended and unanticipated effects.

As Povinelli and Chauncey remark of agency under globalization, "We produce our undoing as we attempt to follow our desires" (1999, 445).[4] In the conclusion, I turn finally to the "unwilled" effects of Japanese women's internationalist narratives and practices when they begin to circulate in global space, implicating other agendas of modernity, emancipation, and desire that arise from Japan's particular position within postcolonial regimes of power.

≋ **Conclusion: Strange Bedfellows**

The migrant is in First World space.—GAYATRI CHAKRAVORTY
SPIVAK, *A Critique of Postcolonial Reason*

A Question of Audience If Japanese women's internationalist practice
is an example of "discrepant cosmopolitanisms" (Clifford 1992, 108),
showing that cosmopolitanism is "neither a Western invention nor a Western privilege" (Robbins 1992, 182), this practice also maintains tense relations with ongoing Western political projects. A humanist resolution to the
tensions of internationalism in an invocation of hybridity and multiplicity
does not account for the continuing (post)colonial hierarchies of legitimacy and power that fix internationalist women in a relationship to the
West and appropriate their narratives for purposes other than their own.
As Gyan Prakash has written, "The concept of multiple-selves . . . cannot
be adequate for conceiving colonial difference" (1997, 497). I suggest this
is true of postcolonial differences as well. In this conclusion, I consider the
real social effects of imaginative agency as it works itself out in actual sites
of postcolonial difference, when fantasies of the eroticized Self/Other
alight in specific encounters and moments of experience, implicating actors and (ethnographic) observers alike.

Because of the social pressures on internationalist women in Japan to
renounce international allegiances in favor of a return to the communal
fold, they are often forced to seek sustenance and legitimation of their
cosmopolitanism from foreign sources. The process of women's internationalism entails above all a disciplining of the body, mind, and voice in
accordance with the "rules" of a predeterminative West, in a version of
what Homi Bhabha (1994) has called "mimicry": "In America I had to

learn to express myself"; "I was forced to think for myself"; "I finally learned to be independent"; "I stopped letting others decide for me." Foreigners, either encountered in Japan or on temporary trips abroad, played the role of audience for this performance of internationalism; they alone could evaluate the performance and legitimate the personal and professional aims that motivated it. The foreigner was the audience to the ongoing performance that sustained internationalism as a coherent identity. As Takahara Etsuko insisted to me, "I spent five years studying in the United States. During that time my professors showed me how to argue, how to critique, how to think about the environment, and be socially aware. I realized, '*I'm* right! *Japan* is wrong!' After that I knew that Japan is the one with the problem, not me. Now, no matter what people say to me here, I'm not swayed. After five years in the United States, I know I'm right." Mori Mayumi, who struggled to continue her studies abroad in the face of intense family disapproval, exclaimed, "For me to go abroad periodically is how I *reconfirm* to myself that I am on the right track. So I make sure I go abroad regularly, and then when I come back to Japan I feel recharged." In this way, internationalism as performance is based on codes of shared knowledge: it requires that women demonstrate the range and correctness of their understandings of Western environments and be affirmed as correct. It is what Vincanne Adams has called a mimetic process, in which women reflect back images of themselves and their "oppression" that are already part of Western cultural understandings (1997, 94–95).

The mimetic nature of internationalism is nowhere better exemplified than in the following dialogue, published as the final chapter of a 1990 book on U.S.-Japan relations written by business consultants Katō Kyōko and Michael Berger. Katō opens the dialogue by forcefully arguing a standard women's internationalism narrative, concluding with the assertion that because of their innate sensitivity to international protocol, women should always represent Japan in trade negotiations with Americans. Berger at once agrees: "Certainly. Unlike a Japanese man, once a Japanese woman recognized the Western style of doing things, she would immediately comply." Katō responds: "We're tough, aren't we?!" Berger: "You certainly are! Japanese men, on the other hand, are all brittle inside because they've been so spoiled by their mothers." Katō goes on: "You know, Mr. Berger, for Japanese women, American men are very easy to negotiate with." Berger:

"Easier than Japanese men?" Katō: "Oh, the two can't possibly be compared! [both laugh]" (270–74). We have returned to the shaming of the Japanese male, but this time in a performative mode. It is an exchange shot through with erotic innuendo. Berger is coyly delighted with Katō's faith in the American male; Katō mirrors back to him what he most wants to believe about himself and the United States. Together they delight in their shared mockery of the dephallicized Japanese man ("all brittle inside").

In *A Critique of Postcolonial Reason* (1999), Gayatri Chakravorty Spivak casts globalization as the latest permutation of imperialism and argues that "imperialism's (or globalization's) image as the establisher of the good society is marked by the espousal of the woman as *object* of protection from her own kind" (291). In the case of the United States, immigration discourse is central to this effect. Lauren Berlant has shown the ways that immigration discourse is a "central technology for the reproduction of patriotic nationalism . . . because the immigrant is defined as *someone who desires America*" (1996, 43; original emphasis). Thus the "immigrant woman" (or potentially immigrant woman) turning her back on her own kind to grasp freedom and opportunity in America has come to serve as one of America's most resonant foundational images, and one increasingly mobilized in the multicultural capitalist imaginary. This is the American (or globalized) version of the European imperialism that, to paraphrase Spivak, "freed Woman to legitimize itself" (1999, 244).[1] Spivak goes on to say that now in the American imaginary, Woman from the non-West is "a particularly privileged signifier, as object and mediator . . . in the market, the favored agent-as-instrument of transnational capital's globalizing reach" (200–201).

Postcolonial feminist critics have objected to Western feminism's tendency to assume that non-Western women are universally "oppressed" in their native lands, calling this assumption a colonizing move that is meant to affirm hierarchies of power between the "advanced" Western woman and her abject Other (Ong 1988; Mohanty 1988; Carby 1982). This is an indispensable critique, but what I wish to explore here is that same assumption on the part of white Western men in eroticized heterosexual rescue fantasies—in other words, the White Man as savior effect (Frankenberg 1997a, 12). For women's "flight to freedom" culminates in the American imagination in the interracial "love" marriage, which is contrasted with the degradation of "arranged marriage" elsewhere. As Dearborn has observed, "Intermarriage between white men and ethnic women becomes a symbolic literalization of the American dream . . . an assertion of melting-pot idealism, of the forging of a 'new man,' of Cinderella success, of love 'regardless of race, creed, or color,' of the promise of America itself" (1986, 103). Japanese and other Asian female immigrants embody a particularly potent version of this intermarriage fantasy (Lye 1995, 272); it is the same fantasy that has propelled Amy Tan and Jung Chang novels to best-seller status as feel-good parables for a multicultural age in which white men are under growing pressure to prove their nonracism.

Bell hooks has trenchantly argued that as one element of this new multiculturalist ethos, some white men "claim the body of the colored Other instrumentally, as unexplored terrain, a symbolic frontier that will be fertile ground for their reconstruction of the masculine norm, for asserting themselves as transgressive desiring subjects" (1992, 24). According to hooks, an intimate relationship with a nonwhite woman serves for these white males as a public rejection of a white supremacist past and an "affirmation of cultural plurality." She goes on, "Not at all attuned to those aspects of their sexual fantasies that irrevocably link them to collective white racist domination, they believe their desire for contact represents a progressive change in white attitudes towards non-whites. They do not see themselves as perpetuating racism" (1992, 24).

Japanese women's internationalist discourses, which similarly valorize interracial intimacy as a symbol of rejection of a Japanese nationalist past, seamlessly merge with such an agenda. For both parties, then, the Japanese woman–white man romance can enable an eroticized assimilationism that makes the United States not only an object of universal female desire but also a multicultural utopia which heralds the end of racist history.

My purpose here, again, is not to cast aspersions on Japanese female–white male couples, but to explain what happens when such *representations* of interracial romance as symbol of a redemptive pluralism and solution to the problem of Japanese male sexism and insularity are recirculated back to Japan. For it is this recirculation, this endlessly repeated feedback loop, that is the very mechanism of deterritorialized desire, the means by which scattered hegemonies are imposed (and potentially resisted) in globalized space. It is this mechanism that allows the Kawachi editorial cited in chapter 2 and elsewhere in the book as a paradigmatic internationalist text to employ as its central legitimating authority not the experiences of actual Japanese women, but American *Time* and *Newsweek* articles, written by American men, about gender discrimination in Japan. But there are other, less obvious means. The musical *Miss Saigon,* for example, which played at the Imperial Theater in 1993, was a major hit among young Japanese women, who overwhelmingly dominated its sold-out performances. This tale of the Vietnamese-prostitute-with-a-heart-of-gold who kills herself for a white G.I. under the leering gaze of her eunuched (Asian) pimp, leaving her half-caste son to be taken by his father to a "better life" in the United States, brought down the house on the night I attended, its audience of women rising en masse to give the performance a fifteen-minute standing ovation.[2] Here the newly reinvigorated trope of *Madama Butterfly* is provided for Japanese women's use, via the imagination of the late-twentieth-century American male Broadway playwright, in narrating a rejection of the Orient/al man.

Another example is the award-winning novel *Ichigensan* (One-timer), written in Japanese by American author David Zoppetti (1997). This novel, which was a best-seller among young women readers, tells the story of a romance between David, an American exchange student, and Kyōko, a young blind Japanese woman. David is rendered powerful by Kyōko's blindness; it is he who is master over the Japanese language and landscape, he who guides a dependent Kyōko across the realm of authentic Japanese-ness. Through her dependence he transcends clumsy, ignorant foreign-ness: "[Kyōko] went beyond nationality or race, she treated me *as a human being*" (121, emphasis added). Meanwhile, David's guidance and attention liberate Kyōko from her lonely, isolated life; together, they create a private world free from the narrow-minded "prejudice" (against foreigners, against the blind) of Japanese society. This novel was so popular that it was made into a hit film in 1999.

There is no more powerful mechanism, however, than that encoded in the pedagogical process itself. An English conversation textbook for use in Japan entitled *Heart to Heart,* written and illustrated by three Western men, features as its central plot line, animating each successive lesson, a budding romance between a white American man and a Japanese woman (Pereira et al. 1992; see Figure 31). The romance, and the textbook, cul-

31. "The connection is perfectly clear." Cover of *Heart to Heart* English textbook. Source: John Pereira, Simon Potter, and Toto Akeru, *Heart to Heart: A Conversation Coursebook for Japanese Students* (Kyoto: City Press, 1992). Reprinted with permission.

32. Clint proposes to Keiko. Illustration from *Heart to Heart* English textbook. Source: John Pereira, Simon Potter, and Toto Akeru, *Heart to Heart: A Conversation Coursebook for Japanese Students* (Kyoto: City Press, 1992), 62.

minate in Clint's marriage proposal to Keiko (resplendent in a formal kimono) and the engaged couple's relocation to America. In their climactic dialogue (which features blank spaces in which students insert the proper vocabulary word chosen from a list), Clint declares to Keiko, "Anyway, gaijin or not, I've always been [myself]. . . . My life is my own and so I can never allow any group or person to control it." (See Figure 32.) Keiko responds, "I've probably been influenced by you, and I, too feel the [same] way. I want to live my life as I see it!" She goes on, "I want to continue working for a better international understanding among people . . . and not just to make Japan a richer country" (112–15). With that, Clint proposes. Through the use of this textbook, one imagines the English conversation classroom itself becoming a venue for the erotic union of Japanese female students' internationalist dreams and white men's agonistic desires.[3]

Recuperative Processes Internationalist women's insistence on a personal flexibility echoes the claims of the global postmodern economy, with its insistence on flexible accumulation and infinitely mobile capital that flourishes according to a logic of downsizing and expendability. In contrast to Ong's (1999) formulation of flexible citizenship, this flexibility is not necessarily radical. At least some segments of the emergent transnational elite class are permitted to enter only insofar as they mimic the practices and priorities of the Eurocenter. This class, to the extent it seeks inclusion in the West, is meant to serve, recalling Spivak's (1999) term, as the Eurocenter's affirmative action alibi.[4] Roger Rouse remarks, "While corporate-liberal multiculturalism echoes many of the idioms of affirmative action, it has clearly appropriated and diverted their more radical impulses. Both corporations and universities have used an emphasis on diversity much less to engage the problems suffered by citizens of color, especially those from the lower reaches of the class structure, than to license the creation of a cosmopolitan professional-managerial class by recruiting . . . from a global pool of talent" (1995, 384).

None have served better as affirmative action alibis than Asian immigrants to the United States (and their Asian American descendants), the so-called model minority. David Palumbo-Liu (1994) has astutely revealed the uses to which Asian Americans have been put by the white mainstream media to "prove" the essentially fair, race-blind nature of American laissez-faire capitalism. His argument applies equally well to elite or would-be elite economic migrants from Asia. Palumbo-Liu's point is that the image of the successful Asian has been "deployed in an eminently programmatic way against other groups. . . . Freeing [Asians] of the burden of their ethnicity and race while retaining (for obvious ideological purposes) the signifier of racial difference: the notion of *self*-affirmative action" (371). At its crudest level, "property" is what is at stake here: Asians have property and defend it against "property-less" blacks: "The supremacy, the ultimate 'soundness,' of the capitalist economics that have disproportionately favored whites over racial and ethnic minorities now seems colorblind because 'yellows' have found it to work in their favor, too" (375).

Spivak also takes up the question of the vexed class privilege in the United States of such "successful" minorities, particularly the figure of what she calls the "financializing female diasporic" (1999, 376). The elite female diasporic is exemplified in her discussion by that paragon of the internationalist Japanese woman, designer Kawakubo Rei. She quotes Kawakubo in a 1984 interview, "I have always felt it important not to be confined by tradition or custom or geography" (Troy 1984, quoted in Spivak 1999, 339), to which Spivak responds, "How does a 1943-born Japanese buy such freedom?" (339). Kawakubo's "plangent female individualism," Spivak notes (352), makes possible an erasure of class that is itself the apotheosis of class hegemony on a global scale.

Of course, in the Japanese women's internationalist discourse on which this book has focused, concerns of capital are superseded by humanist longings that make the West, and the white man, not merely the possessor of all property worth having, but the liberator of the world's oppressed. One author likened an American boss who "rescued" his Japanese female subordinate from being forced by Japanese clients to serve tea to "the fairminded and superior [*yūshūna*] white men who freed the slaves" (Nakajima M. 1996, 196). Takahara Etsuko told me:

> In America you have the American Dream. If you make an effort you can make your dream come true! Americans treat people with respect. I believe this because of the movies I watched when I was a child. I've always watched loads of American movies, all kinds of movies, like cowboy and Indian movies. And in those movies, you know, the whites

would kill the Indians, but at the end, the movie would show that the whites were wrong! Even though the majority of Americans are white, they're not afraid to show what they've done wrong! Same with racism against blacks. White people make movies showing that they are wrong. There's so much justice in America. To me, American movies are symbols of justice!

The mechanisms of democracy and capital have seamlessly merged; a woman's desire for social justice enabled—indeed, produced—by the workings of the global culture industry.

Certainly, internationalist women are not the only Japanese for whom the United States is deployed as a model of justice and opportunity in ways that affirm its centrality and hegemony. Lisa Yoneyama has observed that the United States is often made to serve as a model of genuine democracy and individual rights for many different groups that wish to "object to the failures of democracy in Japan" (1994, 7). She continues, "Litigants fighting for equal treatments as full citizens—such as a Korean minority, a woman, or a Burakumin—often cite the U.S. political culture as a point of reference for a system that is supposedly free from government manipulation or cultural pressure to conform" (7). Yet Yoneyama's point is that there are reactionary political effects when such voices are unself-reflexively relayed back into an American context. Michael Berger, later in the previously introduced dialogue with Katō Kyōko, suggests that there is little or no racial, gender, or age discrimination in the United States. In doing so he aligns himself with Katō's agenda to use the United States as a point of reference to critique gender and age discrimination in Japan; at the same time, Katō's willingness to accept his representations at face value encourages his own constructions of himself and his country as open and nondiscriminatory. What is repressed is any recognition of continuing inequalities in American society, as well as the power relation embedded in a reliance on a Western country as a model for uncritical emulation. As Tani Barlow argues, in the case of some Chinese intellectuals' similar deployment of a mythic modern West against the oppressions of an "autocratic, backward, and primitive" communist China, such discourse must be seen as a form of self-colonization, in which intellectuals gain power only through "the languages of imported Truth" (1991, 226).

Yoneyama writes that such rhetorical manipulations "illustrate the danger involved in the simple transnational transportation of critical discourses from one context to another," and warns us against translating "otherized voices without specifically locating them in relation to potential dominant listeners and their dominant ways of listening" (1994, 8). There are dangers to translations of Japanese women's oppositional discourses into Western/American political contexts for the benefit of an audience that is only too eager to appropriate Asian women's "misery" into affirmation that, after all, the West is the best of all possible worlds.[5]

"Fielding" Ethnography Precisely because the foundations of women's international impulses operate at such taken-for-granted levels, I encountered considerable pressure during fieldwork to desist in my efforts to make them explicit. I was told, more than once, that this was not an appropriate topic of academic inquiry. One potential interviewee I contacted on the phone, a sixty-year-old Christian women's activist who was married to a white man, exploded in anger when I explained my research topic to her: "Well, I'm part of that group, and I don't like that at all. I don't want to be an object of your study! Those are very sad questions you're asking. *Very* sad!!" "Why?" I gasped, dismayed. "Well," she sputtered, "because . . . each person . . ." At a loss for words, she finally burst out, "I think that's a terrible subject of study! I don't think you should study that!" "But," I ventured cautiously, "I think it might be valuable to ask why some Japanese women might seem to prefer the West over Japan." My interlocutor laughed angrily. "And what? You're going to write a *dissertation* about this?? What field could you possibly be in?" "Anthropology," I answered. Another hostile laugh. "So you're going to make some general theory about it?" "No" (defensively). "Well, I don't think you would have any reason to be interested in my work," she said, and with that, hung up. I was left speechless, stunned and dismayed that my topic alone had elicited this degree of anger and distress.

For several weeks following this exchange I contemplated abandoning the project entirely. Ultimately, however, I did not abandon it. I struggled to understand the reasons for such reactions, but I remained convinced that the topic was worth pursuing. That is to say, the very intensity of the reactions my research incited seemed a kind of evidence of the topic's importance. I began to attend more carefully to the responses as part of the study itself.

In this way I came to realize over the course of fieldwork that I was facing an invisible, unspoken code—a code that actively resisted critical scrutiny—about the "rightness" and necessity of the alliance between Japanese women and the West, and in particular the bond between Japanese women and Western men. I was forced to grapple with this code because of my research, but I soon found that it was not simply my research that challenged it. I, myself, as a white woman married to a Japanese man, was unwittingly transgressing it in a way that made people uncomfortable. I certainly did not set out with any such agenda, and I found this interjection of my "private" circumstances into my research persona unappealing. But given the personal nature of my conversations with informants, my own personal circumstances often emerged, and as time passed I could not escape the fact that my marriage to a Japanese man, when revealed, was proving to have a jarring effect on nearly everyone around, disrupting the establishment of a taken-for-granted agreement about the universal desirability of America and American men and the universal abjection of Japan and Japanese men. Indeed, its disruptive power had emerged early on, even before fieldwork commenced, when I told a Japanese female graduate school professor that I had become engaged. She smilingly extended her congratulations, until I told her my fiancé's name. "He's Japanese??" she asked incredulously. After a long pause, smile fading, she remarked, "Well, I guess there's always divorce."

Although at that time I scarcely realized that the code existed, let alone that my husband and I had transgressed it, later, in the field, the nature of our transgression was made explicit. It happened one afternoon in 1993 when we were standing in line at the American Express office in Tora-nomon, Tokyo, waiting to get a cash advance. A young, bilingual Japanese woman stood behind the counter, probably one who had lived and studied abroad for several years, judging by her English skills and internationalist panache. I departed to do some shopping, and my husband progressed to the front of the line, finding himself at her window. He later told me what transpired. Before she would process his request this young woman apparently accosted him, demanding to know if he was married to the white woman she'd seen with him in line. Answered in the affirmative, she crowed, "Oh, you're going to regret it! Don't you *know*," she saw fit to elaborate, "that *Japanese* make the best women? And *Westerners* make the best men!" Regaling Tarō, who was still waiting for his cash advance, with stories of an Italian boyfriend, she finally concluded ominously, "You may think it's fine now, but in ten years you're going to be sorry you didn't marry a *Japanese* woman!"

This was the unspoken code of Tokyo social life. White men and Japanese women belonged together; white women and Japanese men did not. Indeed, white women did not really "belong" at all. During my fieldwork in interracial dating venues such as bars and singles parties, white men I met seemed to feel a special glee in explaining to me the misery of white women in Japan, rejected and unwanted. "I don't envy you," said Gus, a British writer I encountered in Roppongi, "a white woman in Japan." An American journalist married to a Japanese woman told me, "Western women's lives are grim. They hate it here. They're all dying to get laid (excuse the language). They're desperate for a man. They'll latch on to any Western man that gives them the time of day." Jeff, a British translator, told me, "White guys here are really turned off by white women, their weight, their shape—'My god, she's eighteen stone!' And she chomps her food loudly! [laugh] White women certainly become less attractive by comparison."

By no means did all white men in Japan engage in this kind of discourse. It was undoubtedly concentrated in those interracial dating venues that, as I described in chapter 3, were by their very nature meant to exclude white women and Japanese men. Those white men who did hold to these beliefs, however, could barely conceal their outrage at the specter of a white woman happily involved (as opposed to unhappily, which they relished) with a Japanese man; her example had to be eradicated, her motives suspect. James, a thirty-one-year-old financier in a British securities firm, told me, "I've been here five years and I haven't seen more than five Japanese man–Western woman couples. The ones I do see walking around with a Japanese man, I think, 'What's wrong with that woman?' My friends too. We all think she's either stupid or the guy has a lot of money." Only money or mental illness could mediate such an aberrant relation. An American

English teacher told me, "I know one Australian woman who was crazy for Japanese men; I have no idea why. She was a slut anyway, always dragging in guys from the train. So who knows what was going on in her head." The journalist quoted above concluded, "All the Western women here are neurotic. They have some kind of hang up, like they're running away from something at home, or can't make it anywhere else."

The fact of my marriage was evidently so disturbing to some of the white men I met in Tokyo's interracial dating scene that they sometimes seemed intent on baiting me, trying to prod me into a reaction. "You've dated Japanese men, right?" asked Ken, the IBM manager I met on the cruise party. "Are their dicks really as small as they seem?" Although I usually made an effort to retain, for lack of an alternative, the conventional anthropologist's stance of noncommittal tolerance, one day with an English teacher in his mid-forties named Peter, who was married to a Japanese woman, I rose to the bait:

> PETER: Of course, Japanese women like Western men because Japanese men are just not attractive [watches me closely]. You know, they have their mothers take care of them and expect their wives to do the same. Then, if they don't like their wife, they just go back to their mothers [waits for my reaction].
> AUTHOR: Really? I wouldn't know. My husband is really great.
> PETER: [Looks dissatisfied].
> AUTHOR: And of course, white men are so idealized in the media here. I mean, you have to admit there is something of a myth of the white man here.
> PETER: [Angrily] Well, they believe in myths here. It's so easy to pick up a woman here. On the trains or anywhere. If a good-looking one is standing next to me, I don't have to "come on" to her or push or anything. Just a little smile, and she's introducing herself, giving me her phone number.

The price of candor was an angry informant. My small challenge to the code of white male perfection provoked Peter to display "proof": the ease with which he could pick up women on the train.

The spectral presence of my husband in my fieldwork project also affected my ability to build rapport with internationalist women. Some informants undoubtedly approached interviews with me as an opportunity to share the testimony of an "authentic" Western female. As a native of the United States, as an American woman (and, incidentally, one who occupied at least superficially similar age, class, and professional positions as my informants), I was repeatedly called on to field internationalist claims and urged to participate in a shared discourse of allegiance to the West. Because of my marriage, however, as well as a certain (feminist) skepticism I brought with me about the liberatory potential of America, I failed in this role. The resulting tension colored my interviews and influenced my fieldwork in ways that seemed then (and now) both productive and unproductive.

In one sense, the "problems" of my marriage and my skepticism sometimes allowed the sexual code to be made explicit and open for discussion and, in some cases, seemed to provide informants with a means to express ambivalence about the dogma of Western (male) desirability. One informant wrote me after I left the field, "I've enjoyed our conversations; they've made me reconsider the ideal of 'Pax Americana' in my life." This influence seemed less salutary when I was confronted with not-so-subtle urgings from informants to disavow my husband or neutralize his disruptive effect by constructing him as "Americanized" and an "exception to the rule" of Japanese male backwardness. In the interest of building rapport with informants, I reluctantly participated for a time in the exceptionalizing of my husband in ways that permitted the categories of American and Japanese male to remain intact, mutually exclusive, and hierarchically ordered. As time passed, however, such moves became untenable on many levels, both professional and personal. Eventually, I stopped participating in such rapport-building strategies, and my inability to perform in this reflexive process became my primary fieldwork dilemma, one that was never satisfactorily resolved.

The flatness of my responses dumbfounded several of my most highly West-identified informants, leading to a permanent estrangement in one case, with a woman with whom I had been developing a budding friendship. This estrangement grieved and troubled me. I questioned my role: By refusing to collaborate, was I undermining informants' much-needed and deeply invested oppositional efforts? At the time, I wrote in my field journal:

For [my friend] struggling with a Japanese system that ties together race, nation, and the subordination of women into one seamless whole, the rhetoric of "one world" and liberal individualism is a radical act of resistance and defiance. The Western refuge finally found and embraced, now under attack from an unexpected and "in-credible" source—a same-aged white woman who seems to be a clear beneficiary of the goodness of the West, yet who has forfeited the chance to marry a white man. How can a Westerner critique the West? How can a white woman marry a Japanese? Especially in light of the chorus of Western journalists, writers, scholars, and activists who provide the rhetorical fuel for my informants' bombardment of the male-dominated Japanese system . . .

What were my responsibilities as a "native" Western ethnographer? To what extent was I liable for my citizenship in fieldwork? My domestic arrangements? There was no neutral place for me in this fieldwork. I either had to agree with the dogma of Western (male) superiority, or disagree with it—hedging not being an option as time went on—and either choice brought consequences at both personal and professional levels. I was a player in the economy of attraction whether I liked it or not.

And yet, because I was also a researcher and scholar, I found I was accorded yet another role—that of therapist, or confessor, to American men involved with Japanese women. Even before I began fieldwork in Tokyo I had grown accustomed, following talks I gave on yellow cabs in Hawai'i and elsewhere, to having white men from the audience hesitantly approach me, bearing sad and humble stories of unsuccessful affairs with Japanese women, looking, as far as I could tell, for a diagnosis, or at least a confirmation that it "wasn't their fault." My work on yellow cabs bears a long half-life; my articles, abstracts, and paper titles apparently come up under searches for "Japanese women" on the Internet, and over the past eight years I have been contacted with some regularity by a series of white men involved with Japanese women who seem possessed with a need to talk about it. The following is part of an e-mail I received in 1998:

Dear Ms. Kelsky, Being that you are American I will be very direct. . . . I am a 46-year-old white male. To some others I seem much younger. I often date gaksei [*sic; gakusei*, students]. I have been very respectful. Unfortunately I was very wild when I was young and contracted Herpes and Hepatitis B. There is a vacine [*sic*] for B, but I'm afraid I'm stuck with the other. I very much want to marry a *Bejin* [*sic; bijin*, beautiful woman]. I love Japan and the Japanese people. I have many Japanese friends here. I will find a way. *Haji* [shame] is so strong. There must be a young woman who needs me too. Or maybe she's here going to school. I think you get the picture. I truly mean well. Perhaps this is a cause worth fighting for. They come here, contract it, commit suicide or behave and catch something worse. From what I've read about you, you must be right on top of this problem. Do you care? Where is she, this beautiful girl who needs me so? With love, X

This e-mail made me nervous, and I refrained from responding to it, but I was unable to avoid a phone call to my home by another man who had read one of my articles (Kelsky 1994b) and had tracked down my phone number. This man described himself as a professional gigolo in Hawai'i and felt compelled to correct what he saw as several inaccuracies in my work. I will quote only a brief passage from this conversation, which I recorded in written notes with his permission.

I met my permanent sponsor two years ago. She does business in Hawai'i so she is here a lot. She's about forty. The thing I didn't like about your article was that you didn't write about emotional attachment. I'm almost in love with this woman! If there was a rushing car I would throw myself in front of it to save her. It's like that.

She basically wants me to be available to her whenever she wants. She bought me a health club membership and I guess her fantasy is to have this tall athlete with a large penis who she can emotionally feel comfortable with.

She says it's the ultimate yin/yang thing. One of her favorite things to say, when I'm all the way in her and she's going crazy, is, "David, the West is really meeting the East now!" Other girls say things like that too—like "Aren't these good 'international relations'?" Anyway, the main thing is that I am really emotionally bonded to these women, and if anything they are using me. And I really care very much for them. Like I said, I'm willing to die for them.

I repeated to this man that I had never precluded the possibility of affection and love prevailing in relations between white men and Japanese women (although I wondered what it meant to be "almost in love"), but was only concerned to examine the racial and sexual imagery that seemed to surround and enable them. But I never knew exactly how I was supposed to respond to these ghastly intimacies. It seemed that one venerable old question in Japan anthropology, "Who sleeps by whom?" (Caudill and Plath 1966), had been replaced by another: "Who sleeps with whom?" And the ethnographer was not exempt.

What these fieldwork encounters lead me to propose is the need to acknowledge the ways that ethnographers of transnational phenomena are increasingly required to "field" unanticipated (indeed, unanticipatable) and perhaps unpalatable agendas in their research and writing. I fielded internationalist Japanese women's claims about white men and the West, and my responses became part of their encounter with the West, to be accepted or rejected or otherwise interpreted. I fielded white men's claims about Japanese women, and my responses worked, often against my will and intent, to confirm, deny, legitimate, or explain white men's ability to attract. At no time was I a neutral observer; I was not permitted to be.

Lata Mani has written eloquently in her article "Multiple Mediations: Feminist Scholarship in the Age of Multinational Reception" of her own vexed positioning trying to "assess the cultural politics" of those who inquired into her controversial research on *sati* (widow-burning) in India (1989, 1). Describing a troubled encounter at her acupuncturist's office, in which she is caught in the "pincer movement" of his "liberal, relativist, patronising discourse . . . an apparent but ultimately repressive tolerance" (1), Mani demonstrates the difficulty of representing questions of "oppression" or "emancipation" to different listeners with different agendas. Like Mani, I came to dread the question, "So, what is your ph.d. thesis about?" There was no avoiding the "pincer movement" of my interlocutors' stunningly patronizing certainties about the role of the West and the white man in Japanese women's "upward mobility."

Mani notes that in an age of multinational reception, "both readers and writers have had to confront their particularity and history," and argues that such acknowledgments "require an attentiveness to the theoretical and political impulses that shape our projects and an openness to the inevitable fact that different agendas may govern their reception" (1989, 3). This is, of course, what Mani means by "multiple mediations," and what I mean in an ethnographic context by fielding. When the field itself crosses racial and national borders, when conversations about the field topic are routinely conducted across countries and languages, when the ethnographer shares a positioning in the topic that absolutely prevents any fiction of objectivity (or what Mani calls "disinterested knowledges"), and when every interlocutor has an opinion and, more important, an investment in the research outcome, then the shape of ethnography is changed. It is not simply, in the conducting of engaged transnational research, that anthropologists need to conduct "multi-sited" ethnographies (Marcus 1995), but that the ethnographer himself or herself occupies multiple sites, even without leaving "home." It is as if the ethnographer's research and writings are refracted through a kind of funhouse mirror, which sends contorted, distorted reflections across space. It is accountability for the multiple agendas fielded by our research and the multiple sites we are made to inhabit, for the funhouse mirror effect of our writing and speech, that becomes the critical task of the transnational anthropologist.

It seems to me particularly imperative that white ethnographers account for their own "nativeness" in their practice of representation, in both meanings of representing the West in the field and representing the field in the West. Although there has been growing attention to the position of ethnographers who, because of their racial or cultural subject position, identify themselves and are identified with those they study (see Abu-Lughod 1991; Narayan 1993; Visweswaran 1994; Daniels 1984; Kondo 1990), until now the "native" ethnographer has only been problematized as one who is native to his or her non-Western field site. The Western, particularly the white, anthropologist, however, is the native of that West/ modernity that circulates transnationally; he or she is both "native informant" for subjects' knowledge and identity projects that hinged on an idea of whiteness/Westernness, and conduit for the circulation of these projects back to the Western metropolis. To fail to account for that is to reinscribe the unmarked universality of the white Westerner, in anthropology as elsewhere.

Strange Bedfellows Although "alliances" between the ethnographer and his or her subjects have been imagined in some quarters of the discipline as a solution to the historically problematic politics of anthropology, such alliances are not always possible. "We" are not all cosmopolitans in the same way. Progressive intentions do not always yield harmony of interest in the spaces in between countries and racial, sexual, and gendered imaginaries. Following Visweswaran, I found that feminist alliance in the field was mostly a possibility left unachieved, a hope left unfulfilled (1994, 99). As Visweswaran anticipates, this acknowledgment of failure takes one "homeward," rather than away. I could not see the West as my informants saw it. And yet, I do not wish to fall prey to "the unreflective scorn for modernity among Western intellectuals" that, as Robbins has reminded us, actually functions as a kind of "metropolitan self-aggrandizement" (1994, 147). He calls this "kicking away the ladder one has climbed oneself" (147).

With that in mind, I want to be explicit that the fact that Japanese women's internationalist rhetoric feeds Western "vanity" (Berlant 1996) and supports a larger racial/political status quo does not diminish its effectiveness or value as oppositional discourse within a domestic Japanese context. It is one of the very few options available for women to resist multiple interlocking systems of patriarchal control in Japan, and yields possibilities for the enactment of imaginative desire as a kind of social practice whose total effects have yet to be fully grasped. I do not problematize the internationalist option in order to dismiss or repudiate it, but to question what Yoneyama called the problem of "simple transnational transportation of critical discourses from one context to another" (1994, 8). Critiques overlap and contradict one other: women's use of the West to critique Japan disenables political critique of the West; any criticism of West-centrism, meanwhile, undermines the force of women's gendered critique of Japan.

Spivak has characterized elite postcolonial women's place in the Western metropolis as inhabiting the "violent aporia between subject and object status" (1999, 304). The much-vaunted professional opportunities of the international sphere—interpreting, translating, consulting—are at once the "New Empire" (311), but also, in places, tenuous and marginal (especially for Japanese women) to the still powerful national economies of

Japan, the United States, and other countries. The same eroticized alliance between Japanese women and white men that works to interject women into multicultural imaginaries in the United States can also work to further marginalize them in Japan, as yellow cab–derived discrimination against internationalist professional women reveals. Individualistic cosmopolitanism, even a potentially oppositional kind, confronts and finds itself appropriated by continuing geopolitical regimes of power. "Liberation," Mayfair Yang eloquently writes, "is always a prelude to a new insertion into another mode of power" (1997, 311).

Thus, internationalist Japanese women's position is ambiguous in the extreme. The very work of desire is that which is most susceptible to appropriation. Their example shows us the ways that transnational subjects are held responsible for what they want in ways they never intended, cannot anticipate, and perhaps cannot even "imagine."

Cosmopolitan criticism produces its share of strange bedfellows. This is so for cosmopolitan subjects and ethnographers both. How much scrutiny can any of us bear of our most intimate desires, the places of the inscription of fantasy on the body, never free from capital-driven dreams but never wholly contained by them either? Fielding the constantly shifting political agendas of the nation and the transnational imaginary, the intimate spaces where love and desire meet global capital and the continuing seductions of modernity, mobile, striving subjects find themselves embroiled in unanticipated controversies, unrecognized and unrecognizable debates. On the verge of subject and object, they, and we, go on.

Notes

All translations are the author's unless otherwise noted.

Introduction

1   This research is based on fieldwork in Waikiki, Hawai'i in 1991 on the "yellow cabs" phenomenon and in Tokyo in 1993 and 1994 among sixty Japanese women (as well as forty others surveyed through questionnaires) who had internationalist experience through study abroad, work abroad, or employment in foreign-affiliate firms or nongovernmental organizations such as the United Nations. The majority of these women were single, between twenty and forty-five, and bilingual to some degree. About 70 percent had study-abroad experience ranging from six months to four years. Most had been or were currently romantically involved with a white Western man. My fieldwork included sites of Japanese female–foreign male romantic encounters, including Roppongi nightspots, conversation lounges, "friendship parties," and "international dating services," where I also interviewed Japanese and foreign men.

2   I thank Anne Allison for suggesting the term "Occidental longing."

3   Women's internationalist narratives are resolutely heterosexual in nature. Just as Japan is embodied in the Western imaginary by the Japanese woman, the West in women's discourses is embodied by the white man, and international intimacy is imagined as a union of the two. Although there are queer trajectories of desire in operation between Japan and the West, these were not enunciated in women's internationalism. For the lone exception, in which lesbian sexuality is mentioned only to be ridiculed, see Kida (1998, 136–39). For work on queer desire operating between Japan and Western countries, see Hanawa (1996); Treat (1994, 1999); McLelland (2000).

4   It is perhaps ironic that Japanese women claim to be "marginal" given the dominance of the Japanese woman as signifier of a feminized Japan in Western eyes (which I discuss in chapters 1 and 3). Nevertheless, as I show, women's centrality to an external image of Japan does not negate their own insistence on their "internal" marginality.

5   Lynn Stephen, personal communication, February 22, 1999.

6   Kyoko Mori is particularly important in this regard as a writer who almost perfectly balances the conventions of the Japanese-language genre of women's internationalist writing with a larger English-language field of women's postcolonial bildungsroman in the West. See in particular Mori (1997). My gratitude goes to Kimura Naoko for bringing the works of Kyoko Mori to my attention.

Chapter 1. The Promised Land:
A Genealogy of Female Internationalism

1   It is estimated that in 1630, for example, there may have been as many as three hundred Japanese wives and mistresses of foreign men in all of Japan, as well as their children and grandchildren (Leupp 1993, 3). Leupp argues that until 1850, women who consorted with foreigners did not suffer discrimination in Japanese society; according to him, it was only after foreign governments began to seriously erode the Tokugawa Bakufu's authority and threaten Japan's sovereignty that these women were made into scapegoats to bear national humiliation (10).

2   The practice of providing women to visiting foreigners has been called a "national tradition . . . which began over one thousand years ago" (Molasky 1999, 106); see also Duus M. (1979).

3   For full-length English-language biographies of Tsuda Umeko, see Furuki (1991); Rose (1992). In Japanese, see Furuki (1992); Ōba (1990); Yamazaki Takako (1972); Yoshikawa (1956). For Tsuda's writings, see Tsuda (1984); Furuki et al. (1991).

4   An interesting account of the passage of the five girls from Japan to Washington, D.C., is given in Tsuda's later essay for the *Chicago Record* entitled "Japanese Women Emancipated." See Tsuda (1984, 77–84).

5   The Ferris Seminary in Yokohama, for example, established in 1870, was the first school in Japan to offer female education beyond the elementary level. See Bennett, Passin, and McKnight (1958, 156).

6   Tsuda is not credited as coauthor in later editions of this book because of the potential damage to her reputation and prospects in Japan arising from her publication of any writings critical of the status of women there.

7   For influential discussions of Victorian American ideals of female domesticity, see Welter (1966); Lerner (1979, chap. 2). For more recent critical perspectives, see Smith-Rosenberg (1985); Boydston (1991); Lystra (1989).

8   Miyoshi adds, "and I suspect many cannot even now" (1979, 76). See other accounts from the time in P. Duus (1996).

9   For more on the life of Kimura Akebono (whose real name was Kimura Eiko), see Takatsuka (1896); Fukutani (1966). For more on *Fujo no kagami,* see Shiota (1966, 424–25); Hasegawa (1918); Kimura (1950); Kanzaki (1953).

10 This tendency is paralleled in fiction of the time. For a discussion of Western women in Meiji-era novels, see Sawada (1996, chap. 7); see also Miyoshi (1974, 38–43).

11 It is interesting to observe the contrast between Noguchi's depictions of American women based on a lengthy residence in the United States, and his rapturous descriptions of English women based on a short visit in 1913: "The most charming part with them is that, not only do they know how to talk, but also very well understand how to listen to the others, and besides, how to raise and drop their eyelashes" (1914, 156).

12 See also Masaoka (1913); Uemura (1912). For a rare adulatory treatment of Western women from a Christian humanist perspective, see Abe (1910).

13 Of this visit, Ichikawa Fusae, the renowned women's suffrage activist and political leader, was to respond, "It is ridiculous that Mrs. Katō and other female members of the House of Representatives went to MacArthur thanking him for granting Japanese women suffrage! Women's suffrage in the U.S. and Britain was achieved as the result of many women's hard work. We should appreciate such women instead of MacArthur!" (1979, 76–77).

14 For a superb general study of the immediate Occupation period and the "liberation" effect, see Dower (1999). For a good example of ways that "liberation" rhetoric was employed by ordinary women in their memories of the war and Occupation, see also N E T Terebi (1965). Most writers emphasize that legal reforms did not eradicate deeply ingrained "feudalistic" customs regarding women's status, particularly within the family, noting that many of these customs persist to the present day. See Katō S. (1977); Itō (1974, 1990); Yamazaki (1997); Higuchi (1976). It is important to note that there was also a current of anti-American feeling among some women at the time, especially those sympathetic to the socialist and communist movements. Katō Shizue mentions her disagreements with socialist women in meetings of the Fujin Minshu Kurabu (Women's Democracy Club) shortly after the war (1997, 127–36).

15 See Hani (1948); Kawai (1950); Matsuoka (1952); Fujita (1954).

16 The following account of Sakanishi Shiho's life is drawn from Sakanishi Shiho-san Henshū Sewaninkai, eds. (1977). However, Kitayama Setsurō has observed a number of discrepancies between the facts presented in this text and in Sakanishi's own memoirs, *Watakushi no me* (My eyes, 1953). There is reason to believe that after the war, Sakanishi, by then a major pro-American intellectual force, may have chosen to conceal both her 1942 incarceration in a Japanese American relocation camp, as well as aspects of her collaboration with the Japanese war effort after her return to Japan later that year (see Kitayama 1997a, 23–24).

17 Transcripts of the Radio Tokyo propaganda transmissions Sakanishi made in English during the war may be available from the U.S. Foreign Broadcast Monitoring Service, Federal Communications Commission. These were published by the Japanese government's Information Bureau in 1942 for internal circulation and are available in volume 3 of the four-volume collection edited by Kitayama (1997b, 77–108). Sakanishi's abrupt oscillation between pro-Americanism and collaboration with Japanese militarism (and back again) is a fascinating topic meriting further research.

18 For an impassioned analysis of Japanese wives' "slave-like" existence, see Yamakawa (1984, 177–87).

19 In a related vein, accounts of the time frequently remark on Japanese people's encounter with the American comic "Blondie." Ōhori Sueo contrasts the condi-

tions of the Japanese woman, who "spends her days on all fours, like an animal," and Blondie: "Hers was an average American house, but it had a refrigerator that was full of food when they opened the door. The whole house was full of electric appliances, and the housewife's troubles concerned little more than washing the dishes. But what truly astonished the [Japanese] readers was Blondie's hegemony [kyōken] in the home. Authority clearly rested with the wife, and the husband's silence acquiescence to male-female equality was the punch line. No matter what issue of the paper you opened, you never saw Blondie on all fours" (1984, 297–98).

20 On new gender roles for U.S. women during World War II and immediately following, see Anderson (1981); Meyerowitz (1993); Hartmann (1982); May (1988, 1993); Milkman (1997); Evans (2000).

21 See also Ashmead (1946). These representations were paralleled in popular American fiction and film of the time, most notably in the oeuvre of James Michener, particularly the novel *Sayonara* (1953), followed by the 1957 Hollywood film of the same title. See Johnson (1988, 73–91); Simpson (1994, 255–313); Marchetti (1993, 125–75).

22 See also the remarkably similar cartoon by Endō Takeo reproduced in Dower (1999, 135).

23 Japanese fiction of the Occupation period by male authors such as Kojima Nobuo, Ōe Kenzaburō, Nosaka Akiyuki, and Yasuoka Shōtarō reinforced these images of emasculation, shame, and disorientation. See, for example, Kojima (1971). For an analysis of the gendered nature of men's and women's postwar writing, see Molasky (1999); Orbaugh (forthcoming).

24 My gratitude to Mark McLelland for drawing my attention to this important work.

25 Michael Molasky has shown that the name Mizuno Hiroshi (the putative author of *Chastity of Japan*) is a pseudonym and the text itself a work of fiction (see Molasky 1999, 123).

26 This experience is poignantly and powerfully represented in women's fiction from the Occupation, particularly after American censorship restrictions were lifted in 1952. See Hirabayashi (1977); Akagi (1955); Sono (1955); Hiroike (1974); Nakamoto (1953, 1963). For further discussion of women's writing about the Occupation, see Molasky (1999); Orbaugh (forthcoming).

27 On the Occupation comfort women, see Molasky (1999, 103–29); Duus M. (1979, 1985); Inoue S. (1995); Kobayashi and Murase (1971); Yamada M. (1992); Yoshimi (1995); Ozawa (1984); Ōshima (1979); Ienaga (1978, 236–37).

28 I thank Lynn Stephen for suggesting the class inflections of Japanese women's Occupation experience.

29 The names of the interviewees are Wakita Chizuko (first department store clerk), Taniho Fumiko (second department store clerk), Shōju Asako (first dancer), Suda Kiyomi (second dancer), Yamashita Mieko (radio announcer), Chiba Chizuko

(movie company employee), Nishida Tomi (*Shinseikatsu* journalist). The male interviewer is unnamed.

Chapter 2. Internationalism as Resistance

1   There is some recent suggestion in popular media that younger women, those in their early twenties, are returning to an interest in early marriage due to their drastically decreased job prospects in the continuing recession. Whether this trend has any impact on the rising age of average marriage remains to be seen.

2   There are abundant sources on the position of women in Japanese familial and economic institutions. A partial chronological list in English would include Cook and Hayashi (1980); McLendon (1983); Lebra (1984); Lo (1990); Lam (1992); Iwao (1993); Brinton (1993); Molony (1995); Kondo (1990); Allison (2000, 1994); G. Roberts (1994); Fujimura-Fanselow and Kameda (1995); Ogasawara (1998); Robertson (1998a); Kelsky (1999). For an entry into the voluminous Japanese literature, see Ueno (1998, 1994); Funahashi (1996); Kashima (1993); Itō (1998).

3   All names of women interviewed are pseudonyms.

4   Toyoda Masayoshi insists that such a backlash did occur in the form of the "yellow cab" controversy, in which Japanese men attempted to paint all internationally active women as sexually loose and promiscuous in their relations with foreign men. See Toyoda (1994); Kelsky (1996, 1994b).

5   See the following Internet websites (current as of June 2000) for constantly updated versions of women's internationalist discourse: "Yomiuri on-line Ōte Komachi kaigai repōto" (Yomiuri online Ōte Komachi overseas report) (http://www.yomiuri.co.jp/komachi/abroad/index.htm); "Womanjapan.com kaigai de manabō, hatarakō" (womanjapan.com let's study, work abroad) (http://www.womanjapan.com/); "Woman.excite kyariaappu kaigai ryūgaku" (Woman.excite career up study abroad) (http://woman.excite.co.jp/careerup/overseas_study).

6   For a thorough survey of the history of Japanese study abroad, see S. Mori (1994).

7   The number of women who are funded by companies to take MBAS overseas is increasing in recent years. Nevertheless, the number is still small compared to males so funded, and to females who pursue study abroad independently.

8   As in the case of *ryūgaku*, the number of female employees posted abroad by their companies is also growing. However, the number remains small in comparison to men, and to women who seek work opportunities overseas independently.

9   It is useful to turn to census data to trace some of the demographic effects of these patterns of Japanese residence abroad. Japanese Ministry of Foreign Affairs statistics show that in 1998 there were 270,059 Japanese females living or settled in the combined "Western" regions of North America, Western Europe, and Oceania (predominantly Australia and New Zealand), compared to only 224,498 males (Gaimushō 2000). By contrast, in every other region of the world, including Africa, Asia, Latin America, Eastern Europe, and the Middle East, Japanese women

(124,628) were significantly outnumbered by Japanese men (170,349). This gap has existed for the past fifteen years and is growing steadily wider. Indeed, Japanese women's presence worldwide is increasing, whereas men's is diminishing. In 1998, the total number of Japanese women residing long term or permanently abroad increased 2.3 percent, whereas the number of Japanese men actually fell by 0.5 percent (Gaimushō 2000).

10 This distinguishes Japanese women's movements from those of other transmigrant women, such as Filipina domestic maids in Hong Kong and elsewhere, who are forced to relocate abroad out of immediate financial necessity. See Constable (1999, 1997).

11 International sections of Japanese companies are another major venue for English-speaking women. Matsumura Minako, an assistant manager at a Japanese securities firm, told me she was hired to handle *aome kankei* ("blue-eyed relations"; relations with foreign firms). The *kurome kankei* ("black-eyed relations"; relations with Japanese firms) were presumably the responsibility of male workers.

12 It is difficult to find examples of internationalist autobiographical writing by men. Certainly, the genre is not unknown. For example, see Oda (1961); Fujiwara (1977); in the literary realm, Endō (1968). There is also a genre of "internationalist" criticism of Japan by male writers, including Sawada A. and Kadowaki (1990); Sugimoto Y. (1988). However, not only do these books not relate a vision of "masculinity" or gender reform to internationalization, but they do not constitute a genre of writing that compares in breadth or consistency with internationalist writing by women. They also seem to have tapered off in recent years. Of twelve popular books on study abroad that I found at local bookstores over a one-year period between 1993 and 1994, for example, only two were written by men. Whereas the ten written by women were all autobiographical and exhortatory, urging on women the personal and professional benefits of study abroad, the two books by male authors were impersonal and cautionary, focusing on the dangers of study abroad, especially for women, and discouraging Japanese parents from allowing their children to go. The titles of the two books, translated, as I jotted them down in a notebook: *This Is Right, This Is Wrong: The Study Abroad That Students Don't Want to Talk About*, and *Dangerous Study Abroad: 50 Pitfalls of Proud, Weak, and Sleazy Foreign Study*. There are abundant examples of adventure and travel books by young Japanese men about their experiences hiking in the Andes, motorcycling across North America, and exploring the African savannah, to give a few examples, but these books constitute a separate genre, in which the foreign (and it is often not the West) is a bounded and distanced location of temporary exploration/penetration. See Itasaka (1984, 1980); Toi (1983); Shimizu (1990).

13 Mark McLelland (2000) has pointed out that in recent years a parallel phenomenon has emerged in which straight Japanese women have turned to gay Japanese men as their potential allies in a critique of Japanese straight masculinity. According to McLelland, gay men have not welcomed this interest.

Chapter 3. Capital and the Fetish of the White Man

1   An exception was the "beachboys" of Bali: Indonesian men from poverty-stricken regions of Java who looked on Japanese women less as "exotic Orientals" than as economic benefactors.

2   This is not to say that there are no negative stereotypes of white men (and white people more broadly) in Japan. Russell's research has shown that women have also viewed white men as "cold," "passionless," "cunning," and "artificial" (1998, 156). On ambivalent representations of whites in Japan, see also Wagatsuma (1967). Foreigners in general are also associated with disease and contamination (see Buckley 1997b). However, in the young women's popular imaginary I am describing, the akogare-driven image of the white man as romantic object—the "prince on a white horse" (hakuba ni notta ōjisama)—prevails.

3   Similarly, when *Sapio* magazine ran a 1995 survey asking young women to rank their most and least desired lovers by nationality, Americans topped the list and Englishmen followed; Chinese, Southeast Asians, and Iranians ranked at the bottom. See "Ranking of Foreigners Called Common in Japan" (1995).

4   Young, white American men were still, in 1997, writing giddily of their unprecedented popularity in Japan. Exclaims a former paralegal for an American law firm in Tokyo, "I am nowhere near as beautiful as the man Japanese women call 'Brad-o Pitt-o,' but I am six feet five inches and blond, and in Tokyo my Nordic look was enough to win me a little extended eye contact.... The proper attire combined with my height and blondness to create a synergistic effect; I would go to clubs and come home with, at the bare minimum, a telephone number" (Thoreson 1997, 42).

5   The other danger she warns against are lesbians; she devotes a three-page chapter to the perils of the American lesbian temptress for unsuspecting Japanese women (and their parents).

6   For a discussion of changing images of Japanese women in the United States, see Kuzume (1991).

7   Interestingly, in total numbers, far more Japanese men engage in "international marriage" than Japanese women: 20,902 to 7,349 in 1997. However, broken down by spouse nationalities, the rate of Japanese female marriage to *Westerners* far outpaces that of Japanese men, and this gap grows wider by the year. Statistics on Japanese international marriage show that after World War II the number of Japanese women marrying American men (until 1992 the only "Western" classification distinguished in the data) dwarfed the number of Japanese men marrying American women: 1,592 to 64 in 1965. Since 1975, marriages to American men have steadily constituted approximately 20 percent of all female international marriages, while Japanese men's rate of marriage to American women, which represented 4.7 percent of all male international marriages in 1975, has actually fallen off precipitously to a new low in 1997 (the latest year for which data are available) of .08 percent (Kōseishō 2000c). A new breakdown available after 1992 expanding the designated foreign spouse nationalities to include Filipinos/as, Thais, English,

Brazilians, and Peruvians reveals that in 1997, almost 70 percent of Japanese male international marriages were to Filipina, Thai, and Chinese women combined, and only 1.3 percent were to American and English women. By contrast, 22 percent of Japanese female international marriages were to American and English men, and only 1.3 percent were to Chinese, Filipino, and Thai men (Kōseishō 2000c).

8 At this party a middle-aged Japanese woman with whom I had been speaking suddenly asked me, "So, did you find any good men [*sutekina otoko*] here?" "Oh no," I responded hastily. "You see, I'm married!" "Well, so am I!" she exclaimed, "but that doesn't mean you can't make 'friends,' right?" She showed me her wedding ring, which she had removed to her right hand. "They always run away when they see the ring, so I have to put it on the other hand," she told me. "But I don't see why it should make a difference."

9 It is important to distinguish between the fetishization of blonde, Marilyn Monroe images of Western female beauty, reflected in the white female models used in advertising and the objectification of white women more generally, and misgivings about actual Western females as friends, lovers, or wives.

10 *The Way of the Urban Samurai* received positive reviews from a variety of sources. A reader's review posted on the Amazon.com Web site in 1998 called the book "an amusing and accurate view of Japan by a Japanese-American."

11 For a provocative discussion of Japanese racial identifications with whiteness in the early twentieth century, see Ching (1998).

12 Girls' comics (*shōjo manga*) also depend on the figure of the blond, blue-eyed prince riding out on a white steed from his vaguely European castle to rescue the dark-haired damsel. Similar representations can be found in other media, including music videos and even theme parks. See Kelsky (forthcoming).

13 Similarly, Japanese television programs often placed Japanese men in positions of competition and hostility with the foreign world. Of the eight television programs in 1993–1994 that featured Japanese males abroad (compared to twenty-three that featured Japanese women abroad), one was a cartoon for young boys that featured a Japanese male Transformer warrior who traveled through a postnuclear holocaust world accompanied by his loyal Japanese female assistant destroying evil blond male Transformers. Another was an episode of a detective series, *Lullaby Police Detective-'91* (originally aired in 1991), in which a chief of police expressed horror at accidentally speaking English after spending some time in the company of foreigners. The long-running serial *Hotel* also made a running joke of the tensions elicited by a young hotel clerk's ongoing confrontations with a series of unreasonable and volatile foreign male guests.

Chapter 4. (Re)Flexibility in Inflexible Places

1 It is valuable to briefly compare internationalist women and adult female *kikoku-shijo* (children of Japanese expatriates) who have been raised abroad. In the rejec-

tion of akogare and embrace of the Japanese self, disillusioned internationalist women's identity resemble claims those of kikokushijo. The widespread stereotype of kikokushijo is of "half-foreign" Japanese imperfectly integrated into Japanese life and prone to flamboyant dress and behavior, and ostentatious display of foreign-language abilities, foreign mannerisms, and foreign friends. In my fieldwork, however, I found that kikokushijo were the most critical of the West and the most thoroughly identified with Japan of all the women I encountered. While kikokushijo women were willing to employ their native or near-native foreign-language ability for professional advancement, they did not join this with an identification with a liberatory West, and expressed eagerness to reintegrate themselves as seamlessly as possible into Japanese society. Suzuki Kiyoko, a twenty-two-year-old college student who had been raised primarily in Greece and the Philippines, told me, "I never thought of myself as Japanese while I lived abroad, but I rediscovered my Japaneseness in Japan. I don't want to work in a gaishikei. I want to work in a Japanese company and serve tea! And I want to have a typical marriage and be a typical housewife." Kikokushijo also objected to what they saw as the imposition of Western values and practices in Japan. One said: "Recently I find that I dislike Western priorities and logic. Westerners are too logical. The rice importation issue is a good example. It all revolves around Western logic. Japan is forced to conform to Western pressure. Why? For me, Eastern ways of thinking and doing things are the best." Similarly, some kikokushijo saw Japanese people as a nonwhite group victimized by what they saw as a global system of white racism. Matsumura Minako, who had attended high school and college in Canada, told me, "Toronto is a very closed place. The whites, especially the British, completely ignored Asians. They were just unbelievably racist. As though we were simply not part of their universe [bitter laugh]." Kikokushijo, with immediate experience of split identity at a young age and of the wrenching difficulties of multiple adjustments, refused to fetishize the West in a discourse of akogare and transnational upward mobility. Although they had extensive international experience, they were not internationalists.

2   My thanks to Lisa Yoneyama for reminding me of the varieties of feminist activism in Japan.

3   The script of the film is reproduced in Kurihara (1994).

4   Povinelli and Chauncey cite Levinas here: "It is like an animal fleeing in a straight line across the snow before the sound of the hunters, thus leaving the very traces that will lead to its death" (Levinas 1998, 3).

Conclusion: Strange Bedfellows

1   Spivak has elsewhere described this as the trope of the white man saving the brown woman from the brown man (1999, 284).

2   This summary of the plot is drawn from Ryu (1993, 5).

3   This speculation is borne out by quantities of anecdotal evidence from the Tokyo English-teaching scene; see Ma (1996, 80–83).

4   There may be a distinction necessary between transnational elites seeking inclusion in the Eurocenter and those, like the Chinese entrepreneurs described by Aihwa Ong, who appear more concerned to exploit the opportunities of the West primarily for financial gain while retaining a corporate and family base in a home country. See Ong (1999).

5   Anger over the transnational effects of the trope of "Japanese woman's victimhood" apparently motivated the work of the New York–based Japanese group ZIPANGU to produce a bilingual exposé of anti-Japanese stereotypes in the *New York Times* and American media more generally. They turn their particular ire on Japan "experts" Nicholas Kristof and Sheryl WuDunn, who, in their regular columns for the *Times*, obsessively rehearse the victimized status of Japanese women through monotonously regular features on topics such as sexual harassment, sexual assault, and so on. See ZIPANGU (1998, 74–75).

Bibliography

Abe Isō. 1910. *Fujin no risō* (The ideal woman). Tokyo: Hakubunkan.

Abu-Lughod, Lila. 1991. "Writing against Culture." In Richard Fox, ed., *Recapturing Anthropology*. 137–62. Santa Fe, NM: SAR Press.

Adams, Vincanne. 1997. "Dreams of a Final Sherpa." *American Anthropologist* 99:85–98.

Ahmad, Aijaz. 1992. *In Theory: Classes, Nations, Literatures*. London: Verso.

Akagi Keiko. 1955. "Nekusuto doa" (Next door). *Gunzō*, July:74–111.

Akimoto Shin. 1994. "Kokusai kōmuin ni naritai!" (I want to be an international public servant!) *Sankei Shimbun*, 22 February:14.

Akizawa Junko. 1995. *Ibunka ni koi shite* (Falling in love with foreign cultures). Tokyo: Kōsaidō Shuppan.

Allison, Anne. 2000 [1996]. *Permitted and Prohibited Desires: Mothers, Comics, and Censorship in Japan*. Berkeley: University of California Press.

———. 1994. *Nightwork: Sexuality, Pleasure, and Corporate Masculinity in a Tokyo Hostess Club*. Chicago: University of Chicago Press.

AMPO Japan-Asia Quarterly Review, ed. 1996. *Voices from the Japanese Women's Movement*. Armonk, NY: M. E. Sharpe.

Anderson, Karen. 1981. *Wartime Women: Sex Roles, Family Relations and the Status of Women during World War II*. Westport, CT: Greenwood Press.

Andressen, Curtis A., and Kumagai Keiichi. 1996. *Escape from Affluence*. Queensland, Australia: Centre for the Study of Australia-Asia Relations, Faculty of Asian and International Studies, Griffith University.

Appadurai, Arjun. 1996. *Modernity at Large: Cultural Dimensions of Globalization*. Minneapolis: University of Minnesota Press.

———. 1991. "Global Ethnoscapes: Notes and queries for a transnational anthropology." In Richard G. Fox, ed., *Recapturing Anthropology*. 191–210. Santa Fe, NM: New School of American Research Press.

"Are Yellow Cabs Real?" 1993. *Transpacific*, July–August:53–89.

Ariyoshi Sawako. 1977. "NOBODY ni tsuite" (About nobody). In Sakanishi Shiho-san Henshū Sewaninkai, eds., *Sakanishi Shiho-san* (Miss Sakanishi Shiho). 221–23. Tokyo: Kokusai Bunka Kaikan.

Asahi Jānaru, ed. 1984. *Onna no sengoshi I: shōwa nijūnendai* (Women's postwar history: 1945–1955). Tokyo: Asahi Shimbunsha.

Ashmead, John. 1946. "Japs Look at the Yanks." *Atlantic Monthly*, April:86–91.

Asian Women United of California, ed. 1989. *Making Waves: An Anthology of Writings by and about Asian-American Women*. Boston: Beacon Press.

Bacon, Alice Mabel. 1902 [1891]. *Japanese Girls and Women*. Boston: Houghton, Mifflin.

Bando, Mariko Sugahara. 1991 [1977]. *Japanese Women, Yesterday and Today*. About Japan Series 5. Tokyo: Foreign Press Center.

Barlow, Tani. 1991. Zhishifenzi [Chinese Intellectuals] and Power. *Dialectical Anthropology* 16:209–232.

Beard, Mary R. 1953. *The Force of Women in Japanese History*. Washington, DC: Public Affairs Press.

Befu, Harumi. 1993. "Nationalism and *Nihonjinron*." In Harumi Befu, ed., *Cultural Nationalism in East Asia: Representations and Identity*. Berkeley: Institute of East Asian Studies, University of California.

Bennett, John W., Herbert Passin, and Robert K. McKnight. 1958. *In Search of Identity: The Japanese Overseas Scholar in America and Japan*. Minneapolis: University of Minnesota Press.

Berlant, Lauren. 1996. "The Face of America and the State of Emergency." In Cary Nelson and Dilip Parameshwar Gaonkar, eds., *Disciplinarity and Dissent in Cultural Studies*. 397–440. New York: Routledge.

Bhabha, Homi. 1994. "Of Mimicry and Man: The Ambivalence of Colonial Discourse." In *The Location of Culture*. 85–92. New York: Routledge.

Blair Teruko. 1991. *Ōsutoraria ni dakarete* (Embraced by Australia). Tokyo: TV Asahi Publishing.

Boydston, Jeanne. 1991. *Home and Work: Housework, Wages and the Ideology of Labor in the Early Republic*. New York: Oxford University Press.

Brennan, Timothy. 1997. *Cosmopolitanism Today*. Cambridge, MA: Harvard University Press.

———. 1989. *Salman Rushdie and the Third World*. New York: St. Martin's Press.

Brinton, Mary C. 1993. *Women and the Economic Miracle: Gender and Work in Postwar Japan*. Berkeley: University of California Press.

Buckley, Sandra. 1997a. *Broken Silence: Voices of Japanese Feminism*. Berkeley: University of California Press.

———. 1997b. "The Foreign Devil Returns: Packaging Sexual Practice and Risk in Contemporary Japan." In Lenore Manderson and Margaret Jolly, eds. *Sites of Desire and Economic Pleasure: Sexualities in Asia and the Pacific*. 262–92. Chicago: University of Chicago Press.

Busch, Noel. 1947. "Tokyo Geisha." *Life*, 17 March:61–70.

Carby, Hazel. 1982. "White Women Listen! Black Feminism and the Boundaries of Sisterhood." In Centre for Contemporary Cultural Studies, ed., *The Empire Strikes Back*. 211–35. Birmingham, England: Centre for Contemporary Cultural Studies, University of Birmingham.

Carter, Isabel Ray. 1965. *Alien Blossom: A Japanese-Australian Love Story*. Melbourne, Australia: Lansdowne Press.

Caudill, William, and David W. Plath. 1966. "Who Sleeps by Whom? Parent-Child Involvement in Urban Japanese Families." *Psychiatry* 29: 344–66.

Chapman, Christine. 1993. "A Japanese Woman Looks East and West." *International Herald Tribune*, 12 July:20.

Ching, Leo. 1998. "Yellow Skin, White Masks: Race, Class, and Identification in Japanese Colonial Discourse." In Kuan-Hsing Chen, ed., *Trajectories: Inter-Asia Cultural Studies*. 65–86. New York: Routledge.

Chow, Claire S. 1998. *Leaving Deep Water: The Lives of Asian American Women at the Crossroads of Two Cultures*. New York: Dutton.

Chow, Rey. 1993. *Writing Diaspora: Tactics of Intervention in Contemporary Cultural Studies*. Bloomington: Indiana University Press.

Chūsonji Yutsuko. 1991. *Change Your Program: Jibunkaizōshugi* (Change your program: Self-improvement-ism). Tokyo: Magazine House.

Clifford, James. 1994. "Diasporas." *Cultural Anthropology* 9:302–38.

——. 1992. "Traveling Cultures." In Lawrence Grossberg, Cary Nelson, and Paula Treichler, eds., *Cultural Studies*. 96–112. London: Routledge.

Clifford, James, and George E. Marcus, eds. 1986. *Writing Culture: The Poetics and Politics of Ethnography*. Berkeley: University of California Press.

Constable, Nicole. 1999. "At Home but Not at Home: Filipina Narratives of Ambivalent Returns." *Cultural Anthropology* 14, no. 2:203–28.

——. 1997. *Maid to Order in Hong Kong: Stories of Filipina Workers*. Ithaca, NY: Cornell University Press.

Cook, Alice, and H. Hayashi. 1980. *Working Women in Japan: Discrimination, Resistance and Reform*. Cornell, NY: Cornell University Press.

Cornyetz, Nina. 1994. "Fetishized Blackness: Hip-Hop and Racial Desire in Contemporary Japan." *Social Text*, October:114–39.

Creighton, Millie R. 1995. "Imaging the Other in Japanese Advertising Campaigns." In James G. Carrier, ed., *Occidentalism: Images of the West*. 135–60. Oxford: Clarendon Press.

Crockett, Lucy Herndon. 1949. *Popcorn on the Ginza: An Informal Portrait of Postwar Japan*. New York: William Sloan Associates.

Daniel, E. Valentine. 1984. *Fluid Signs: Being a Person the Tamil Way*. Berkeley: University of California Press.

Day Takako. 1991. "Amerika de jiritsu o mezasu nihonjoseitachi no yume to genjitsu: hakujindansei no 'yasashisa' ga 'fugainasa' ni kawaru toki" (The dream and reality of Japanese women who seek independence in America: When white men's "kindness" turns to "unreliability"). *Kokusai kekkon o kangaeru kai nyūzurettā* (Association for international marriage newsletter) 128, 25 September:8–9 [Originally published in *Asahi Journal*, 2 August 1991:20–23].

Dearborn, Mary V. 1986. *Pocahontas's Daughters: Gender and Ethnicity in American Culture*. New York: Oxford University Press.

Deleuze, Gilles, and Félix Guattari. 1996. *Anti-Oedipus: Capitalism and Schizophrenia*. Trans. Robert Hurley, Mark Seem, and Helen R. Lane. Minneapolis: University of Minnesota Press.

Dower, John. 1999. *Embracing Defeat: Japan in the Wake of World War II*. New York: Norton.

Duus Masayo. 1985. *Makkāsā no futatsu no bōshi: Tokushu ian shisetsu RAA o meguru senryōshi no sokumen* (MacArthur's two hats: A side view of Occupation history from the perspective of the RAA and the special comfort facilities). Tokyo: Kōdansha.

——. 1979. *Haisha no okurimono: Kokusaku ianfu o meguru senryōka hishi* (Gift of the defeated: The secret Occupation history of the official comfort women). Tokyo: Kōdansha.

Duus, Peter. 1996. *The Japanese Discovery of America: A Brief History with Documents*. Boston: Bedford Books.

Dyer, Richard. 1988. "White." *Screen* 29, no. 4 (autumn):44–64.

Ebi Naomi. 1994. *Hon kon ni koi shita kyaria gāru* (Career girls who fell in love with Hong Kong). Tokyo: Sandokei Shuppankyoku.

Ebisaka, Takeshi. 1988. "Men, Women and Divorce." *Japan Echo* 15:45–47.

Ebron, Paulla, and Anna Lowenhaupt Tsing. 1995. "In Dialogue? Reading across Minority Discourses." In Ruth Behar and Deborah Gordon, eds., *Women Writing Culture*. 390–411. Berkeley: University of California Press.

Edwards, Walter. 1989. *Modern Japan through Its Weddings: Gender, Person and Society in Ritual Portrayal*. Stanford, CA: Stanford University Press.

Endō Shūsaku. 1968. *Ryūgaku* (Study abroad). Tokyo: Shinchōsha.

Errington, Frederick. 1987. "Reflexivity Deflected: The Festival of Nations as an American Cultural Performance." *American Ethnologist* 14, no. 4:654–67.

Esperitu, Yen Le. 1997. *Asian-American Women and Men: Labor, Laws, and Love*. Thousand Oaks, CA: Sage Press.

Evans, Sara. 2000. " 'Rosie the Riveter': Women and War Work during World War II." In Linda K. Kerber and Jane Sherron De Hart, eds., *Women's America: Refocusing the Past*. 5th ed. 442–47. New York: Oxford University Press.

Fanon, Frantz. 1967. *Black Skin, White Masks*. Trans. Charles Lam Markmann. New York: Grove Press.

Farman, Abou. 1992. "An Archaeology of Inter-racial Relations." *FUSE* 15, no. 3 (winter):7–11.

Forum for Citizen's Television. 1991. *Terebi ga utsushidasu "gaikoku" to nihon no kokusaika* ("Foreignness" depicted on television and Japan's internationalization). Kanagawa, Japan: Kawamura Insatsu.

Foucault, Michel. 1978. *The History of Sexuality*. Vol. 1: *An Introduction*. Trans. Robert Hurley. London: Penguin Books.

Fox, Richard G., ed. 1991. *Recapturing Anthropology*. Santa Fe, NM: New School of American Research Press.

Fox-Genovese, Elizabeth. 1982. "Placing Women's History in History." *New Left Review* 133 (May–June):5–29.

Frankenberg, Ruth. 1997a. "Introduction: Local Whiteness, Localizing Whiteness." In

Ruth Frankenberg, ed., *Displacing Whiteness: Essays in Social and Cultural Criticism*. 1–33. Durham, NC: Duke University Press.

——, ed. 1997b. *Displacing Whiteness: Essays in Social and Cultural Criticism*. Durham, NC: Duke University Press.

——. 1993. *White Women, Race Matters: The Social Construction of Whiteness*. Minneapolis: University of Minnesota Press.

Fujikawa Hiroko. 1992. *Konnichiwa eirian: Suchuwādesu ikka ni kita gaijintachi* (Hello alien: The foreigners who came to a stewardess's home). Tokyo: Shimizu Shoin.

Fujimura-Fanselow, Kumiko, and Atsuko Kameda. 1995. *Japanese Women: New Feminist Perspectives on the Past, Present, and Future*. New York: Feminist Press/City University of New York.

Fujita, Taki. 1954. *Japanese Women in the Postwar Years*. Tokyo: Nihon Taiheiyō Mondai Chōsakai.

Fujiwara Masahiko. 1977. *Wakaki sūgakusha no Amerika* (A young mathematician in America). Tokyo: Shinchōsha.

Fuke Shigeko. 1991. *Kaisha o yamete, ryūgaku shimasu* (I will quit the company and study abroad). Tokyo: Daiyamondosha.

——. 1990. *Miserarerete nyū yōku* (Beguiled by New York). Tokyo: Shinshindō.

Fukutani Sachiko. 1966. "Kimura Akebono." In Saisho Atsuko, ed., *Meiji bungaku zenshū 81: Meiji joryū bungakushū, 1* (Complete Collection of Meiji Literature 81: Meiji Women's Literature, 1). 440. Tokyo: Chikuma Shoten.

Funabashi Kuniko. 1996. *Jendā ga yattekita* (Gender has arrived). Tokyo: Mokuseisha.

Furuki Yoshiko. 1992. *Tsuda Umeko: Hito to shisō* (Tsuda Umeko: The individual and her ideas). Tokyo: Shimizu Shoin.

——. 1991. *The White Plum: A Biography of Ume Tsuda, Pioneer in the Higher Education of Japanese Women*. New York: Weatherhill.

Furuki Yoshiko et al., eds. 1991. *The Attic Letters: Ume Tsuda's Correspondence to Her American Mother*. New York: Weatherhill.

"Gaikokujin kara mita anata no otonado" (Your maturity from a foreigner's perspective). 1988. *Cosmopolitan Japan*, June:36–41.

Gaimushō (Ministry of Foreign Affairs). 2000. "Kaigai zairyū hōjinsū tōkei 1999 nendoban" (Number of Japanese residing abroad, fiscal 1999 statistical data). Gaimushō tōkei jōhō (Ministry of Foreign Affairs statistical information). Http://www.mofa.go.jp/mofaj/toko/tokei/hojin99/index.html.

Glick-Schiller, Nina, Linda Basch, and Christina Szanton Blanc. 1995. "From Immigrant to Transmigrant: Theorizing Transnational Migration." *Anthropological Quarterly* 68, no. 1:48–63.

Godzich, Wlad. 1993. Foreword. In Doris-Louise Haineault and Jean-Yves Roy, eds., *Unconscious for Sale: Advertising, Psychoanalysis, and the Public*. Trans. Kimball Lockhart with Barbara Kerslake. ix–xix. Minneapolis: University of Minnesota Press.

Goodman, David. 1990. *Japan's "International Youth": The Emergence of a New Class of Schoolchildren*. Oxford: Clarendon Press.

263 ≈ Bibliography

Gotō, Kayoko. 1994. *New York Career Scene.* Tokyo: Magazine House.

Gotō Tsutomu. 1965. *Anata no shiranai toki ni: Sengo zankoku monogatari* (A time you didn't know about: Postwar tales of cruelty). Tokyo: Daiwa Shobō.

———. 1953. *Zoku nihon no teisō* (Chastity of Japan continued). Tokyo: Sōjūsha.

Grewal, Inderpal, and Caren Kaplan. 1994. "Introduction: Transnational Feminist Practices and Questions of Postmodernity." In Inderpal Grewal and Caren Kaplan, eds., *Scattered Hegemonies: Postmodernity and Transnational Feminist Practices.* 1–33. Minneapolis: University of Minnesota Press.

———, eds. 1994. *Scattered Hegemonies: Postmodernity and Transnational Feminist Practices.* Minneapolis: University of Minnesota Press.

Gupta, Akhil, and James Ferguson. 1997a. "Beyond 'Culture': Space, Identity, and the Politics of Difference." In Akhil Gupta and James Ferguson, eds., *Culture, Power, Place: Explorations in Critical Anthropology.* 33–52. Durham, NC: Duke University Press.

———. 1997b. "Discipline and Practice: 'The Field' as Site, Method, and Location in Anthropology." In Akhil Gupta and James Ferguson, eds., *Anthropological Locations: Boundaries and Grounds of a Field Science.* 1–46. Berkeley: University of California Press.

———, eds. 1997a. *Culture, Power, Place: Explorations in Critical Anthropology.* Durham, NC: Duke University Press.

———. 1997b. *Anthropological Locations: Boundaries and Grounds of a Field Science.* Berkeley: University of California Press.

"Haisenka no seikatsu" (Daily life in defeat). 1984 [1945]. *Shinseikatsu.* Reprinted in *Dokyumento shōwa nijūnen hachigatsu jūgonichi: senryōka no nihonjin, zōhoban* (Document 15 August 1945: Japanese under the Occupation, expanded edition). 220–34. Tokyo: Sōshisha.

Hall, Stuart. 1994. "Cultural Identity and Diaspora." In Francis Barker, Peter Hulme, and Margaret Iverson, eds., *Colonial Discourse, Postcolonial Theory.* 392–403. Manchester, England: Manchester University Press.

———. 1993. "Culture, Community, Nation." *Cultural Studies* 7, no. 2:349–63.

Hamada Keiko. 1999. "Amerika de hataraku: jitsuryoku shakai o ikiru nihonjin josei" (Working in America: Japanese women who live in the merit-based society). *AERA,* 29 November; http://www.asahi.com/paper/aic/Mon/d_aera/19991122.html.

Hanawa, Yukiko. 1996. "Inciting Sites of Political Interventions: Queer n' Asian." *Positions* 4, no. 3:459–90.

Hani, Setsuko. 1948. *The Japanese Family System: As Seen from the Standpoint of Japanese Women.* Tokyo: Nihon Taiheiyō Mondai Chōsakai.

Hannerz, Ulf. 1996. "Cosmopolitans and Locals in World Culture." In *Transnational Connections.* 102–11. London: Routledge.

Harada Tōichirō. 1912. *Nyūyōku* (New York). Tokyo: Seikyōsha.

Hartmann, Susan M. 1982. *The Home Front and Beyond: American Women in the 1940s.* Boston: Twayne Publishers.

Harton, Ron. 1989. "Gaijin zuki nihon gyaru no seikōdo" (The sex lives of Japanese girls who like gaijins). Trans. Yasuda Yōko. *Fujin Kōron*, 20 September:178–88.

Harvey, David. 1989. *The Condition of Postmodernity.* Cambridge, MA: Blackwell.

Hasegawa Katsuyuki. 1991. *Karuchā shokku saizensen: Nihonjin no shiranai nihon no sugao* (On the frontlines of culture shock: The true Japan the Japanese don't know about). Tokyo: Cosmo Books.

Hasegawa Shigure. 1918. *Bijinden* (Biographies of beautiful women). Tokyo: Tōkyōsha.

"Hataraku josei kaigai shinshutsu: jitsuryoku shakai ni akogare" (Working women's overseas advance: Longing for merit-based societies). 1993. *Nihon Keizai Shimbun*, 17 December:15.

"Hawai nihon ryūgakusei no ygōka naru benkyōburi" (Japanese students' extravagant "pretend study" in Hawai'i). 1989. *Shūkan Gendai*, August:150–52.

Hayami Yukiko. 1993. "Kyaria josei wa gaishikei mezasu" (Career women aim for foreign affiliates). *AERA*, 7 September:60–63.

"Heroine: nihon no josei wa tsuyoi nē" (Heroine: Japanese women are strong, aren't they?). 1993. *FOCUS*, 17 September:8.

Higuchi Keiko. 1976. "Kazoku seido no kaikaku" (The reform of the family system). In Ienaga Saburō, ed., *Senryō to saisei: Shōwa no sengoshi, dai-1 kan* (Occupation and rebirth: Postwar Showa history, part I). 97–111. Tokyo: Jakubunsha.

Hirabayashi Taiko. 1977 [1952]. "Hokkaidō Chitose no onna" (Women of Chitose, Hokkaido). In *Hirabayashi Taiko zenshū 5* (Collected works of Hirabayashi Taiko). 427–36. Tokyo: Ushio Shuppansha.

Hirano, Kyoko. 1992. *Mr. Smith Goes to Tokyo: Japanese Cinema under the American Occupation, 1945–1952.* Washington, DC: Smithsonian Institution Press.

Hiroike Akiko. 1974 [1953]. "Onriitachi" (The steady girls). In Joryū Bungakusha Kai, eds., *Gendai no joryū bungaku I* (Contemporary women writers I). 193–212. Tokyo: Mainichi Shimbunsha.

Hisada Megumi. 1993. "Kanojo no baai: jōba ni eigo ni biseinen, igirisuteki naru mono, tokoton aishiteru" (In her case: Horseback riding, English, beautiful young men, and everything English, she loves it all). *Nikkei Woman*, September:130.

"H.K. Job Seminars Lure Women." 1994. *Daily Yomiuri*, 20 May:3.

Hoberecht, Earnest. 1947. *Tokyo Romance.* New York: Didier Publishers.

"Honkon mezasu kyaria josei" (Career women aiming for Hong Kong). 1994. *Asahi Shimbun*, 24 January:17.

hooks, bell. 1997. "Representing Whiteness in the Black Imagination." In Ruth Frankenberg, ed., *Displacing Whiteness: Essays in Social and Cultural Criticism.* 165–79. Durham, NC: Duke University Press.

———. 1992. "Eating the Other." In *Black Looks: Race and Representation.* 21–40. Boston: South End Press.

Hoshino, Ai. 1929. "The Education of Women." In Nitobe Inazo, ed., *Western Influences in Modern Japan*, Part 2. 1–19. Tokyo: Japanese Council, Institute of Pacific Relations.

Hoyano Hatsuko. 1991. "AERA ripōto, tenshoku: sukauto ni nerawareru gaishikei no onnatachi (AERA report, changing jobs: Foreign affiliate women targeted by scouts). *AERA*, 6 August:65.

Huddleston, Jackson. 1990. *Gaijin Kaisha: Running a foreign business in Japan.* Armonk, NY: M. E. Sharpe.

Ichikawa Fusae. 1979. "Watakushi no fujin undō: Senzen kara sengo e" (My women's movement: From before the war to after). Interview by Inamaru Giichi. In Kodama Katsuko and Itō Yasuko, eds., *Kindai nihonshi e no shōgen* (Introduction to modern Japanese history). 49–110. Tokyo: Domesu.

——. 1976. "Fujin sanseiken (Women's suffrage)." In Ienaga Saburō, ed., *Senryō to Saisei: Shōwa no sengoshi, dai-1 kan* (Occupation and rebirth: Postwar Showa history, part 1). 83–96. Tokyo: Jakubunsha.

ICS (Center for International Cultural Studies and Education). 1998. *ICS ryūgaku hakusho* (ICS study abroad white paper). Tokyo: ICS Kokusai Bunka Kyōiku Center.

Ieda Shōko. 1991a. *Ierō kyabu: Narita o tobitatta onnatachi* (Yellow cabs: The women who took off from Narita airport). Tokyo: Kōyū Shuppan.

——. 1991b [1985]. *Ore no hada ni muragatta onnatachi* (The women who flocked to my skin). Tokyo: Shōdensha.

Ienaga, Saburō. 1978. *The Pacific War: World War II and the Japanese, 1931–1945.* New York: Random House.

Igarashi Yoshikuni. 1998. "The Bomb, Hirohito, and History: The Foundational Narrative of United States–Japan Postwar Relations." *Positions* 6, no. 2:261–302.

Igata Keiko. 1993. *Itsuka igirisu ni kurasu watashi* (Someday I shall live in England). Tokyo: Furōraru Shuppan.

Iizuka Makiko. 1993. *Kyabu ni mo norenai otokotachi* (The guys who can't even hitch a ride on a cab). Tokyo: Harashobō.

Inage Noriko. 1989. *Watashi no Amerika taizaiki* (Diary of my stay in America). Tokyo: Kōgakusha.

Inamasu Tatsuo. 1993. " 'Shōshi shakai' no kīman toshite no dankai junia" (Baby-boomers junior as the key to "low birth rate society"). *Nikkei Image Climate Forecast*, January:4–7.

Inoue Kiyoshi. 1967. *Shinpan nihon joseishi* (Japanese women's history, new ed.). Tokyo: San'ichi Shobō.

Inoue Setsuko. 1995. *Senryōgun ianjo: Kokka ni yoru baishun shisetsu* (Occupation comfort stations: State-established prostitution facilities). Tokyo: Shinhyōron.

Inoue Teruko. 1994. *Nihon no feminizumu/Feminism in Japan* (Japanese feminism/feminism in Japan). 6 vols. Tokyo: Iwanami Shoten.

Ishida Yōko, ed. 1997. *Marugoto onna no tenki* (Complete woman's turning point). Tokyo: Asupekuto.

Ishigaki, Ayako [Matsui, Haru]. 1940. *Restless Wave: An Autobiography.* New York: Modern Age Books.

Ishikawa Sachiko. 1992. *Kokusai kekkon* (International marriage). Tokyo: Simul Press.

Ishimoto Shizue. 1984 [1935]. *Facing Two Ways: The Story of My Life.* Stanford, CA: Stanford University Press.

Itasaka Gen. 1984. *Itasaka Gen no amerikan rūru* (Itasaka Gen's American rules). Tokyo: Daiyamondosha.

———. 1980. *Harukanaru rinkaku: Amerika* (Distant neighbor: America). Tokyo: Kōdansha.

Itō Yasuko. 1998. *Tatakau josei no nijusseiki* (Women's fight in the twentieth century). Tokyo: Yoshikawa Kōbunkan.

———. 1990. "Haisenzengo ni okeru seikatsu ishiki no hen'yō" (Changes in women's daily life perspectives before and after the defeat). In Joseishi Sōgō Kenkyūkai, ed., *Nihon josei seikatsushi 5: Gendai.* (Japanese women's daily life history. Vol. 5: The contemporary era). 1–34. Tokyo: Tokyo Daigaku Shuppan kai.

———. 1987. "Sengo kaikaku to josei kaihō" (Postwar reforms and women's liberation). In Wakita Haruko, Hayashi Reiko, and Nagahara Kazuko, eds., *Nihon joseishi* (Japanese women's history). 274–77. Tokyo: Yoshikawa Kōbunkan.

———. 1974. *Sengo nihon joseishi* (Postwar Japanese women's history). Tokyo: Ōtsuki Shoten.

Ivy, Marilyn. 1995. *Discourses of the Vanishing: Modernity, Phantasm, Japan.* Chicago: University of Chicago Press.

Iwao, Sumiko. 1993. *The Japanese Woman: Traditional Image and Changing Reality.* New York: Free Press.

Iyer, Pico. 1991. *The Lady and the Monk: Four Seasons in Kyoto.* New York: Knopf.

JAC Shingapōru and Parutī, eds. 1998. *Kyaria in shingapōru* (Career in Singapore). Tokyo: JAC.

"Japanese Best Seller." 1947. *Life,* April 7:107–10.

John, Mary. 1996. *Discrepant Dislocations: Feminism, Theory, and Postcolonial Histories.* Berkeley: University of California Press.

Johnson, Sheila K. 1988. *The Japanese through American Eyes.* Stanford, CA: Stanford University Press.

Joseishi Sōgō Kenkyūkai, ed. 1990. *Nihon josei seikatsushi 5: Gendai* (History of Japanese women's daily life. Vol. 5: The contemporary era). Tokyo: Tokyo Daigaku Shuppan kai.

Kabbani, Rana. 1986. *Europe's Myths of Orient: Devise and Rule.* London: Macmillan.

"Kaigai kyōryoku no dantai ni ninki" (Popularity of overseas cooperative agencies). 1993. *Asahi Shimbun,* 28 May:3.

Kajiwara Hazuki. 1991. "Kōron shuron: hitomae de no kisu (Debate: kissing in public). *AERA,* 6 August:58.

Kanzaki Kiyoshi. 1953. *Bungaku kyōshitsu* (Literature course). Tokyo: Tōyō Shokan.

Kashima Takashi. 1993 [1989]. *Otoko to onna, kawaru rikigaku: katei, kigyō, shakai.* (Men and women, changing power: Family, company, society). Tokyo: Iwanami Shoten.

Kasumi. 1992. *The Way of the Urban Samurai: The Japanese Male Exposed.* Rutland, VT: Tuttle.

Katō Kyōko. 1985. *Konna Amerika o shittemasuka?* (Do you know this side of America?). Tokyo: Chūkō Bunkō.

Katō Kyōko, and Michael Berger. 1990. *Nihonjin o shiranai amerikajin, amerikajin o shiranai nihonjin* (The Americans who don't know the Japanese, and the Japanese who don't know the Americans). Tokyo: TBS Britannica.

Katō Mikio. 1984. "Kaigai ryūgaku" (Overseas study). In Asahi Jānaru, ed., *Onna no sengoshi I: Shōwa nijūnendai* (Women's postwar history 1: 1945–1955). 276–83. Tokyo: Asahi Shimbunsha.

Katō Shizue. 1997. *Katō Shizue: Aru josei seijika no hansei* (Katō Shizue: Life of a woman politician). Tokyo: Nihon Tosho Sentā.

——. 1977. "Josei daigishi tanjō" (Birth of the woman representative). In Tsubota Itsuo, ed., *Senryōka no jidai: Shōwa nihonshi 9* (The Occupation Era: Japan's Showa history 9). 103. Tokyo: Akatsuki Kyōiku Tosho Kabushikigaisha.

—— [Ishimoto Shizue]. 1984 [1935]. *Facing Two Ways: The Story of My Life.* Stanford, CA: Stanford University Press.

Kawachi, Kazuko. 1994. "Female Students Fight Uphill Battle for Jobs." *Daily Yomiuri,* 1 August:6.

Kawai, Michi. 1950. *Sliding Doors.* Tokyo: Keisen Jogaku En.

——. 1939. *My Lantern.* Tokyo: Kyo Bun Kwan (Kyōbunkan).

Kawataki Kaori. 1993. *Kokusai renai zukan* (Pictures of international marriage). Tokyo: Kōsaidō.

——. 1992. *Kokusai kekkon monogatari* (Tales of international marriage). Tokyo: Kōsaidō.

Kelley, Frank, and Cornelius Ryan. 1947. *Star-Spangled Mikado.* New York: Robert M. McBride.

Kelsky, Karen. Forthcoming. "Theme Park Japan and the Colonial Subject/Object." In Tamar Gordon, ed., *Theme Parks and Cultural Centers: Logics, Economies, and Identities.* Durham, NC: Duke University Press.

——. 1999. "Gender, Modernity, and Eroticized Internationalism in Japan." *Cultural Anthropology* 14, no. 2 (May):229–55.

——. 1996. "Flirting with the Foreign: Interracial Sex in Japan's 'International' Age." In Rob Wilson and Wimal Dissanayake, eds., *Global/Local: Cultural Production in the Transnational Imaginary.* Durham, NC: Duke University Press.

——. 1994a. "Intimate Ideologies: Transnational Theory and Japan's 'Yellow cabs.' " *Public Culture* 6, no. 3 (spring):465–78.

——. 1994b. "Postcards from the Edge: The 'Office Ladies' of Tokyo." *U.S.-Japan Women's Journal English Supplement* 6:3–26.

Kida, Megumi. 1994. "From Here On I Want to Value Heart-to-Heart Communication." *Hiragana Times* 95 (September):46.

Kida Midori. 1998. *Joseitachi yo! Amerika e itte dō suru no?* (Women! What do you want from America?) Tokyo: PHP Kenkyūjo.

Kimura, Akebono. 1988a. "A Mirror of Womanhood, Part 1." Trans. Margaret Mitsutani. *The Magazine* (Publicity magazine for Esso Oil Co., Japan) 3, no. 5:50–55.

——. 1988b. "A Mirror of Womanhood, Part 2." Trans. Margaret Mitsutani. *The Magazine* (Publicity magazine for Esso Oil Co., Japan) 3, no. 6:51–54.

———. 1996 [1889]. *Fujo no kagami* (Mirror of womanhood). In Saisho Atsuko, ed., *Meiji bungaku zenshū 81: Meiji joryū bungakushū*, Vol. 1. 200–245. Tokyo: Chikuma Shobō.

———. 1896. *Fujo no kagami* (Mirror of womanhood). Tokyo: Okamoto Masa.

Kimura Sōta. 1950. *Ma no utage* (The magic banquet). Tokyo: Asahi Shimbunsha.

Kirishima Yōko. 1990. *Rinjūki nōto: jinsei no aki o ikiru* (Deathbed notes: Living the autumn of life). Tokyo: Sekai Bunkasha.

———. 1987. *Anata nimo kono shiokaze o, ki no nioi o* (You too will feel this ocean breeze and smell the trees). Tokyo: Bungei Shunjū.

———. 1982. *Onna ga habataku toki: ai, jiyū, tabi no nōto* (When a woman spreads her wings: Notes on love, freedom, and travel). Tokyo: Kadokawa Shoten.

———. 1975 [1971]. *Sabishii amerikanjin* (The lonely American). Tokyo: Bungei Shunjū.

Kiriyama Hideki. 1994. *Nihonjin kaizō kōza: Zainichi gaikokujin ga honne de kataru* (Lessons on reforming the Japanese: Foreigners in Japan speak from the heart). Tokyo: Tōyō Keizai Shimbunsha.

Kitayama Setsurō, ed. 1997a. *Taiheiyō sensō hōsō senden shiryō, dai-1-kan: Bugaihi: "kaigaihōsō kōenshū," dainigo* (Radio propaganda materials from the Pacific War. Vol. 1: Restricted: "Overseas radio transmissions," collection 2). Tokyo: Ryokuin Shobō.

———. 1997b. *Taiheiyō sensō hōsō senden shiryō, dai-3-kan: Bugaihi: "kaigaihōsō kōenshū," daiyongo* (Radio propaganda materials from the Pacific War. Vol. 3: Restricted: "Overseas radio transmissions," collection 4). Tokyo: Ryokuin Shobō.

Kiyooka, Eiichi, ed. 1988. *Fukuzawa Yukichi on Japanese Women: Selected Works*. Tokyo: University of Tokyo Press.

Kobayashi Daijiro and Murase Akira. 1971. *Kokka baishun meirei monogatari* (The story of state-ordered prostitution). Tokyo: Yūzankaku.

Koike Jun'ichi. 1990. "Nyū yōku itte toku shitai: Amerika eijūken wa kōshite tsukame!" (I want to take advantage of New York: Here's how to get hold of an American green card). *Weekly Themis*, 24 January:24–27.

Kojima Nobuo. 1971 [1954]. "Amerikan sukūru" (The American school). In *Kojima Nobuo zenshū 4*. 218–44. Tokyo: Kōdansha.

Kokuni Aiko. 1990. *Anata no shiranai rondon* (The London you don't know). Tokyo: Meisō Shuppan.

Kondo, Dorinne. 1997. *About Face: Performing Race in Fashion and Theater*. New York: Routledge.

———. 1990. *Crafting Selves: Power, Gender and Discourses of Identity in a Japanese Workplace*. Chicago: University of Chicago Press.

Kōseishō (Ministry of Health and Welfare). 2000a. "Gōkei tokushu shusseiritsu no nenjisuii" (Combined average birthrates, yearly trends). *Kōseishō tōkei jōhō* (Ministry of Health and Welfare statistical information). Http://www.mhw.go.jp/toukei/index.html.

———. 2000b. "Fūfu no heikin kon'innenrei no nenjisuii" (Average married couples' age of marriage, yearly trends). *Kōseishō tōkei jōhō* (Ministry of Health and Welfare statistical information). Http://www.mhw.go.jp/toukei/index.html.

———. 2000c. "Fūfu no kokusekibetsu in mita kon'inkensū no nenjisuii" (Number of marriages based on nationality of spouses, yearly trends). Kōseishō tōkei jōhō (Ministry of Health and Welfare statistical information). Http://www.mhw.go.jp/toukei/index.html.

Kosugi Shunya. 1998. *Nijūkyūsai wa kyaria no tenki* (29 is the turning point for careers). Tokyo: Daiyamondosha.

Kudo Akiko. 1990. "Gaijin no otoko denakereba sekkusu dekinai onna" (The women who can have sex only with foreigners). *Fujin Kōron*, 20 June:408–11.

Kurata Yasuo. 1953. *Meoto ryūgaku: Amerika tsūshin* (Husband-wife study abroad: Report from America). Tokyo: Rokko Shuppansha.

Kurihara Nanako. 1994. *Nyū yōku jibun sagashi monogatari: Okotteru onna wa utsukushii!* (Finding myself in New York: Angry women are beautiful!) Tokyo: WAVE Shuppan.

———. 1993. *Rukkingu foa Fumiko* (Looking for Fumiko; English title: *Ripples of Change*). Videocassette, 57 min., color, 1/2 inch. New York: Women Make Movies.

Kuzume Yoshi. 1991. "Images of Japanese Women in U.S. Writings and Scholarly Works, 1860–1990: Formation and Transformation of Stereotypes." *U.S.-Japan Women's Journal* (English Supplement) 1 (August):6–50.

LaCerda, John. 1946. *The Conqueror Comes to Tea: Japan under MacArthur*. New Brunswick, NJ: Rutgers University Press.

Lachman, Alice Wahl. 1998. "Beyond the Gate: The U.S. Graduate Education and Reentry Experiences of Japanese Women." Ph.D. diss., University of Oregon.

Lam, Alice. 1992. *Women and Japanese Management: Discrimination and Reform*. New York: Routledge.

Lavie, Smadar, and Ted Swedenberg. 1996. "Introduction: Displacement, Diaspora, and Geographies of Identity." In Smadar Lavie and Ted Swedenberg, eds., *Displacement, Diaspora, and Geographies of Identity*. 1–26. Durham, NC: Duke University Press.

Lebra, Takie. 1984. *Japanese Women: Constraint and Fulfillment*. Honolulu: University of Hawai'i Press.

Lerner, Gerda. 1979. *The Majority Finds Its Past: Placing Women in History*. New York: Oxford University Press.

Leupp, Gary P. 1993. "Nichiōkan no kokusaikekkon to konketsu 1543–1868: sengoku-kinsei ni okeru minzoku ishiki, sei, kaikyū" (Japanese-European marriage and race mixing 1543–1868: Ethnic consciousness, sex, and class in the Sengoku and early modern periods). Paper presented at the Historical and Contemporary Constructions of Gender Conference, Osaka, Japan, 1 August.

Levinas, Emmanuel. 1998. "Is Ontology Fundamental?" In *Entre Nous: On Thinking-of-the-Other*. Trans. Michael B. Smith and Barbara Harshav. 1–24. New York: Columbia University Press.

Lo, Jeannie. 1990. *Office Ladies and Factory Women: Life and Work at a Japanese Company*. Armonk, NY: M. E. Sharpe.

Loti, Pierre. 1916 [1888]. *Japan: Madame Chrysanthème*. Trans. Laura Ensor. New York: J. Pott.

Lye, Colleen. 1995. "*M. Butterfly* and the Rhetoric of Antiessentialism: Minority Discourse in an International Frame." In David Palumbo-Liu, ed., *The Ethnic Canon: Histories, Institutions, and Interventions*. 260–89. Minneapolis: University of Minnesota Press.

Lystra, Karen. 1989. *Searching the Heart: Women, Men, and Romantic Love in Nineteenth Century America*. New York: Oxford University Press.

Ma, Karen. 1996. *The Modern Madame Butterfly: Fantasy and Reality in Japanese Cross-Cultural Relationships*. Tokyo: Charles E. Tuttle.

Makino [Markino] Yoshio. 1912a. *My Idealed [sic] John Bullesses*. Toronto: Musson Book Co.

———. 1912b. *When I Was a Child*. Boston: Houghton, Mifflin.

Malkki, Liisa. 1997. "News and Culture: Transitory Phenomena and the Fieldwork Tradition." In Akhil Gupta and James Ferguson, eds., *Anthropological Locations: Boundaries and Grounds of a Field Science*. 86–101. Berkeley: University of California Press.

———. 1994. "Citizens of Humanity: Internationalism and the Imagined Community of Nations." *Diaspora* 3, no. 1:41–68.

Mani, Lata. 1989. "Multiple Mediations: Feminist Scholarship in the Age of Multinational Reception." *Inscriptions* 5 (*Traveling Theories, Traveling Theorists*): 1–23.

Maraini, Fosco. 1959. *Meeting with Japan*. New York: Viking.

Marchetti, Gina. 1993. *Romance and the "Yellow Peril": Race, Sex, and Discursive Strategies in Hollywood Fiction*. Berkeley: University of California Press.

Marcus, George. 1995. "Ethnography in/of the World System: The Emergence of Multi-Sited Ethnography." *Annual Review of Anthropology* 24:95–117.

Marks Toshiko. 1999. *Tondemonai hahaoya to nasakenai otoko no kuni nippon* (Japan, country of ridiculous mothers and pathetic men). Tokyo: Sōshisha.

———. 1993. *Yutori no kuni igirisu to narikin no kuni nippon* (England the rich, Japan the nouveau riche). Tokyo: Sōshisha.

———. 1992. *Otona no kuni igirisu to kodomo no kuni nippon* (England, country of adults; Japan, country of children). Tokyo: Sōshisha.

———. 1986. *Eikoku kizoku ni natta watakushi* (I became a British aristocrat). Tokyo: Sōshisha.

Masaoka Yūichi. 1913. *Beikoku oyobi beikokujin* (America and Americans). Tokyo: Niyōsha.

Massey, Doreen. 1994. *Space, Place, and Gender*. Minneapolis: University of Minnesota Press.

Matsubara Junko. 1989. *Eigo dekimasu* (I can speak English). Tokyo: Bungei Shunjū.

———. 1988. *Kurowassan shōkōgun* (The croissant syndrome). Tokyo: Bungei Shunjū.

Matsui, Machiko. 1995. "Gender Role Perceptions of Japanese and Chinese Female Students in American Universities." *Comparative Education Review* 39, no. 3:356–78.

———. 1994. "Nihonjosei no beikoku ryūgaku taiken: Seibetsu yakuwari bunka kara no bōmei" (Exiles from a sexist culture: Japanese female students' experiences in the United States). *Joseigaku nenpō* (Annual report of the women's studies society) 15: 128–39.

Matsui, Yayori. 1989. *Women's Asia*. London: Zed.

Matsuoka, Yōko. 1952. *Daughter of the Pacific*. New York: Harper.

May, Elaine Tyler. 1993. "Rosie the Riveter Gets Married." *Mid-America* 75, no. 3:269–82.

———. 1988. *Homeward Bound: American Families in the Cold War Era*. New York: Basic Books.

McKnight, Robert, and John W. Bennett. 1956. "Liberation or Alienation: The Japanese Woman Student in America." *International Institute of Education News Bulletin* 31: 38–53.

McLelland, Mark. 2000. *Male Homosexuality in Modern Japan: Cultural Myths and Social Realities*. Richmond, England: Curzon.

McLendon, James. 1983. "The Office: Way Station or Blind Alley?" In David Plath, ed., *Work and Lifecourse in Japan*. 156–82. Albany: State University of New York Press.

Mears, Helen. 1948. *Mirror for Americans: Japan*. Boston: Houghton Mifflin.

Meyerowitz, Joanne. 1993. "Beyond the Feminine Mystique: A Reassessment of Postwar Mass Culture, 1946–1958." *Journal of American History* 79, no. 4: 1455–482.

Michener, James. 1953. *Sayonara*. New York: Fawcett Crest.

Milkman, Ruth. 1997. *Gender at Work: The Dynamics of Job Segregation by Sex during WWII*. Urbana: University of Illinois Press.

Milne, Lisa. 1994. "The Manic Art of Kusama: Japan's Most Celebrated Outsider Not Slowing Down." *Daily Yomiuri*, 20 May:11.

Mishima Sumie. 1953. *The Broader Way: A Woman's Life in the New Japan*. Westport, CT: Greenwood.

———. 1941. *My Narrow Isle: The Story of a Modern Woman in Japan*. New York: John Day.

Mishima, Yukio. 1977. *The Way of the Samurai: Yukio Mishima on Hagakure in Modern Life*. Trans. Kathryn Sparling. New York: Basic Books.

Miyakawa, Masuji. 1910. *Life of Japan*. New York: Neale Publishing.

Miyamoto Michiko. 1988. *Amerika no koibito* (American lover). Tokyo: Sōonsha.

———. 1985. *Watashi wa eigo ga daisuki datta* (I always loved English). Tokyo: Bungei Shunjū.

Miyauchi Sai. 1993. "Kyō o irodotta gokusaishiki no yūbe" (A brilliant evening that showed off the colors of Kyoto). *Le Coeur* (November):273.

Miyazaki Chieko. 1997. "Hansamuna gaikokujin dansei wa hontōni 'risō no dārin' ka?" (Is a handsome foreign man really your "ideal sweetheart"?). In Ishida Yōko, ed., *Marugoto onna no tenki: Itsukara demo yarinaosō* (The complete women's turning point: It's never too late to get your life in order). 134–45. Tokyo: Asupekuto.

Miyoshi, Masao. 1991. *Off Center: Power and Cultural Relations between Japan and the United States*. Cambridge, MA: Harvard University Press.

———. 1979. *As We Saw Them: The First Japanese Embassy to the United States (1860)*. Berkeley: University of California Press.

———. 1974. *Accomplices of Silence: The Modern Japanese Novel*. Berkeley: University of California Press.

Mizuno Hiroshi. 1953. *Nihon no Teisō: Gaikokuhei ni okasareta joseitachi no shuki* (Chastity of Japan: The memoirs of women raped by foreign soldiers). Tokyo: Sojūsha.

Mizuta Noriko. 1993. "Ikokujin toshite no josei" (Woman as foreigner). *Josei Jōhō,* May:31 [Originally published in *Yomiuri Shimbun,* 5 April 1993].

Moeran, Brian. 1996. *A Japanese Advertising Agency: An Anthropology of Media and Markets.* Honolulu. University of Hawai'i Press.

Mohanty, Chandra. 1988. "Under Western Eyes: Feminist Scholarship and Colonial Discourses." *Feminist Review* 30:61–88.

Molasky, Michael. 1999. *The American Occupation of Japan and Okinawa: Literature and Memory.* London: Routledge.

Molony, Barbara. 1995. "The Employment Law in Japan." *Signs* (winter): 268–302.

Mori, Kyoko. 1997. *Polite Lies: On Being a Woman Caught between Cultures.* New York: Henry Holt.

Mori, Shunta. 1994. "The Social Problems of Students Returning to Japan from Sojourns Overseas: A Social Constructionist Study." Ph.D. diss., University of California at Santa Cruz.

Mori Yōko. 1988. *Famirī repōto* (Family report). Tokyo: Shinchō Bunko.

Murota Yasuko. 1987. "Kanaami ni karamitsuita kanashii yokubō" (Sad desires entangled in wire fences). *Asahi Jānaru,* 13 November:5–9.

Nagamine Konomi. 1999. " 'Chikyū no dokodemo shigotoba': Kokusai kōmuin" (A job anywhere in the world: International public servants). *Yomiuri Shimbun,* 14 November; http://www.yomiuri.co.jp/komachi/news/index.htm.

Nakajima Arika. 1994. "Shakai kōken, beikokuryū de shinpū" (American style brings new life to social contribution). *Nihon Keizai Shimbun,* 13 July:40.

Nakajima Midori. 1996. *Onna wa wakai hō ga ii?!* (A woman must be young?!). Tokyo: Ariadone Kikaku.

Nakamoto Takako. 1963. "The Only One" (trans. of "Kichi no onna"). In Jay Gluck, ed., *Ukiyo: Stories of the "Floating World" of Postwar Japan.* 159–73. New York: Vanguard.

——. 1953. "Kichi no onna" (Women of a base town). *Gunzō,* July: 102–27.

Nakane, Chie. 1973 [1970]. *Japanese Society.* Rutland, VT: Tuttle.

Nakaya Tetsuya. 1994. "Kokusai kōryū pātī hanazakari" (International exchange parties are in full bloom). *Hiragana Times* 97 (November): 6–12.

Nandy, Ashis. 1983. *The Intimate Enemy: The Loss and Recovery of Self under Colonialism.* New Delhi: Oxford University Press.

Narayan, Kirin. 1993. "How Native Is a Native Anthropologist?" *American Anthropologist* 95, no. 3:671–87.

"Naze motenai, nihonjin dansei?" (Why are Japanese men so unpopular?). 1994. *Hiragana Times* 98 (December):6–11.

NET Terebi, ed. 1965. *Hachigatsu jūgonichi to watakushi* (August 15 and me). Tokyo: Shakai Onsōsha.

NHK Shuzaihan. 1990. *Kyaria appu: nyū yōku ni kakeru onnatachi* (Career up: Women who bet on New York). Tokyo: Nihon Hōdō Shuppan Kyōkai.

Nihon Keizai Shimbunsha, eds. 1998. *Onnatachi no shizukana kakumei: "Ko" no jidai ga hajimaru* (Women's quiet revolution: The dawn of the individualist era). Tokyo: Nihon Keizai Shimbunsha.

Noda Kaori. 1992. *Nyū yōku kara no saiyō tsūchi: sugao no wākingu uōman sutōrī* (Employment report from New York: The real working woman's story). Tokyo: Daiyamondosha.

Noguchi, Yone. 1914. *The Story of Yone Noguchi, Told by Himself.* London: Chatto and Windus.

Nonaka Hiiragi. 1993 [1992]. *Chokoretto ogazumu* (Chocolate orgasm). Tokyo: Fukutake Shoten.

Nonini, Donald M. 1997. "Shifting Identities, Positioned Imaginaries: Transnational Traversals and Reversals by Malaysian Chinese." In Aihwa Ong and Donald M. Nonini, eds., *Ungrounded Empires: The Cultural Politics of Chinese Transnationalism.* 203–27. New York: Routledge.

Nonini, Donald, and Aihwa Ong. 1997. "Chinese Transnationalism as Alternative Modernity." In Aihwa Ong and Donald Nonini, eds., *Ungrounded Empires: The Cultural Politics of Chinese Transnationalism.* 3–33.

Ōba Minako. 1990. *Tsuda Umeko.* Tokyo: Asahi Shimbunsha.

Oda Makoto. 1961. *Nandemo mite yarō* (Let's see everything). Tokyo: Kawade Shobō.

Ogasawara, Yuko. 1998. *Office Ladies and Salaried Men: Power, Gender, and Work in Japanese Companies.* Berkeley: University of California Press.

Ōhashi Terue. 1993. *Mikonka no shakaigaku* (Sociology of nonmarriage). Tokyo: Nihon Hōsō Shuppan Kyōkai.

Ōhori Sueo. 1984. " 'Sōmeina josei' to deatta toki" (The time I met a "wise woman"). In Asahi Jānaru, ed., *Onna no sengoshi I: Shōwa nijūnendai* (Women's postwar history 1: 1945–1955). 293–300. Tokyo: Asahi Shimbunsha.

"OL, joshidaisei kaigairyokō no seika hōkoku" (OL, girl college students overseas travel sex report). 1988. *Shūkan Hōseki,* August:218–21.

Ong, Aihwa. 1999. *Flexible Citizenship: The Cultural Logics of Transnationality.* Durham, NC: Duke University Press.

———. 1988. "Colonialism and Modernity: Feminist Representations of Women in Non-Western Societies." *Inscriptions* 3–4:79–93.

Ong, Aihwa, and Donald Nonini, eds. 1997. *Ungrounded Empires: The Cultural Politics of Chinese Transnationalism.* New York: Routledge.

Orbaugh, Sharalyn. Forthcoming. *The Japanese Fiction of the Allied Occupation, 1945–1952.* Stanford: Stanford University Press.

Ōshima Yukio. 1979. " 'Kokusaku baishun' no tenmatsu" (An account of official prostitution). In Tsubota Itsuo, ed., *Nihonjosei no rekishi 13: Senchū sengo no josei* (The history of Japanese women 13: Women in wartime and postwar periods). 92–94. Tokyo: Akatsuki Kyōiku Tosho Kabushikigaisha.

O'Toole, Thomas. 1993. "Fast Track Career Women Chase Promotions by Earning MBAs Abroad." *Nikkei Weekly,* 14 June:20.

" 'Otto to no bekkyō' o nozomu sanjūdai dokushin OL ga zōka?" (Increase in number of single OLs in their 30s who want to "live apart from husband"?). 1998. *Nikkan Gendai,* 3 December; http://www.ngendai.com.

Ōya Sōichi, Takagi Tatsuo, and Nakaya Ken'ichi. 1957. "Taiheiyō no ryōgan" (Both sides of the Pacific). *Chūō Kōron,* August: 166–75.

Ozaki, Takeshi. 1993. "United Nations Looks to Japanese Career Women." *Nikkei Weekly,* 7 June:21.

Ozawa Nobuo. 1984. "Panpan" (Panpan girls). In Asahi Jānaru, ed., *Onna no sengoshi I: Shōwa nijūnendai* (Women's postwar history 1: 1945–1955). 19–27. Tokyo: Asahi Shimbunsha.

Palumbo-Liu, David. 1994. "Los Angeles, Asians, and Perverse Ventriloquisms: On the Functions of Asian America in the Recent American Imaginary." *Public Culture* 6:365–81.

Parrott, Lindsay. 1946. "Now a Japanese Woman Can Be a Cop. *New York Times Magazine,* 2 June: 18, 56.

——. 1945. "Out of Feudalism: Japan's Women." *New York Times Magazine,* 28 October: 10–11.

Pereira, John, Simon Potter, and Toto Akeru. 1992. *Heart to Heart: A Conversation Coursebook for Japanese Students.* Kyoto: City Press.

Pharr, Susan J. 1987. "The Politics of Women's Rights." In Robert E. Ward and Sakamoto Yoshikazu, eds., *Democratizing Japan: The Allied Occupation.* 221–52. Honolulu: University of Hawai'i Press.

Povinelli, Elizabeth, and George Chauncey. 1999. "Thinking Sexuality Transnationally." *GLQ* 5: 439–50.

Prakash, Gyan. 1997. "Postcolonial Criticism and Indian Historiography." In Anne McClintock, Aamir Mufti, and Ella Shohat, eds., *Dangerous Liaisons: Gender, Nation, and Postcolonial Perspectives.* 491–500. Minneapolis: University of Minnesota Press.

Pratt, Mary Louise. 2000. "Postcoloniality: An Incomplete Project or an Irrelevant One?" Talk given at the University of Oregon Comparative Literature Speaker Series, Eugene, 4 May.

Rabinow, Paul. 1986. "Representations Are Social Facts: Modernity and Post-Modernity in Anthropology." In James Clifford and George E. Marcus, eds., *Writing Culture: The Poetics and Politics of Ethnography.* 234–61. Berkeley: University of California Press.

"Ranking of Foreigners Called Common in Japan." 1995. *Honolulu Advertiser,* 21 November: A10.

Rifkin, Alan. 1993. "Asian Women, L.A. Men." *Buzz,* September:73–112.

Robbins, Bruce. 1999. "Introduction, Part 1: Actually Existing Cosmopolitanism." In Bruce Robbins and Pheng Cheah, eds., *Cosmopolitics: Thinking and Feeling beyond the Nation.* Durham, NC: Duke University Press.

——. 1994. "Upward Mobility in the Postcolonial Era: Kincaid, Mukherjee, and the Cosmopolitan au Pair." *Modernism/Modernity* 1, no. 2: 133–51.

——. 1992. "Comparative Cosmopolitanism." *Social Text* 31–32:169–86.

Roberts, Glenda. 1994. *Staying on the Line: Blue Collar Women in Contemporary Japan*. Honolulu: University of Hawai'i Press.

Roberts, Walter. 1993. "Ghost in the Machine." *Tokyo Today*. December:64–65.

Robertson, Jennifer. 1998a. "It Takes a Village: Internationalization and Nostalgia in Postwar Japan." In Stephen Vlastos, ed., *Mirror of Modernity: Invented Traditions of Modern Japan*. 110–29. Berkeley: University of California Press.

——. 1998b. *Takarazuka: Sexual, Political and Popular Culture in Modern Japan*. Berkeley: University of California Press.

——. 1992. "The Politics of Androgyny in Japan: Sexuality and Subversion in the Theater and Beyond." *American Ethnologist* 19, no. 3:419–42.

Rofel, Lisa. 1997. "Rethinking Modernity: Space and Factory Discipline in China." In Akhil Gupta and James Ferguson, eds., *Culture/Power/Place: Explorations in Critical Anthropology*. 155–78. Durham, NC: Duke University Press.

Rose, Barbara. 1992. *Tsuda Umeko and Women's Education in Japan*. New Haven: Yale University Press.

Ross, Karen. 1996. *Black and White Media: Black Images in Popular Film and Television*. Cambridge, MA: Polity Press.

Rouse, Roger. 1995. "Thinking through Transnationalism." *Public Culture* 7, no. 2:353–402.

Russell, John. 1998. "Consuming Passions: Spectacle, Self-Transformation, and the Commodification of Blackness in Japan." *Positions* 6, no. 1:113–77.

——. 1995. "Consuming Passions: Spectacle, Liminality, and the Commodification of Blackness in Japan." Paper presented at the 47th annual meeting of the Association for Asian Studies, 6–9 April. Washington, DC.

Ryu, Marcus. 1993. "Invisible Men: Woes of Today's Asian-American Man." *Nassau*, 4 November:5.

"Ryūgaku taikenki: OL ryūgaku watashi no baai" (Study-abroad experiences: OL study abroad, my case). 1992. *URASHIMER*, September: 6–7.

Said, Edward. 1984. "Reflections on Exile." *Granta* 13 (autumn): 157–72.

——. 1978. *Orientalism*. New York: Random House.

Saisho Atsuko, ed. 1966. *Meiji bungaku zenshū 81: Meiji joryū bungakushū, 1* (Complete collection of Meiji literature 81: Meiji women's literature, 1). Tokyo: Chikuma Shoten.

Saitō Minako. 1993. *Chōichiryūshugi* (Super top-classism). Tokyo: Magazine House.

"Saitō Minako no 'atsugeshō' o hippagasu" (Tearing the "thick makeup" off Saitō Minako). 1993. *Shūkan Bunshun*, 28 October: 208–11.

Sakai, Naoki. 1997. *Translation and Subjectivity: On Japan and Cultural Nationalism*. Minneapolis: University of Minnesota Press.

——. 1989. "Modernity and Its Critique: The Problem of Universalism and Particularism." In Masao Miyoshi and H. D. Harootunian, eds., *Postmodernism and Japan*. 93–122. Durham, NC: Duke University Press.

Sakakibara Yoshitaka. 1984. "A Study of Japanese Students at the University of Southern California, 1946–1980." Ph.D. diss., University of Southern California.

Sakanishi Shiho. 1956. *Seikatsu no chie* (Wisdom of life). Tokyo: Kindai Seikatsusha.

——. 1953. *Watakushi no me* (My eyes). Tokyo: Yomiuri Shimbunsha.

——. 1950 [1946]. *Amerika no josei* (The American woman). Tokyo: Kadokawa Shoten.

——. 1947. *Chi no shio* (Salt of the earth). Kyoto: Takagiri Shoten.

——. 1946. *Amerika no nichijō seikatsu* (American everyday life). Tokyo: Nihonbashi Shoten.

Sakanishi Shiho-san Henshū Sewaninkai, eds. 1977. *Sakanishi Shiho-san* (Miss Sakanishi Shiho). Tokyo: Kokusai Bunka Kaikan.

Sakuma Rika. 1992. "Imaya kokusaishakai de ikiru nara gōrudokādo yori gurīn kādo?" (To live in international society you need a Green Card, not a Gold Card). *Marco Polo*, February:64–68.

Sarratt, George. 1992. *Nyū yōku no kagai jugyō* (New York after school lessons). Tokyo: Kōyū Shuppan.

Sasaki Izumi. 1997. "Borantia katsudō ga watashi no ikikata wo kaeta" (Volunteering changed my life). In Ishida Yōko, ed., *Marugoto onna no tenki* (Complete woman's turning point). 58–71. Tokyo: Asupekuto.

Sasaki Kaori. 1993. " 'Yaruki' OL wa amerika o mezasu" (OLs with ambition head for America). *President*, September:216–21.

Satō, Kyōko. 1993. "Women Find Opportunities in U.N." *Japan Times*, 2 September:3.

Sawada Akio and Kadowaki Kōji. 1990. *Nihonjin no kokusaika: Chikyū shimin no jōken o saguru* (The internationalization of the Japanese: Exploring the criteria of the global citizen). Tokyo: Nihon Keizai Shimbunsha.

Sawada, Mitziko. 1996. *Tokyo Life, New York Dreams: Urban Japanese Visions of America, 1890–1924*. Berkeley: University of California Press.

Seo Manami. 1993. "Tsūyaku, honyaku: josei muki? dansei muki?" (Interpreting, translating: Are women better suited than men?). *Tsūyaku/Honyaku Jānaru* (Interpreting/translating journal), December:11–24.

Shah, Sonia, ed. 1997. *Dragon Ladies: Asian American Feminists Breathe Fire*. Boston: South End Press.

Shimizu Ikutarō. 1990 [1989]. *Sakujitsu no tabi: Raten amerika kara supein e* (Yesterday's journey: From Latin America to Spain). Tokyo: Chūō Kōronsha.

Shiohara Akira. 1994. "Nipponjin no eikaiwa shijōshugi no gu" (The stupidity of Japanese worship of English). *SPA!* June:36–45.

Shiota Ryōhei. 1966. "Kimura Akebono." In Saisho Atsuko, ed., *Meiji bungaku zenshū 81: Meiji joryū bungakushū, 1* (Complete collection of Meiji literature 81: Meiji women's literature, 1). Tokyo: Chikuma Shoten.

Sievers, Sharon L. 1983. *Flowers in Salt: The Beginnings of Feminist Consciousness in Modern Japan*. Stanford, CA: Stanford University Press.

Simpson, Caroline Sue. 1994. "American Orientalisms: The Gender and Cultural Politics of America's Postwar Relationship with Japan." Ph.D. diss., University of Texas at Austin.

Smith-Rosenberg, Caroll. 1985. *Disorderly Conduct: Visions of Gender in Victorian America*. New York: Knopf.

Sodei Rinjirō. 1985. *Haikei makkāsā gensuisama: Senryōka no nihonjin no tegami* (Greetings, Supreme Commander MacArthur: Japanese letters from the Occupation). Tokyo: Ōtsuki Shoten.

Sono Ayako. 1955. "Good Luck for Everybody!" *Gunzō*, November:61–79.

"Sonzai riyūnaki monotachi" (Things that have no reason to exist). 1993. *SPA!*, December–January:53–59.

Sōrifu Tōkeika. 1999. *Nihon tōkei nenkan 2000* (Japan statistical yearbook 2000). Tokyo: Japan Statistical Association.

"SPA! Ura guddo dezain taishō" (SPA! anti–good design top prize). 1994. *SPA!*, 25 May:47–55.

Spickard, Paul R. 1989. *Mixed Blood: Intermarriage and Ethnic Identity in Twentieth-Century America*. Madison: University of Wisconsin Press.

Spivak, Gayatri Chakravorty. 1999. *A Critique of Postcolonial Reason: Toward a History of the Vanishing Present*. Cambridge, MA: Harvard University Press.

——. 1990a. "The Making of Americans, the Teaching of English, the Future of Colonial Studies." *New Literary History* 21, no. 4:781–98.

——. 1990b. *The Post-Colonial Critic*. New York: Routledge.

——. 1985. "Three Women's Texts and a Critique of Imperialism." In Henry Louis Gates, ed., *"Race," Writing, and Difference*. 262–80. Chicago: University of Chicago Press.

Sugimoto, Etsu Inagaki. 1926. *A Daughter of the Samurai*. New York: Doubleday.

Sugimoto Yoshio. 1988. *Shinka shinai nihonjin e* (To the Japanese who don't advance). Tokyo: Jōhō Sentā.

Taga Mikiko. 1991. *Nyū yōku de yumesagashi* (Finding our dreams in New York). Tokyo: Jijitsūshinsha.

Tajima Yōko. 1994. *Koi o shimakure: Watashi no taikenteki ren'airon* (Loving out of bounds: My personal theory of love). Tokyo: Tokuma Shoten.

——. 1993. "Sunday nikkei: Otoko e no messēji, otoko ni totte, onna wa 'gaijin'" (Sunday Nikkei: Message to men, in men's eyes women are foreigners). *Nihon Keizai Shimbun*, 27 June:19.

Takahashi Eiko. 1995. *Kokusaijin nyūmon: sekai ni tsūjiru kurashi to manā* (Primer for internationalists: Lifestyle and manners accepted by the world). Tokyo: Tabata Shoten.

Takahashi Fumiko. 1989. *Gaikokujin dansei to tsukiau hō* (How to date a foreign man). Tokyo: Shufu to seikatsusha.

Takahashi Nobuko. 1979. *Junēbu nikki: Remanko no mieru ofisu de* (Geneva diary: From an office overlooking Lake Leman). Tokyo: Nihon Rōdō Kyōkai.

Takahashi Toshie. 1989. *Wataru Amerika, oni wa nashi* (No demons on the road to America). Tokuma Shoten.

Takahashi Yuichi. 2000. "Gaishi no aranami, tomadou shokuba" (Workplaces reeling in the rough seas of foreign investment). *Sankei Shimbun*, 19 January; http://www.sankei.co.jp/main/html.

Takata Kiyoko. 1995. *Little Bridge across the Pacific: Amerika de kurashite Nihon ga mieta* (Little bridge across the Pacific: Living in America I came to see Japan). Tokyo: Akashi Shoten.

Takatsuka Kiyoko [pseud. Uemura Kiyoka]. 1896. "Kimura Eiko joshi no shōden" (Short biography of the life of Kimura Eiko). In Kimura Akebono, *Fujo no kagami* (Mirror of womanhood). 1–3. Tokyo: Okamoto Masa.

Tamanoi, Mariko Asano. 1990. "Women's Voices: Their Critique of the Anthropology of Japan." *Annual Review of Anthropology* 19:17–37.

Tanabe Atsuko. 1993. *Onna ga gaikoku de hataraku toki* (When a woman works overseas). Tokyo: Bungei Shunjū.

Tanaka, Michiyo. 1993. "Yellow Cabs: A Suspicious Definition." *Transpacific*, July–August:88–89.

Tanaka Nobuhiko. 1998a. "Gaishikei kigyō de hataraku" (Working at the foreign-affiliate corporation). In *Kokusaiha no tenshoku saizensen* (On the front lines of job hunting for the internationally oriented). 11–89. Tokyo: SPACE ALC.

———. 1998b. "Jiyū ni ikiru: Jiyū janakereba, jinseijanai" (Living free: No freedom, no life). In *Kokusaiha no tenshoku saizensen* (On the front lines of job hunting for the internationally oriented). 94–135. Tokyo: SPACE ALC.

———. 1998c. "Manabi no datsuraku" (The pleasures of learning). In *Kokusaiha no tenshoku saizensen* (On the front lines of job hunting for the internationally oriented). 137–68. Tokyo: SPACE ALC.

Tanaka Sumiko. 1984. "Fujin sanseiken" (Women's suffrage). In Asahi Jānaru, ed., *Onna no sengoshi I: Shōwa nijūnendai* (Women's postwar history 1: 1945–1955). 55–64. Tokyo: Asahi Shimbunsha.

Tanimura Shiho. 1996. *Kekkon shinai kamoshirenai shōkōgun, danseiban* (The "I may not marry" syndrome, men's edition). Tokyo: Shufu no Tomosha.

———. 1991. "Chōsha intabyū" (Author interview). *Cosmopolitan Japan*. January:126.

———. 1990. *Kekkon shinai kamoshirenai shōkōgun* (The "I may not marry" syndrome). Tokyo: Shufu no Tomosha.

Taylor, Sully. 1994. "Book review of Alice Lam, *Women and Japanese Management: Discrimination and Reform* (New York: Routledge, 1992)." *Journal of Asian Studies* 53, no. 1: 216–18.

Thoreson, Tyler. 1997. "American Gigolo." *Swing* 3, no. 4:42.

Tobin, Joseph. 1992. "Introduction: Domesticating the West." In Joseph Tobin, ed., *Remade in Japan: Everyday Life and Consumer Taste in a Changing Society*. 1–41. New Haven, CT: Yale University Press.

Toi Jūgatsu. 1983. *Yuku michi wa, kaze: Hokubei tairiku ojūdan baiku ichimanyonsenkiro* (I

ride the wind: 14,000-kilometer journey across the North American continent). Tokyo: Kadokawa Shoten.

"Tora no i ni makenai namaiki" (A brashness unintimidated by authority). 1987. *Asahi Shimbun*. 18 June:4.

"Tōsei 'dōji tsūyaku' jijō: minzoku, bunka no hashiwatashiyaku desu" (The state of "simultaneous interpreting" in the present day: Acting as bridges for peoples and cultures). 1994. *Tokyo Shimbun*, 26 February:14.

Toyoda Masayoshi. 1994. *Kokuhatsu! Ierō kyabu* (Yellow cabs exposed!). Tokyo: Sairyūsha.

Treat, John Whittier. 1999. *Great Mirrors Shattered: Homosexuality, Orientalism, Japan.* New York: Oxford University Press.

——. 1994. "AIDS Panic in Japan: Or, How to Have a Sabbatical in an Epidemic." *Positions* 2, no. 3:629–79.

Troy, Carol. 1984. "Like the Boys." *Village Voice*, 14 February:37, 41.

Tsuda Umeko. 1984. *Tsuda Umeko monjo* (The writings of Tsuda Umeko). Ed. Furuki Yoshiko, Ueda Akiko, and Mary Althaus. Kodaira: Tsuda Juku Daigaku.

Uemura Tora. 1912. *Beikoku jijō: Tobeisha hikkei* (The situation in America: A handbook for the America-bound). Tokyo: Naigai Shuppanki.

Ueno Chizuko. 1998. *Nashonarizumu to jendā* (Nationalism and gender). Tokyo: Seidosha.

——. 1994. *Kindai kazoku no seiritsu to shūen* (The rise and fall of the modern family). Tokyo: Iwanami Shoten.

——. 1988. "The Japanese Women's Movement: The Countervalues to Industrialism." In Gavan McCormack and Yoshio Sugimoto, eds., *The Japanese Trajectory: Modernization and Beyond.* 167–85. Cambridge, England: Cambridge University Press.

UPDATE, ed. 1990. *Onna wa chikyū o aishiteru: sekai de katsuyaku suru Nihon no joseitachi* (Women love the earth: Japanese women active in the world). Tokyo: Hon no Ki Publishers.

Visweswaran, Kamala. 1994. *Fictions of Feminist Ethnography.* Minneapolis: University of Minnesota Press.

Vorakitphokatorn, Sairudee, et. al. 1993. "AIDS Risk in Tourists: A Study on Japanese Female Tourists in Thailand." *Journal of Population and Social Studies* 5 (1–2):55–84.

Wagatsuma, Hiroshi. 1967. "The Social Perception of Skin Color in Japan." *Daedalus* (spring):407–43.

Welter, Barbara. 1966. "The Cult of True Womanhood." *American Quarterly* 18:151–74.

White, Linda. 1997. "Three Steps Behind: Representations of Japanese Women in *Looking for Fumiko*." Paper presented at the Western Conference of the Association of Asian Studies, Boulder, CO, 22–24 October.

White, Merry. 1988. *The Japanese Overseas: Can They Go Home Again?* New York: Free Press.

"White Male Qualities." 1971. In Amy Tachiki, Eddie Wong, and Franklin Odo, eds., *Roots: An Asian American Reader.* Los Angeles: UCLA Asian American Studies Center.

"Women Translators Gaining More Clout." 1993. *Daily Yomiuri*, 16 October:3.

Yamada Eimi. 1985. *Beddotaimu aizu* (Bedtime eyes). Tokyo: Kawade Shobō Shinsha.

Yamada Meiko. 1992. *Senryōgun ianfu: Kokusaku baishun no onnatachi no higeki* (Comfort women of the Occupation troops: The tragedy of women subjected to the national prostitution policy). Tokyo: Kōjinsha.

Yamakawa Kikue. 1984. *Yamakawa Kikue: Josei kaihōronshū* (Yamakawa Kikue: Collected works on women's liberation). Ed. Suzuki Yūko. Tokyo: Iwanami Shoten.

Yamamoto Michiko. 1993a. *Amerika gurashi no ikikata bijin: kyūkutsuna Nihon ni sumanai onnatachi* (Lifestyle beauties living in America: The women who won't live in oppressive Japan). Tokyo: Aki Shobō.

——. 1993b. *Deyōka Nippon, onna 31 sai: Amerika, chūgoku o yuku* (Shall I leave Japan? A woman at 31 travels America and China). Tokyo: Kōdansha.

Yamamoto, Traise. 1999. *Masking Selves, Making Subjects: Japanese American Women, Identity, and the Body*. Berkeley: University of California Press.

Yamamuro Tamiko. 1947. *Wakai josei no ikikata* (Young women's lifestyles). Tokyo: Shakai Kyōiku Sōgōkaihen.

Yamanaka Keiko. 1993. "Book review of Mary Brinton, *Women and the Economic Miracle: Gender and Work in Postwar Japan* (Berkeley: University of California Press, 1993)." *Journal of Asian Studies* 52, no. 4:1005–1007.

Yamazaki, Takako. 1989. "Tsuda Ume: 1864–1929." In Benjamin C. Duke, ed., *Ten Great Educators of Modern Japan: A Japanese Perspective*. 125–47. Tokyo: University of Tokyo Press.

——. 1972. *Tsuda Umeko*. Tokyo: Yoshikawa Kōbunkan.

Yamazaki Tomoko. 1997. *Nihon no feminizumu: Nihon josei no hatsugen no rekishi* (Japanese feminism: A history of Japanese women's voices). Tokyo: Ōzorasha.

Yang, Mayfair Mei-hui. 1997. "Mass Media and Transnational Subjectivity in Shanghai: Notes on (Re)cosmopolitanism in a Chinese metropolis." In Aihwa Ong and Donald M. Nonini, eds., *Ungrounded Empires: The Cultural Politics of Modern Chinese Transnationalism*. 287–322. New York: Routledge.

Yoneyama, Lisa. 1994. "Japanese Studies and the Locations of Criticism." Paper presented at Internationalizing Cultural Studies Conference, East-West Center, Honolulu, Hawai'i, 12–16 December.

Yoshida Emiko. 1993. "Cosmo essayist club: Ryūgaku shite, gonen ga tatte" (Cosmo essayist club: study abroad, five years later). *Cosmopolitan Japan*, 20 June:118.

Yoshikawa Riichi. 1956 [1931]. *Tsuda Umeko den* (Story of Tsuda Umeko). Tokyo: Tsuda Juku Dōsōkai.

Yoshimi Yoshiaki. 1995. *Jūgun ianfu* (Military comfort women). Tokyo: Iwanami Shinsho.

"Young Workers Flocking Abroad to Find More Challenging Jobs." 1994. *Daily Yomiuri*, 19 April: 9.

ZIPANGU. 1998. *Warawareru nipponjin: "Nyū yōku taimuzu" ga egaku fukashigina nippon* (The ridiculed Japanese: Bizarre Japan as it appears in the New York Times) [English title: *Japan Made in U.S.A.*]. New York: ZIPANGU.

Žižek, Slavoj. 1989. *The Sublime Object of Ideology*. London: Verso.

Zoppetti, David. 1997. *Ichigensan* (One-timer). Tokyo: Shūeisha.

Index

Enlightenment, 120, 123, 218

Equal Employment Opportunity Law (EEOL), 2, 93–94

Essentialism, 10; and fieldwork, 31; in women's internationalist identity, 8–9

Ethnography: cosmopolitan, 27, 30; humanist concern of, 24; Japanese reactions to, 237–44; location-work in, 32; normativity in, 28–29; objectivity in, 244–45; and researcher/subject alliances, 246–47; as a source of knowledge of the West, 30–31

Eurocenter, 11, 234, 258 n.4

Exclusion. *See* Marginality

Exiles, characteristics of, 201

Fairy tales, 148–49

Fanon, Frantz, 81

Fantasy, 52, 75, 80, 125, 247; and desire, 27, 148; heterosexual rescue in United States, 229–30; as social practice, 13; Western, of Japanese men, 180; Western, of Japanese women, 174; of white men, 149, 150, 191, 195; and whiteness, 188, 200; in women's images of America, 46, 54, 148, 223–24

Farman, Abou, 186, 187

Female diasporic, elite, 235

Feminine Mystique, 62–63

Feminism, 24, 229; and ethnography, 246

Feminist activism: and criticism of Japanese men, 219–20; vs. dependency, 219; effectiveness of, in Japan, 219; vs. internationalism, 217–18, 219–25; and the West as emancipatory, 223–24

Ferguson, James, 31, 32

Ferris Seminary (Yokohama), 250 n.5

Feudalism, 55; in the Meiji family system, 38, 46; in women's views of Japan, 4, 8, 37, 44, 54

Fieldwork, 29, 237–47; and "fielding," 31–33, 34, 244–45

Flexibility, and accumulation, 12, 13; and citizenship, 12–13; and women's adaptability, 117–20, 202, 234–35

Foreign-affiliate firms (gaishikei): gaishikei-fication of Japanese firms, 114–15; gender inequality at, 207; work in, as internationalist resistance, 100, 114–17, 115, 254 n.11

Foreign language study, 2, 100–102. *See also* English study

Foucault, Michel, 10

Frankenberg, Ruth, 147, 155

Fujin Minshu Kurabu (Women's Democracy Club), 251 n.14

Fujioka Wakao, 130

Fujita Taki, 43

Fuke Shigeko, 90, 93, 98–99, 127, 128, 130

Fukuzawa Yukichi, 39

Funamoto Emiko, 222

Furuki Yoshiko, 41

Gaishikei. *See* Foreign-affiliate firms (gaishikei)

Gender inequality, in the workplace, 206–8

Gender relations, traditional: critique/rejection of, 2–4, 8; Japanese women–Westerners alliance as threat to, 37; transformations in, 1; Western deliverance from, 86, 98–100, 99

Gilmour, Leonie, 53

Girls' comics, 256 n.12

Girls' School of English. *See* Tsuda Daigaku; Tsuda Juku

Global culture, 13, 236

Globalization, 12, 13, 16–17, 24, 249 n.6, 257 n.1; and agency, 225–26; and imperialism, 229

Godzich, Wlad, 24, 224

Goodman, David, 105

Gotō, Kayoko, 202

Meiji Restoration, 35, 55–56; foreign legitimation of, 227–28; and individualism/personhood, 44; limits of, 205–8; media's promotion of, 10–12; of men vs. women, 7–8; as mimetic, 227–29; and the Occupation, 36, 37; and raising up Japanese womanhood, 38; and rashamen (mistresses of foreigners), 35, 250 nn.1–2; scale of, 5; and translators, 100–101; use of term, 5–6. *See also* Internationalism, as resistance; *See also* Occupation, and liberation of women; Occupation, sexual nexus of; Study abroad

Internationalism, as resistance, 85–132; and adaptability of women, 117–21; and alienation of women, 120–21; via autobiographical texts by women, 86, 87, 254 n.12; backlash against, 97, 253 n.4; and the consciousness gap, 87, 88–91; and delayed marriage, 88–89, 94; and economic recession, 87–88; and the EEOL, 93–94; via English study, 100–102; and expendable income of women, 85; and the individualistic lifestyle, 87, 89–91, 97, 106, 116–17; by minority of women, 86–87; narratives of, 97–100; and number of men vs. women living abroad, 253–54 n.9; and opportunities for women, 86–87; and personhood, 88, 101–2; and professional frustrations, 91–96; and space, 98; and upward mobility, 123–24, 132, 186; and Western deliverance from traditional gender relations, 86, 98–100, 99; via work abroad, 96–97, 97, 100, 106–14, 253–54 nn.8–10; via work in foreign-affiliate firms, 100, 114–17, 115, 254 n.11; via work in international organizations, 100, 111–14. *See also* New self (atarashii jibun); Study abroad

Internationalist writing, 45–46, 52–54. *See also* Fuke Shigeko; Mishima Sumie; Mori, Kyoko; Mori Yōko; Yamamoto Michiko

Internationalization (kokusaika), 5, 127, 214

International organizations, 100, 111–14

Interpreters, 100

Ise Momoyo, 112

Ishigaki Ayako (Haru Matsui), 45–46

Ishihara, Yuriko, 81–84

Itō Yasuko, 56

Ivy, Marilyn: on cultural relativism, 29; on the "Discover Japan" campaign, 130; on internationalization, 5; on Japan vs. the foreign, 30; on male vs. female travelers, 9–10; on the realm of the masculine native, 119; on volkisch unity, 120

Iwao, Sumiko, 90

Iyer, Pico, 180–81

Japan, Country of Ridiculous Mothers and Pathetic Men (Marks T.), 125

Japanese Constitution, 55

Japanese Girls and Women (Tsuda U. and Bacon), 42, 250 n.6

Japanese men: critique/repudiation of, 21–22, 165–66; as emasculated/abject/sexually inadequate, 71, 74, 80, 83, 181–86, 182–83, 185, 228–29, 252 n.23; exclusion/representation of, and the new self, 125, 127–28, 128–29; feminist critique of, 219–20; in foreign-affiliate firms, 115–16; gay, 254 n.13; and gender relations, yellow cabs' critique of, 138–40, 141, 156; as hating foreigners, 127; as infantilized, 182–84; internationalist criticism of Japan by, 254 n.12; Japanese women rejected by, 209–10; in the Occupation, 71, 73, 74,

Upward mobility, 17, 123–24, 132, 156, 186, 187, 210, 212, 244

Visweswaran, Kamala, 24, 217, 246
voluntarism, 112–13
Vorakitphokatorn, Sairudee, 142

The Way of the Urban Samurai (Kasumi), 181, 182–83, 256 n.10
West: criticism of, 213–15, 256–57 n.1; as emancipatory, 36–37, 43, 44–45, 86, 98–100, 99, 223–24; as fantasy, 7, 10–11, 223–24; freedom of, 121–23
White, Merry, 110
White men, 4, 8, 17, 33, 170–71, 172, 249 n.3; and akogare, 198–201; and assimilation, 175; vs. black men, 142–43, 145, 146–47; commodification of, 152, 154, 155, 156–57, 198–99, 255 nn.3–4; as fetish objects, repudiation of, 215; importance as husbands/employers, 145–46, 146; at international singles parties, 177–78, 256 n.8; vs. Japanese men, 151–52, 153, 154; Japanese women's critique of, 199–200; and marginality of Japanese women, 169–70; and military victory/world dominance, 83; and the new self, 128–30, 131, 132; and personhood, 200; in pornography, 149, 150, 151; postwar magnetism, of, 81; and race/sex, 146–49, 154, 155–56, 186–87; and rage against Japan, 54; as rescuers, 229–31, 232–33, 234, 235–36; scarcity of, 178–79, 199–200; sexual access to women of other races, 80; stereotypes of, 145, 175–76, 255 n.2; and upward mobility, 186; the West as embodied in, 134; and white women, 154, 155. See also *How to Date a Foreign Man* (Takahashi F.); *The Lonely American* (Kirishima); Sexual involvement, with white men; White men, global market-

ing of; *Women! What Do You Want from America?* (Kida); Yellow cabs
White men, global marketing of, 187–98; and authority, 188–91; and Japanese women–white men pairings, 191–93, 192, 256 n.12; prevalence of white foreigners on Japanese television, 187; and sexual adequacy of Japanese vs. white men, 193–95, 256 n.13; and transnational meanings, 196–98; and white men as infantile/subdued, 195–96, 197. See also White men: commodification of
Whiteness, 27, 145, 148; in Japanese television commercials, 187–88
White women: fetishization of models, 256 n.9; objectification of, 188–90, 190, 256 n.9; and white men, 154, 155. See also American women
Woman, as signifier of Japan, 8–9, 16, 18, 249 n.4
Women! What Do You Want from America? (Kida), 156–57, 167–70, 255 n.5
Women's magazines, 127–28
Women's rights. See Occupation, and liberation of women
The Women Who Flocked to My Skin (Ieda), 137–38
Work abroad, 2, 249 n.1; as internationalist resistance, 96–97, 97, 100, 106–14, 253–54 nn.8–10; for men vs. women, 7–8
WuDunn, Sheryl, 258 n.5

Yamada Eimi, 142; *Bedtime Eyes*, 137, 138
Yamakawa Kikue, 43, 59
Yamamoto, Traise, 174, 180
Yamamoto Michiko, 86; on arriving in America, 108; on the en masse environment, 96; on the good life, 90; on her journey to the West, 122; on marriage and the Green Card, 210–11; on

Yamamoto Michiko (*cont.*)
 marrying for a Green Card, 212; on
 OLS, 92; on the space of Japan vs. West,
 98
Yamanaka Keiko, 91
Yamazaki Tomoko, 55–56
Yang, Mayfair, 11, 247
Yasashisa (kindness, gentleness, chivalrousness), 138
Yasuoka Shōtarō, 252 n.23
Yellow cabs, 8, 31–32, 133–56, 144, 253
 n.4; and black men, 134–35, 137–38,
 139, 142; as consumers of the exotic,
 135–36; and critique of Japanese men/
 gender relations, 138–40, 141, 156; and
 female sexual agency, 139–40, 141–42;
 and financing of affairs, 136, 137; and
 the Ierō Kyabu o Kangaeru Kai, 140–
 42, 147, 187; vs. internationalist
 women, 152; locations for encounters
 by, 136, 255 n.1; male accounts of, 136–
 37; media sensationalization of, 134–
 35, 140; and the OL life- style, 135; public outcry over, 137; study of, 242–43;
 usage of the term, 134, 140–41; and
 white men, commodification of, 152,
 154, 155, 255nn.3–4; and white men,
 importance as husbands/employers,
 145–46, 146; and white men, in pornography, 149, 150, 151; and white men,
 stereotypes of, 145, 255, n.2; and white
 men, vs. black men, 142–43, 145, 146–
 47; and white men, vs. Japanese men,
 151–52, 153, 154; and whiteness/ West-
 ernness/race, 146–49, 154, 155–56;
 and yasashisa of foreign men, 138
Yoneyama, Lisa, 236, 237, 246
Yoshimura Fumiharu, 178–80

ZIPANGU, 258 n.5
Žižek, Slavoj, 26
Zoppetti, David: *Ichigensan*, 231

Karen Kelsky is Assistant Professor of
Anthropology at the University of Oregon.

Library of Congress Cataloging-in-Publication Data
Kelsky, Karen.
Women on the verge : Japanese women,
Western dreams / Karen Kelsky.
p. cm. — (Asia-Pacific)
Includes bibliographical references and index.
ISBN 0-8223-2805-4 (cloth : alk. paper)
ISBN 0-8223-2816-X (pbk. : alk. paper)
1. Women—Japan—Social conditions.
2. Women—Employment—Japan. 3. Women—
Japan—Identity. 4. Women—Employment—
Foreign countries. I. Title. II. Series.
HQ1762.K45 2001   305.42'0952—dc21   2001033378